THE BUILDING OPPOSITE volume 1

L'immeuble en flammes

I met Vanyda in front of a building that was up in flames.

It was in January 2003. We had planned an evening with Kan Takahama and some friends at Fred Boot's apartment in Paris, but an absent-minded neighbor on the first floor forgot some beans on the stove so we had to go party somewhere else.

It wasn't the flames that made me realize there had been a fire - it was already extinguished - but an unusual to-do on the sidewalk : several firemen who were watching over the area and the residents who'd been told to wait outside for instructions. And the residents chatted pleasantly - muffled conversations, half-amused, half-anxious, concerned, an occasional burst of laughter - among people who live on the same landing and haven't had to wait for a fire to get to know and talk to each other.

A year earlier, when I visited Fred Boot for the first time, it had already struck me: "Wow, the people here really know each other. They seem like friends, they chat, they call upon each other, they squabble... The kind of place where the outgoing girl next door has a secret crush on the shy guy who lives on the first floor". And I had thought: "It's like Escalier C by Jean-Charles Tachella!".

Six months later I would have said: "It's like The Building Opposite by Vanyda!"

I discovered The Building Opposite - not yet the superb volume now published by la Boîte à Bulles but an 80 page self-published first version - at the start of summer 2002. Fred Boot -him again?-

saw the work in the Cartoonist and immediately sent me a copy. According to him the creator was, what, about twenty years old? I was amazed! Over the years I have seen many talented young artists come and go. But gifted storytellers... Not one! Well, yes, just the same, one, a young woman: Kan Takahama! With Vanyda that makes two. Two young women. Strange isn't it? Is it only women who dare start telling real stories from their 20s? I mean, stories with real people and real tea bags in boiling water, real toothpaste kisses, real doors that only open when you have the real key.

In the charred building's downstairs bar we were singing Areski and Brigitte Fontaine's C'est normal with the neighbors when Vanyda walked in. And here was another surprise! This young spinner of real stories with her huge wheelie (this evening being a Parisian stopover between her home town, Lille, and the Angoulême Festival, she had brought her building with her) was very, very pretty! Hence my concern while writing these lines. "Why do you only draw pretty, young Japanese girls?" I was asked, not without a touch of malice, by a female student of French at the University of Jochi who had come to interview me for a report she was preparing. A little later she persisted: "Your latest book was written together with Kan Takahama, a mangaka who is also very young and very pretty, was this by chance?". What would she think today if she were to read my introduction to The Building Opposite? "You admire the album of an artist who is very young and very pretty. Do you do this on purpose or what?".

Frédéric Boilet
Tokyo, November 19, 2003

Vanyda

THE BUILDING OPPOSITE volume 1

FANFARE / PONENT MON

Characters

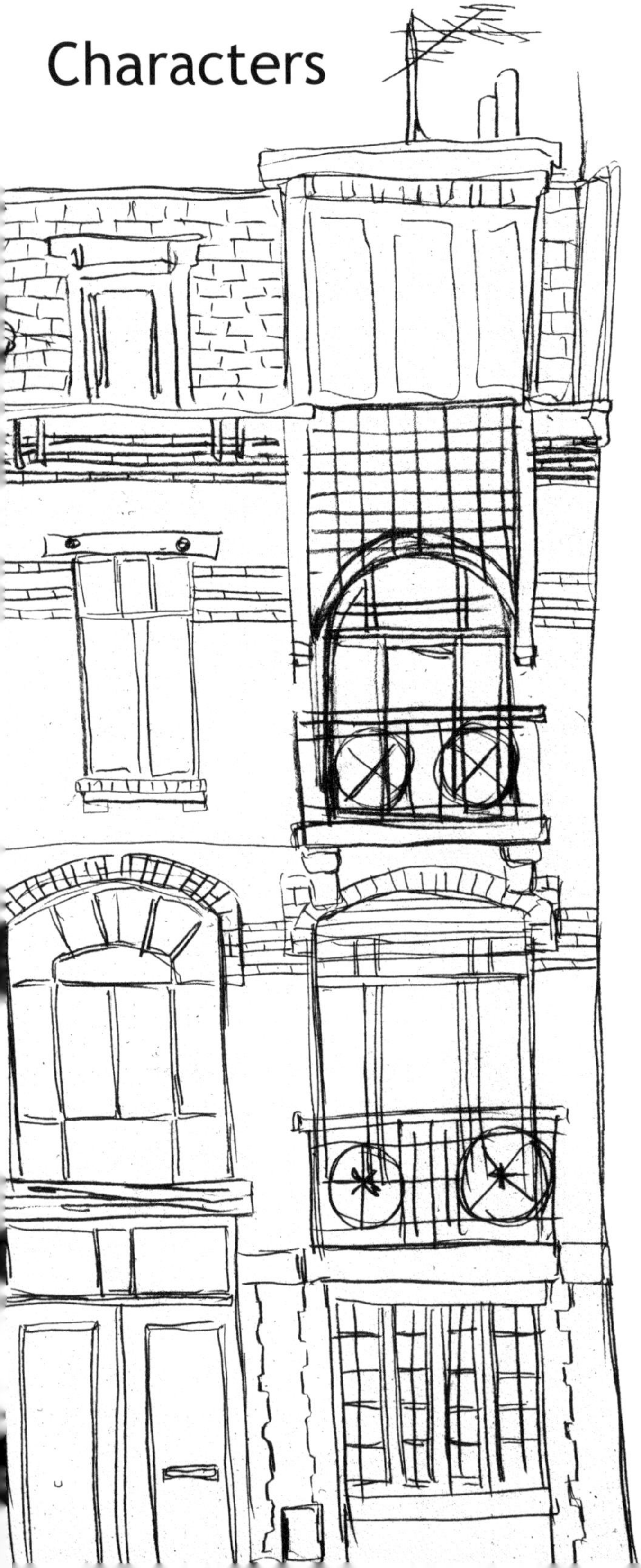

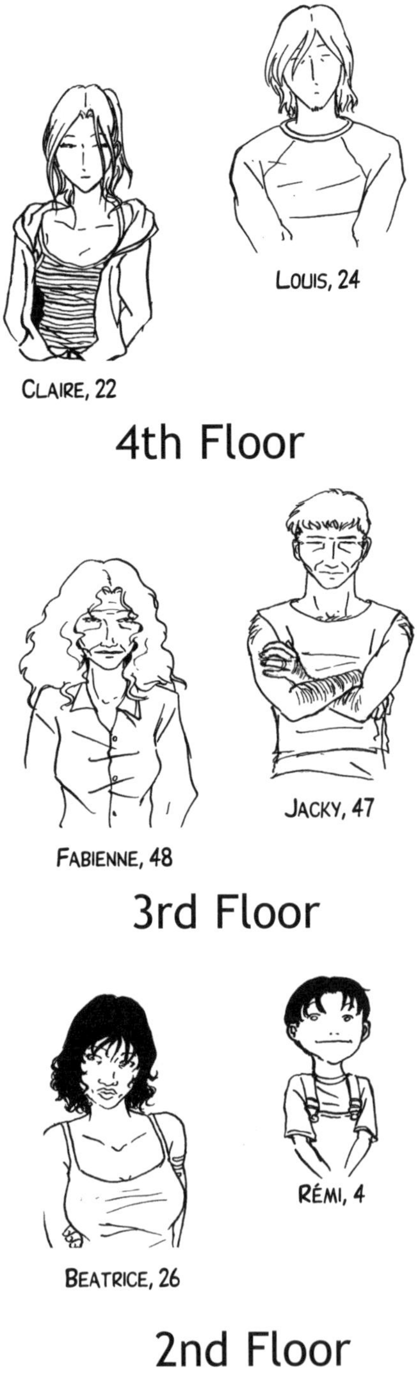
Claire, 22
Louis, 24
4th Floor
Fabienne, 48
Jacky, 47
3rd Floor
Beatrice, 26
Rémi, 4
2nd Floor

Chapter 1
Chronic pains

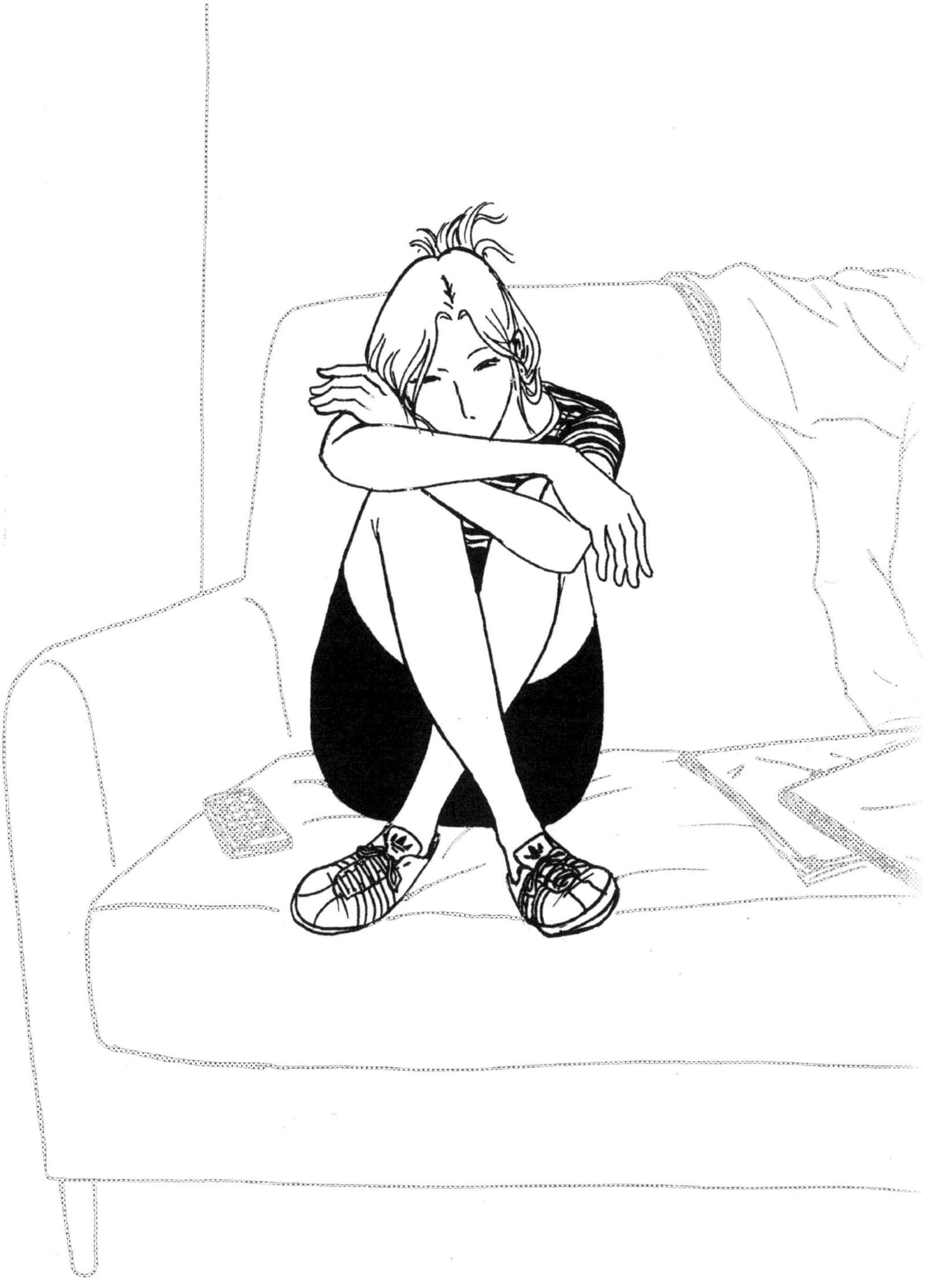

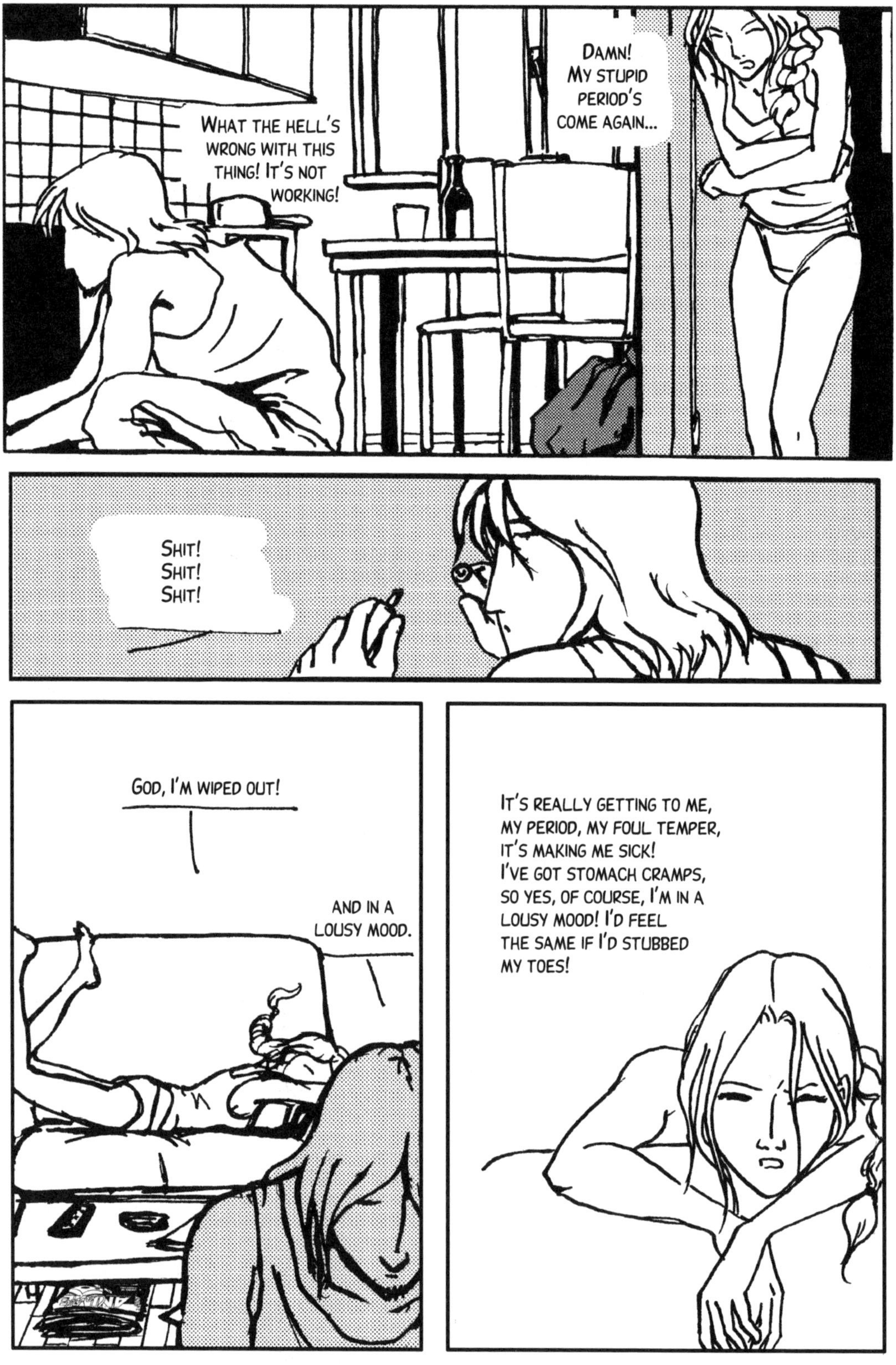
What the hell's wrong with this thing! It's not working!
Damn! My stupid period's come again...
Shit! Shit! Shit!
God, I'm wiped out!
And in a lousy mood.
It's really getting to me, my period, my foul temper, it's making me sick! I've got stomach cramps, so yes, of course, I'm in a lousy mood! I'd feel the same if I'd stubbed my toes!

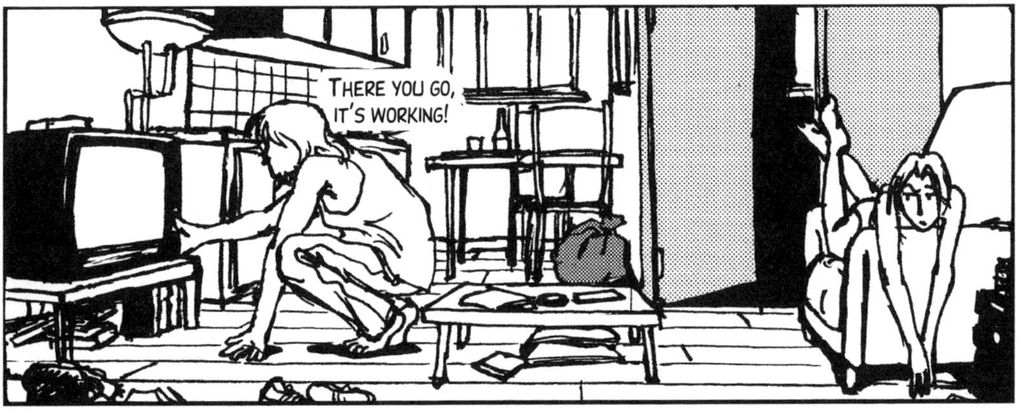
THERE YOU GO, IT'S WORKING!

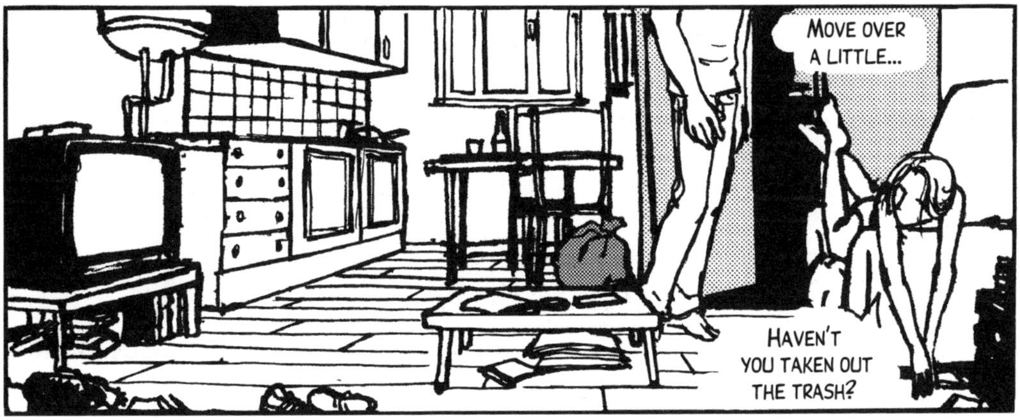
MOVE OVER A LITTLE...
HAVEN'T YOU TAKEN OUT THE TRASH?

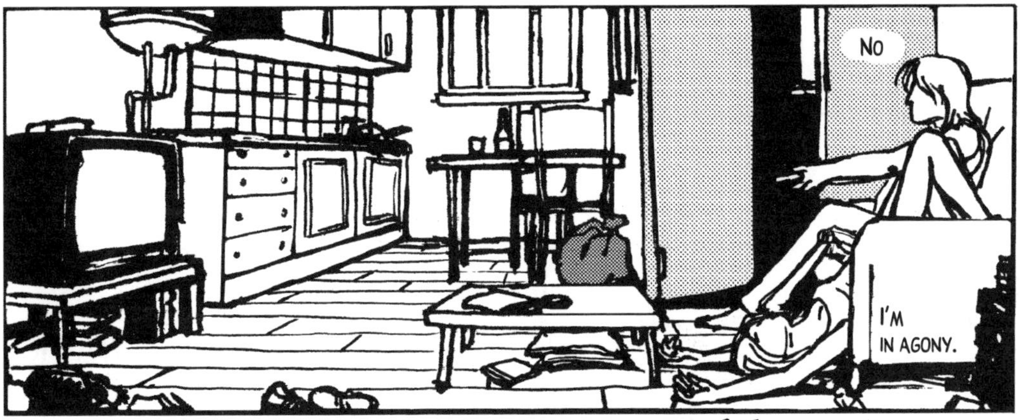
NO
I'M IN AGONY.

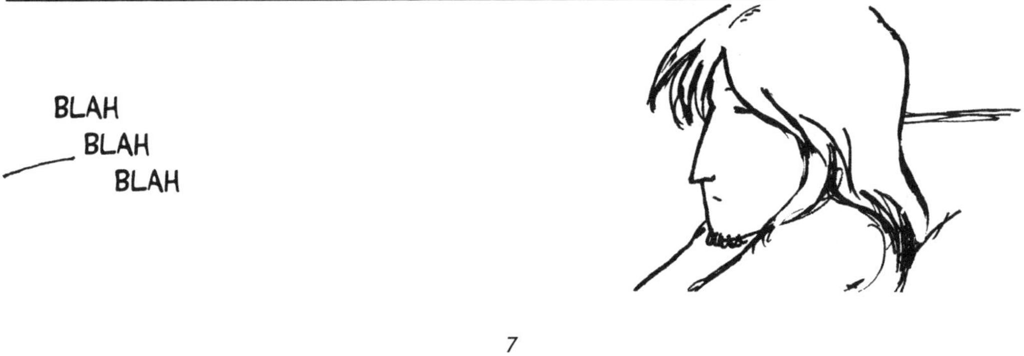
BLAH
BLAH
BLAH

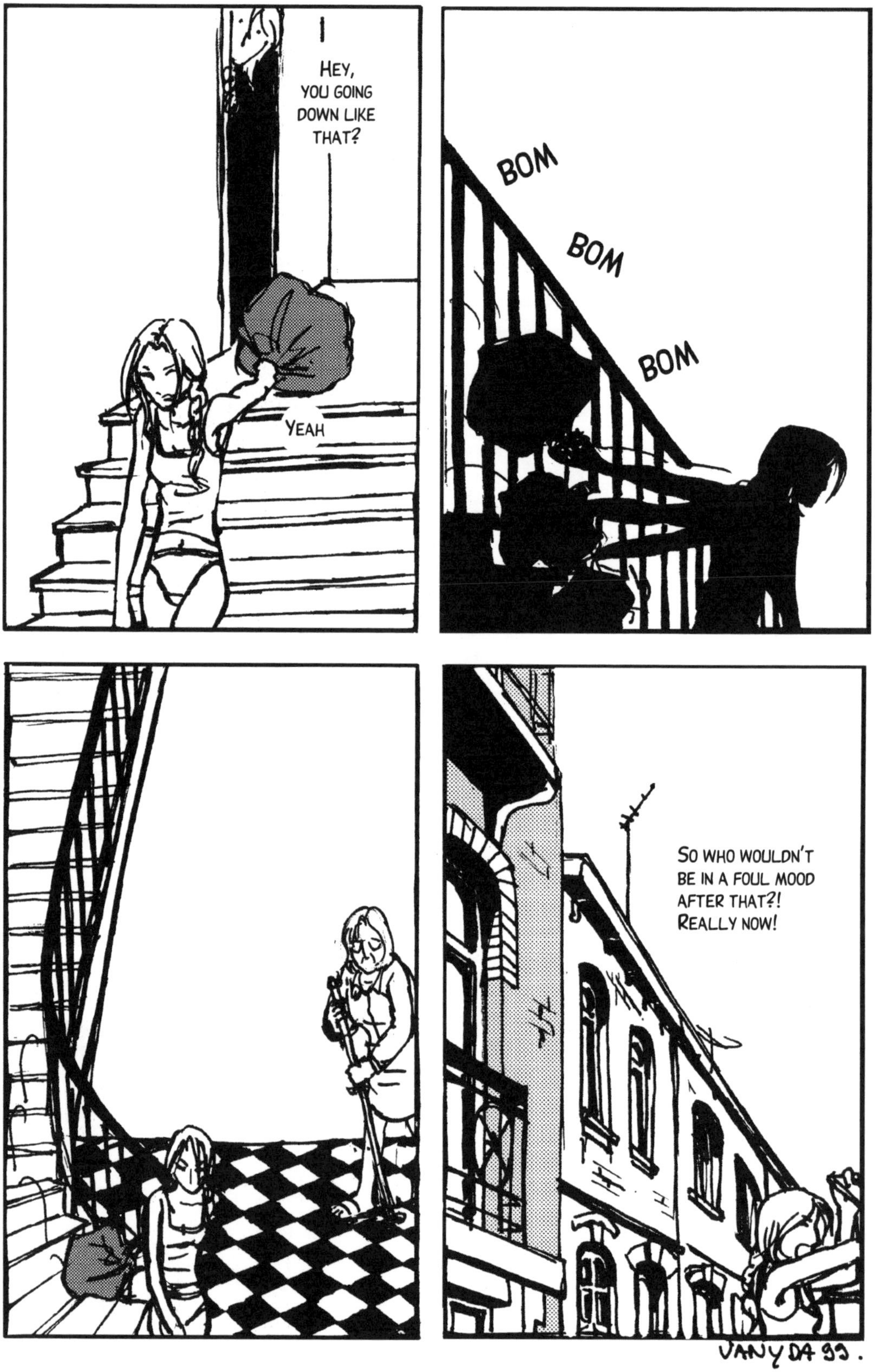
HEY, YOU GOING DOWN LIKE THAT?
YEAH
BOM
BOM
BOM
SO WHO WOULDN'T BE IN A FOUL MOOD AFTER THAT?! REALLY NOW!
VANYDA 99.

Chapter 2
No more Coke!

THERE'S NO COKE LEFT!
TOO BAD, HAVE SOMETHING ELSE!!

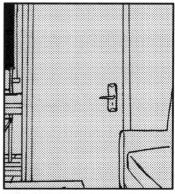

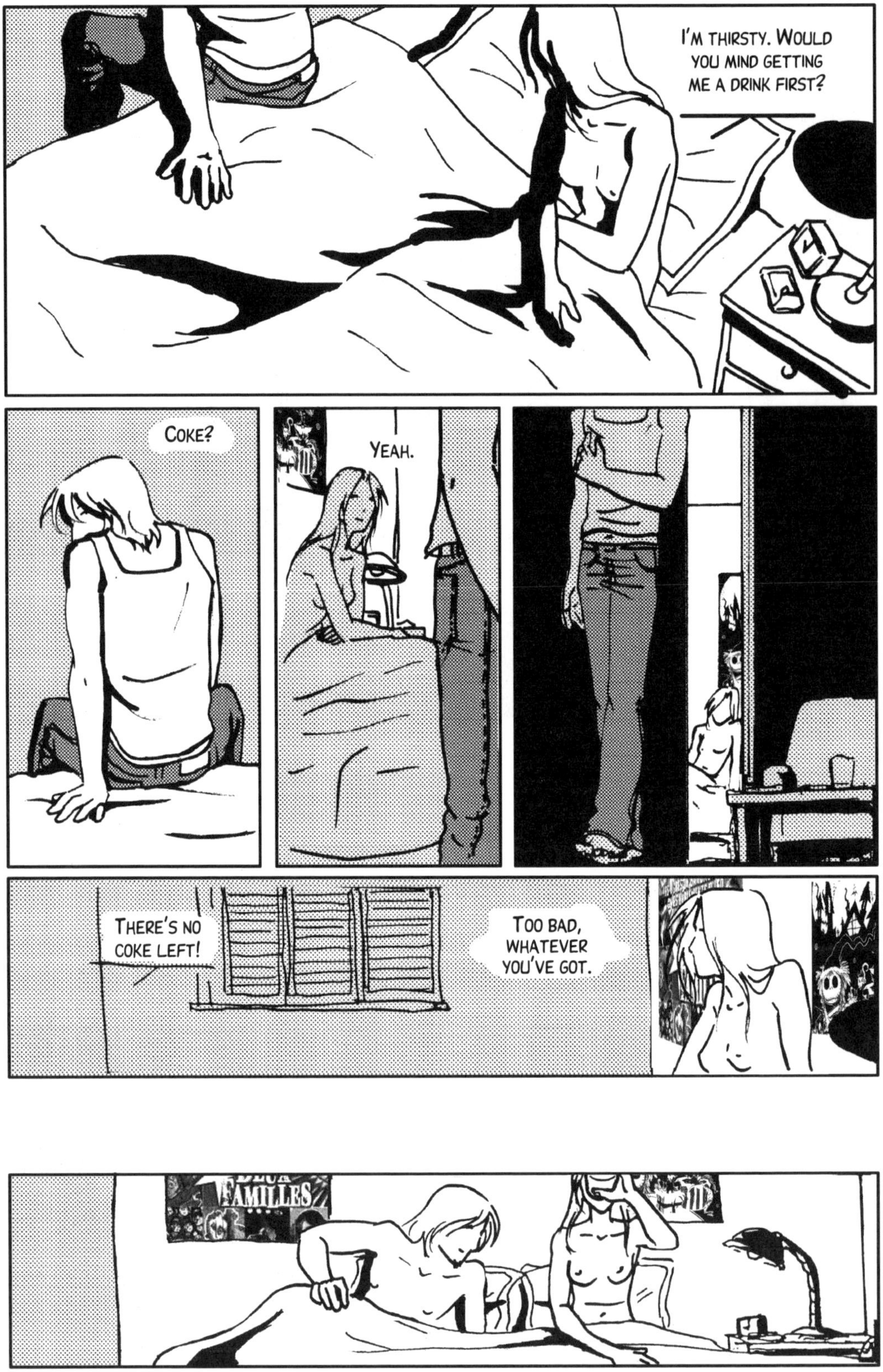
I'M THIRSTY. WOULD YOU MIND GETTING ME A DRINK FIRST?
COKE?
YEAH.
THERE'S NO COKE LEFT!
TOO BAD, WHATEVER YOU'VE GOT.
FAMILLES

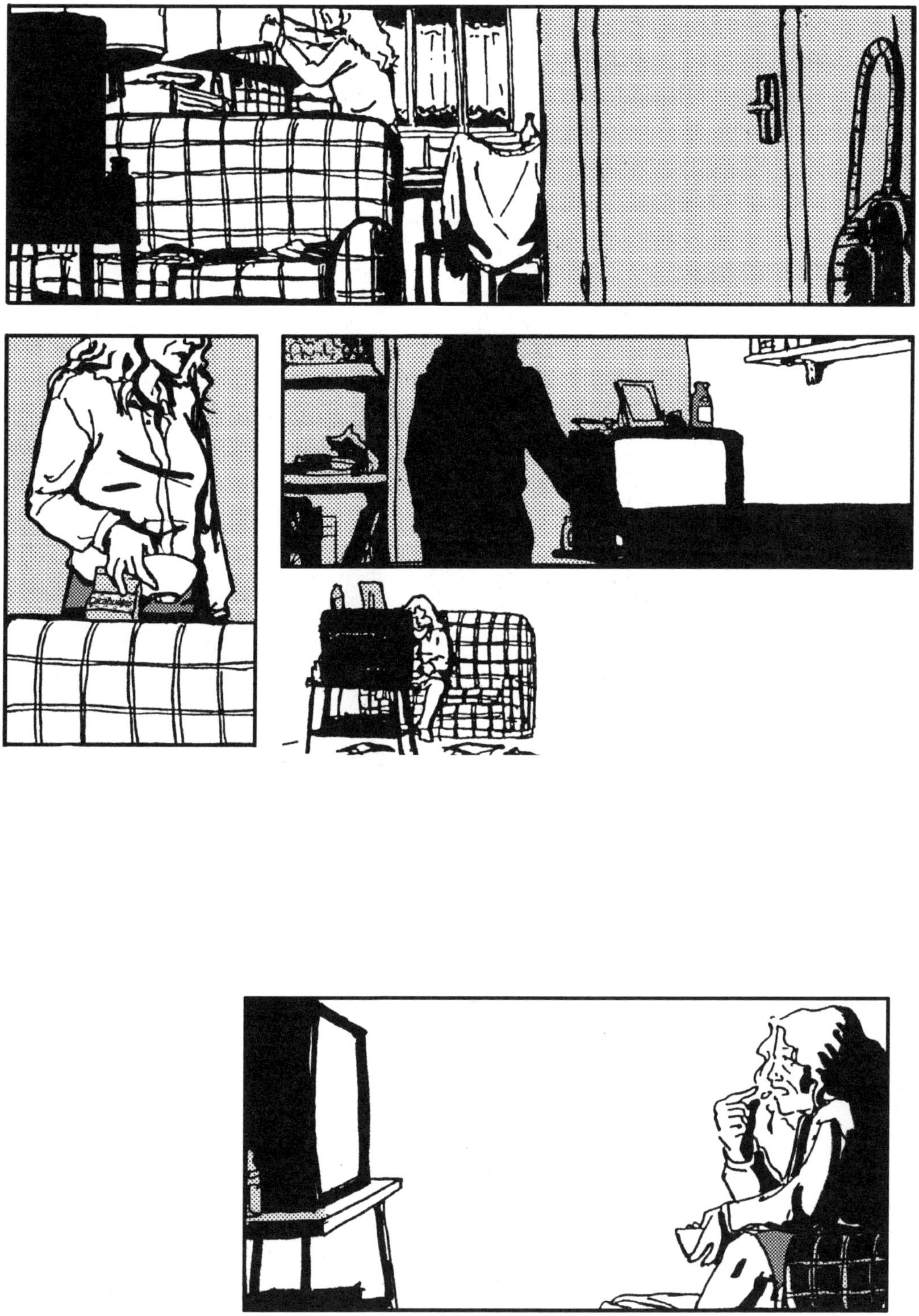

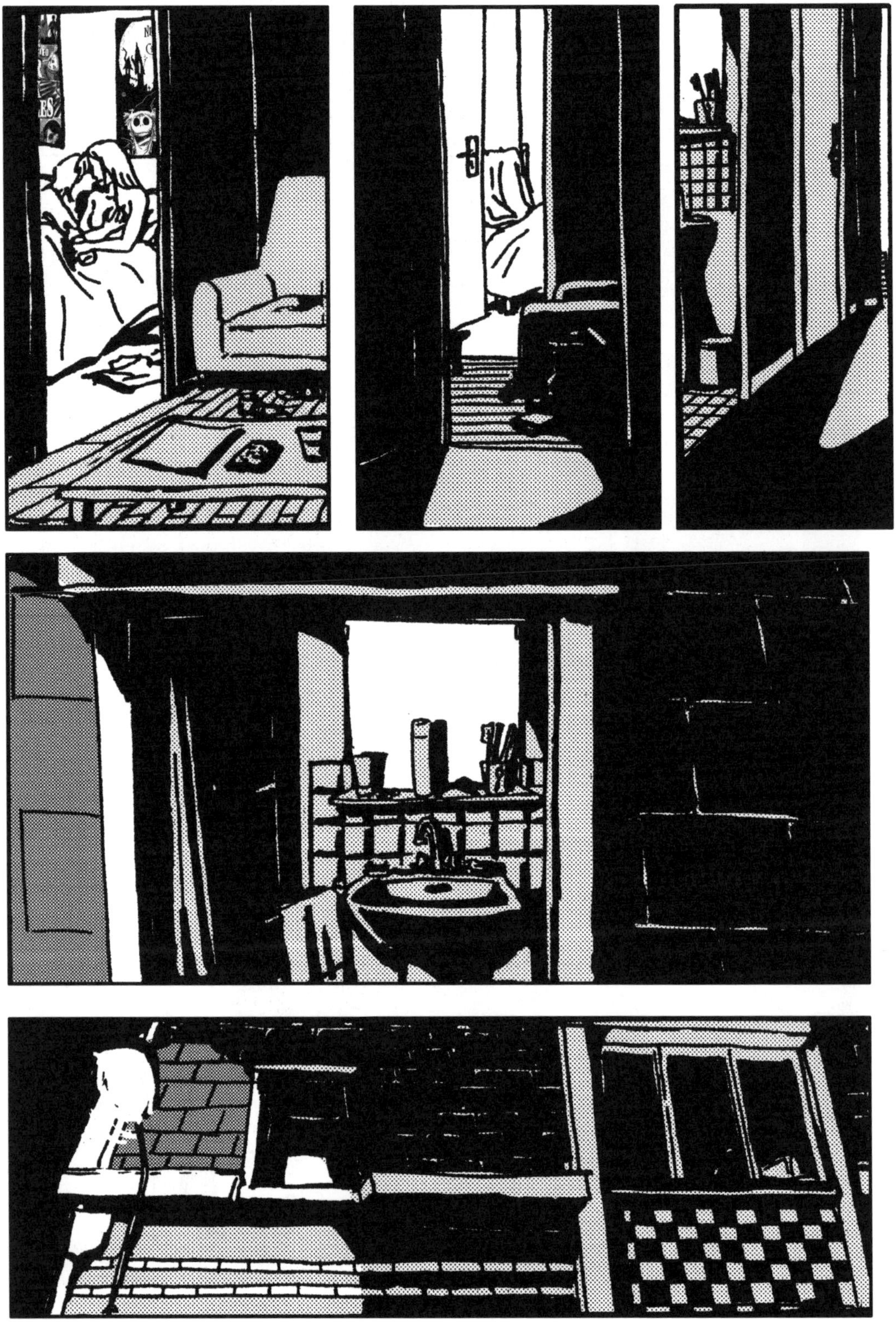

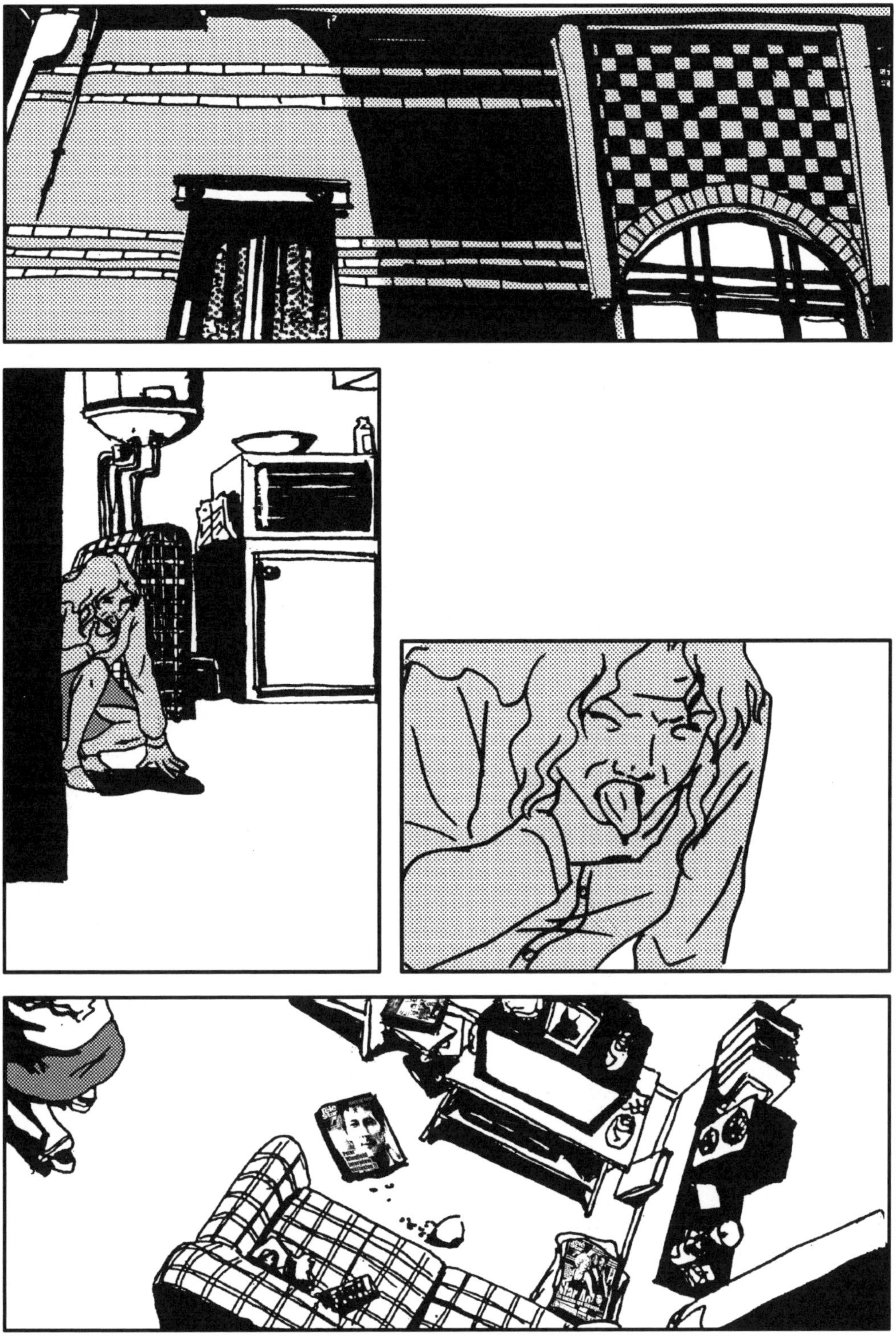

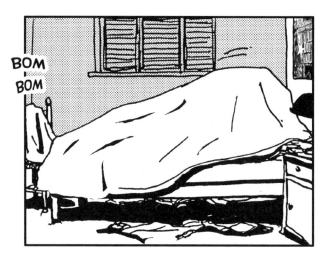

BOM
BOM

BOM
BOM

?

WE EXPECTING ANYONE?

NO

UH, YES?

...!

WHAT'S THE MATTER?

...!

WHO IS IT?

IT'S THE NEIGHBOR! SHE SEEMS TO HAVE...

... A REAL BIG PROBLEM!

...

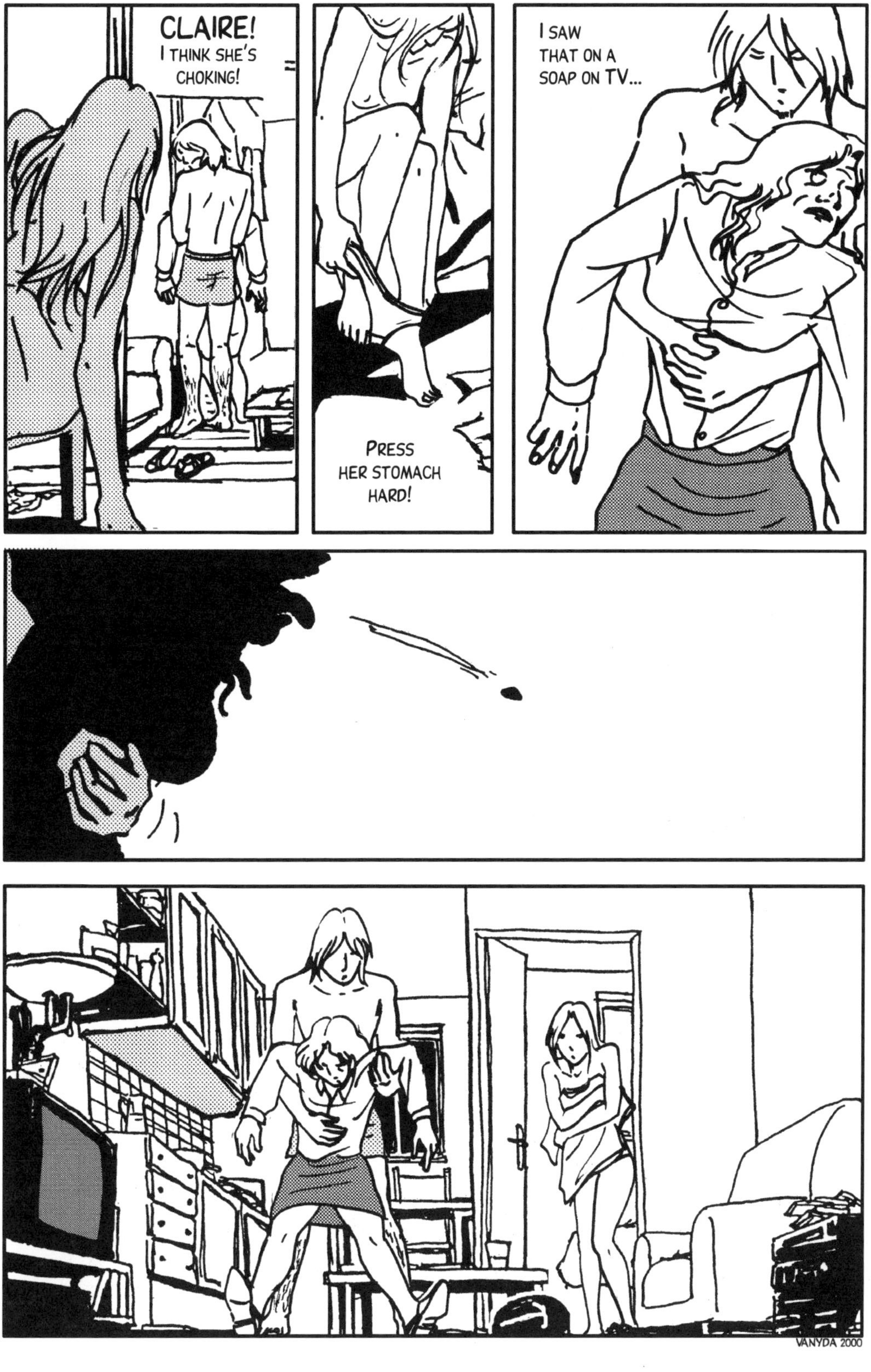
CLAIRE!
I THINK SHE'S CHOKING!
PRESS HER STOMACH HARD!
I SAW THAT ON A SOAP ON TV...
VANYDA 2000

Chapter 3
Sketches
(One Saturday morning)

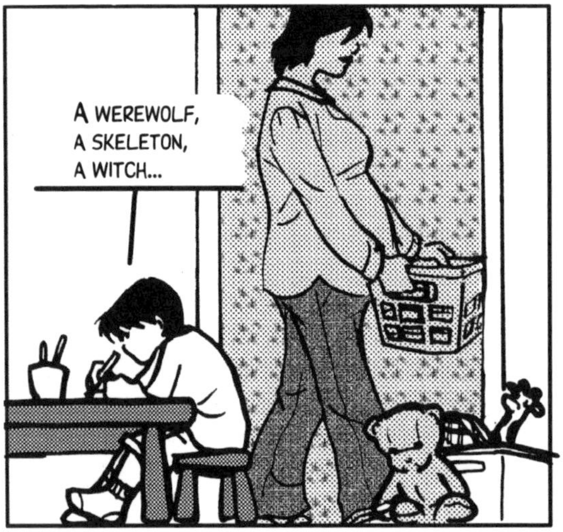
A WEREWOLF,
A SKELETON,
A WITCH...

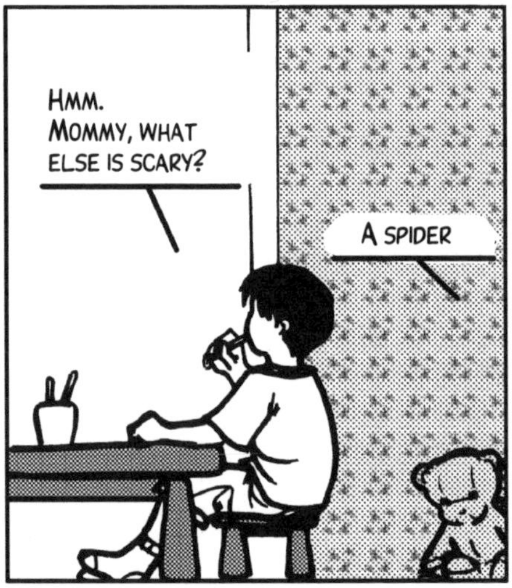
HMM.
MOMMY, WHAT
ELSE IS SCARY?
A SPIDER

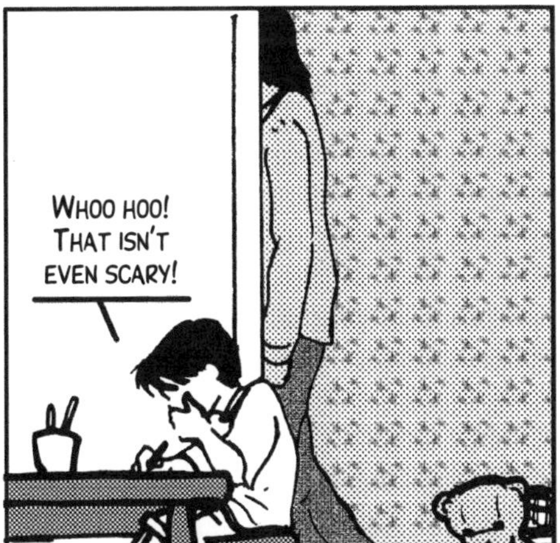
WHOO HOO! THAT ISN'T EVEN SCARY!
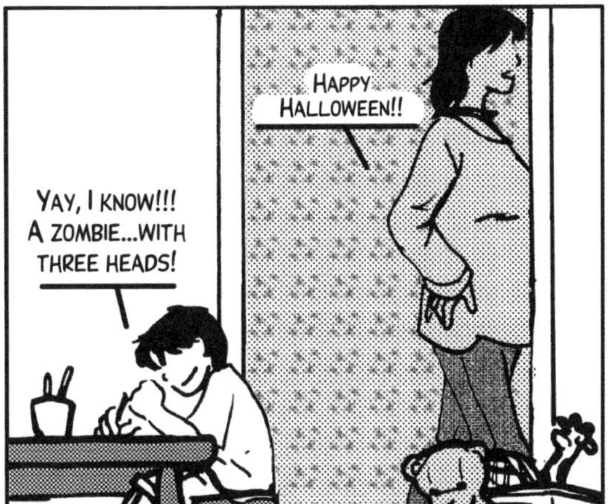
HAPPY HALLOWEEN!!
YAY, I KNOW!!! A ZOMBIE...WITH THREE HEADS!

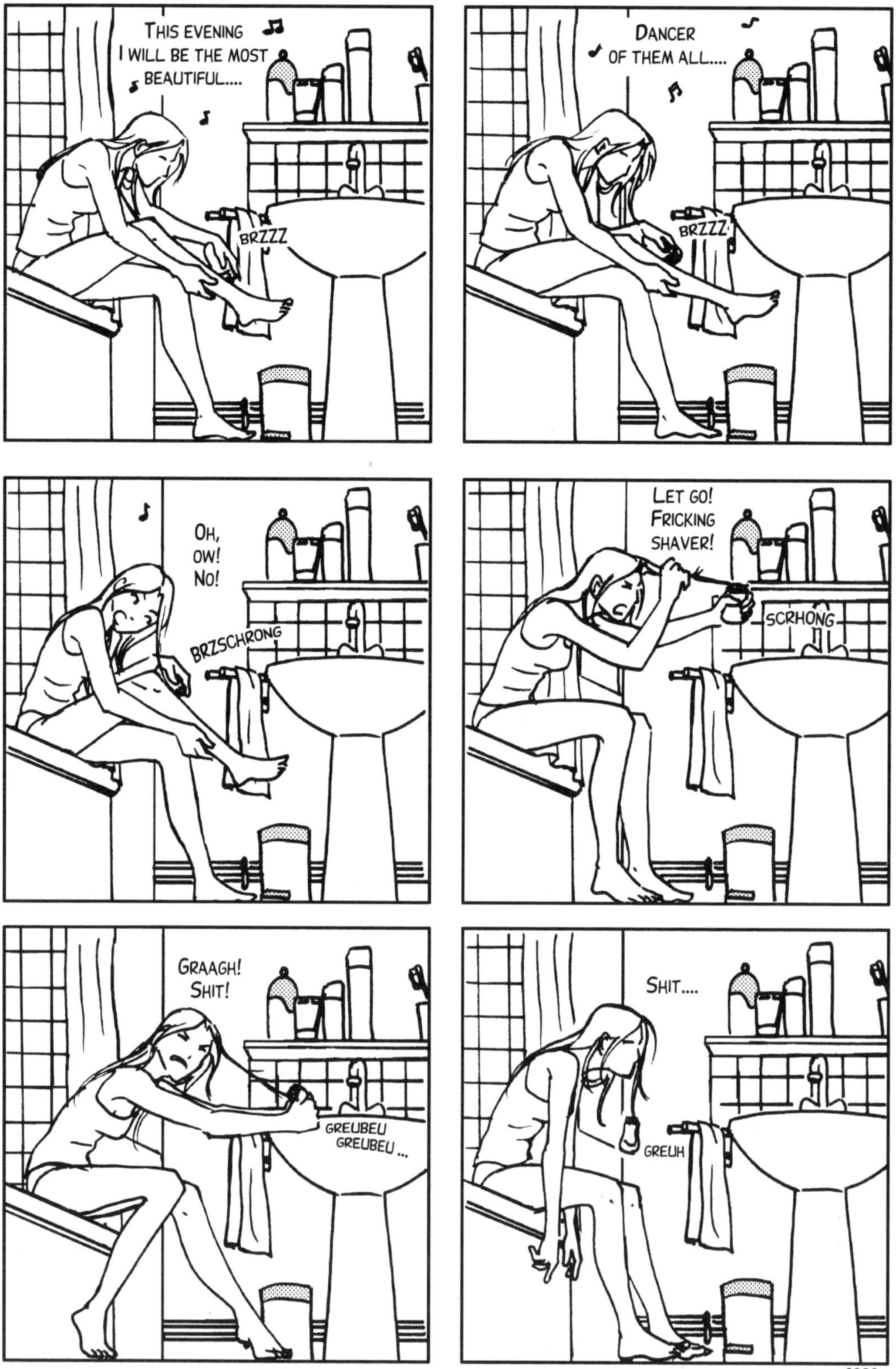
THIS EVENING I WILL BE THE MOST BEAUTIFUL....
BRZZZ
DANCER OF THEM ALL....
BRZZZ
OH, OW! NO!
BRZSCHRONG
LET GO! FRICKING SHAVER!
SCRHONG
GRAAGH! SHIT!
GREUBEU GREUBEU ...
SHIT....
GREUH
VANYDA 2000

Chapter 4
A Tale of Peanuts
(One Saturday evening)

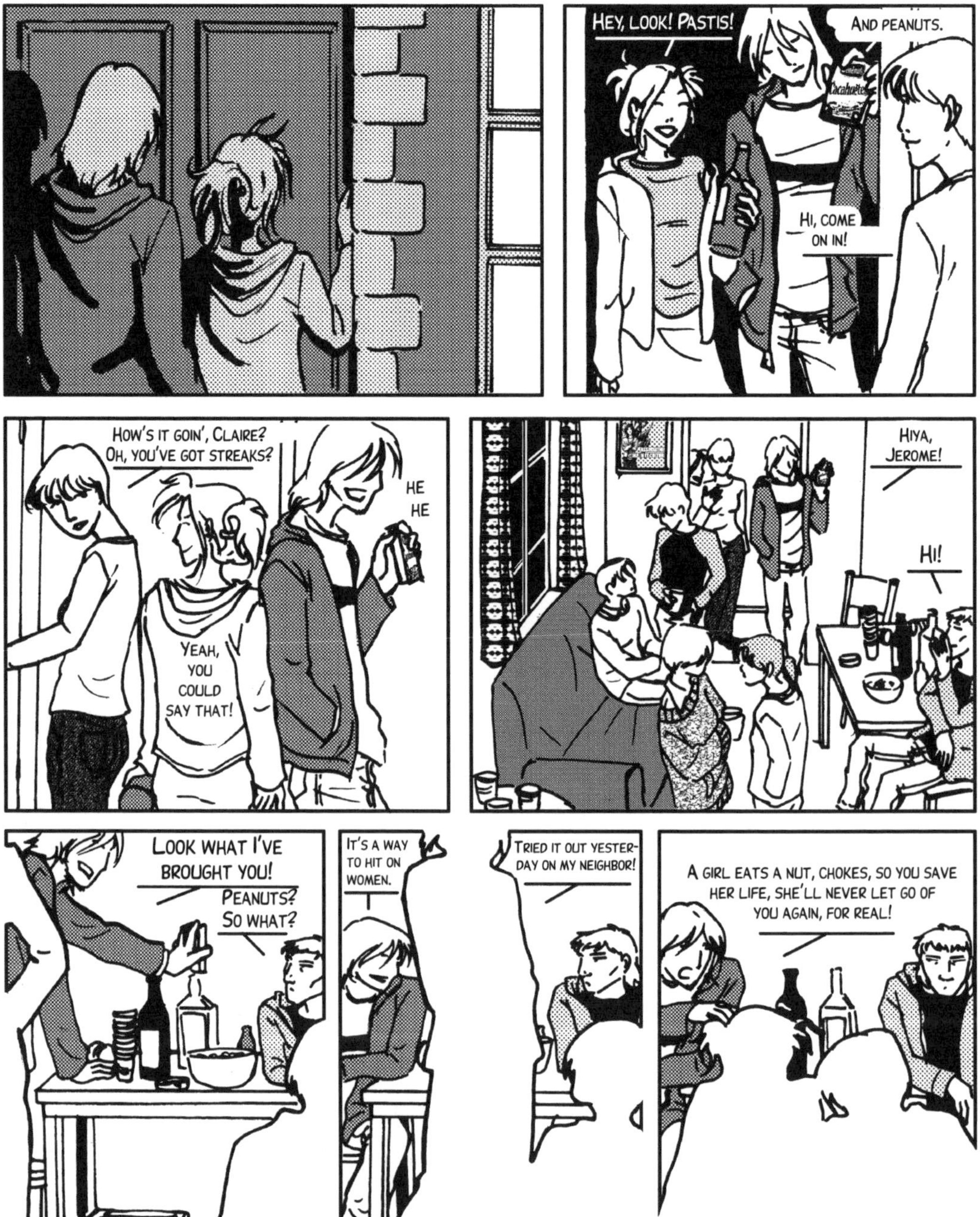
HEY, LOOK! PASTIS!
AND PEANUTS.
Cacahuètes
HI, COME ON IN!
HOW'S IT GOIN', CLAIRE? OH, YOU'VE GOT STREAKS?
HE HE
YEAH, YOU COULD SAY THAT!
HIYA, JEROME!
HI!
LOOK WHAT I'VE BROUGHT YOU!
PEANUTS? SO WHAT?
IT'S A WAY TO HIT ON WOMEN.
TRIED IT OUT YESTERDAY ON MY NEIGHBOR!
A GIRL EATS A NUT, CHOKES, SO YOU SAVE HER LIFE, SHE'LL NEVER LET GO OF YOU AGAIN, FOR REAL!

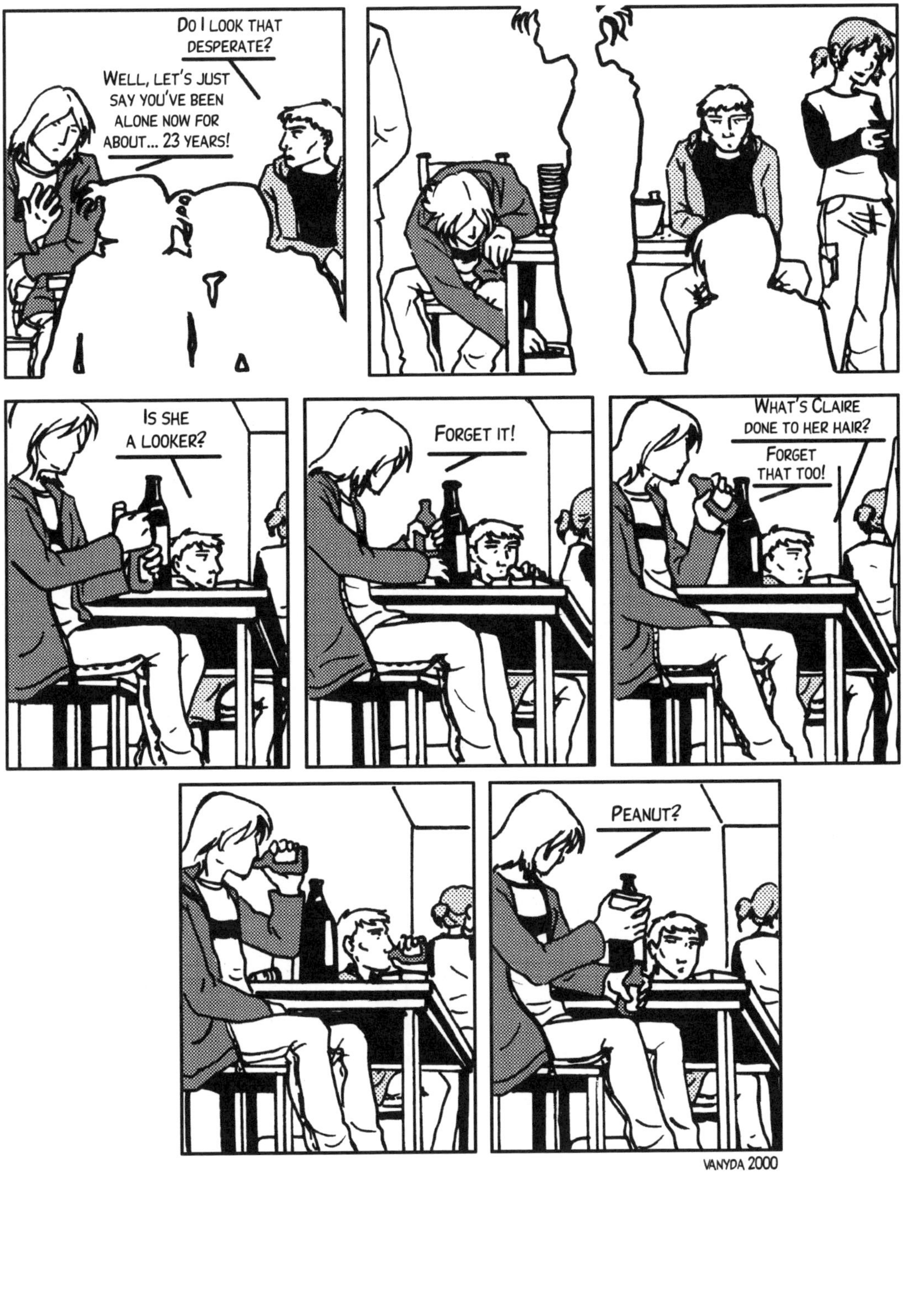
DO I LOOK THAT DESPERATE?
WELL, LET'S JUST SAY YOU'VE BEEN ALONE NOW FOR ABOUT... 23 YEARS!
IS SHE A LOOKER?
FORGET IT!
WHAT'S CLAIRE DONE TO HER HAIR?
FORGET THAT TOO!
PEANUT?
VANYDA 2000

Chapter 5
Just like every
Sunday....

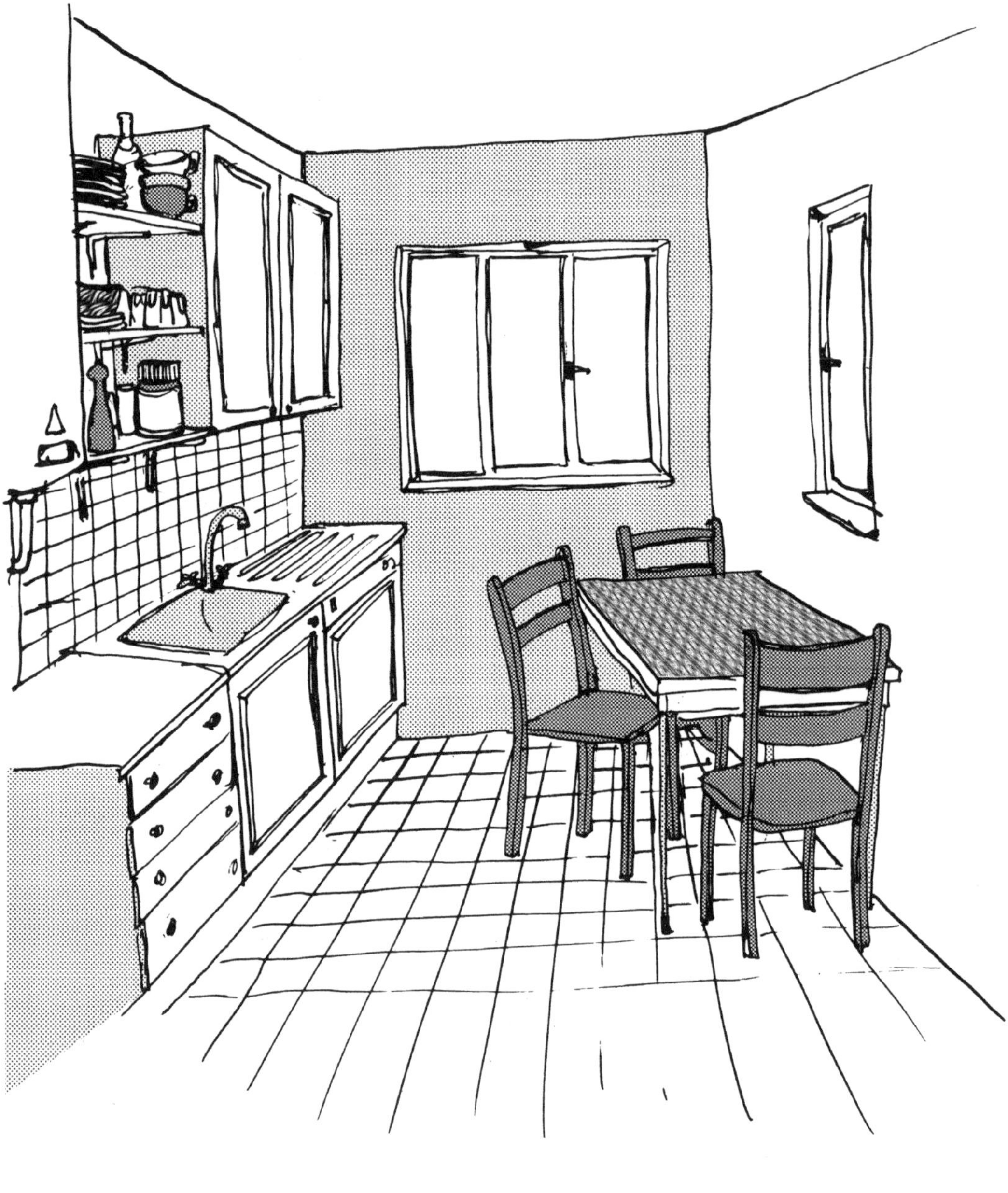

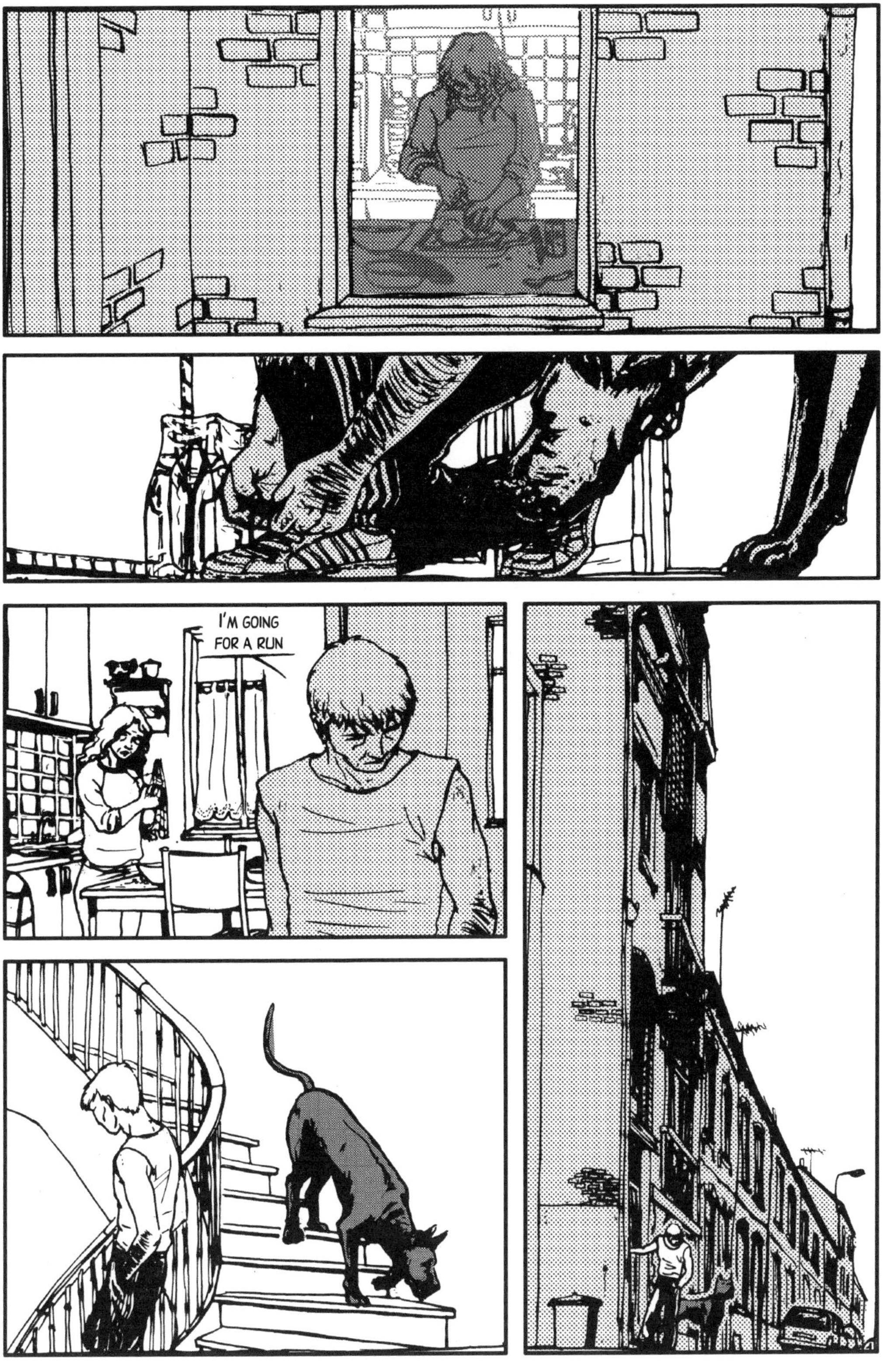
I'M GOING FOR A RUN

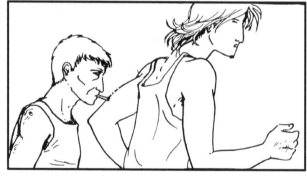

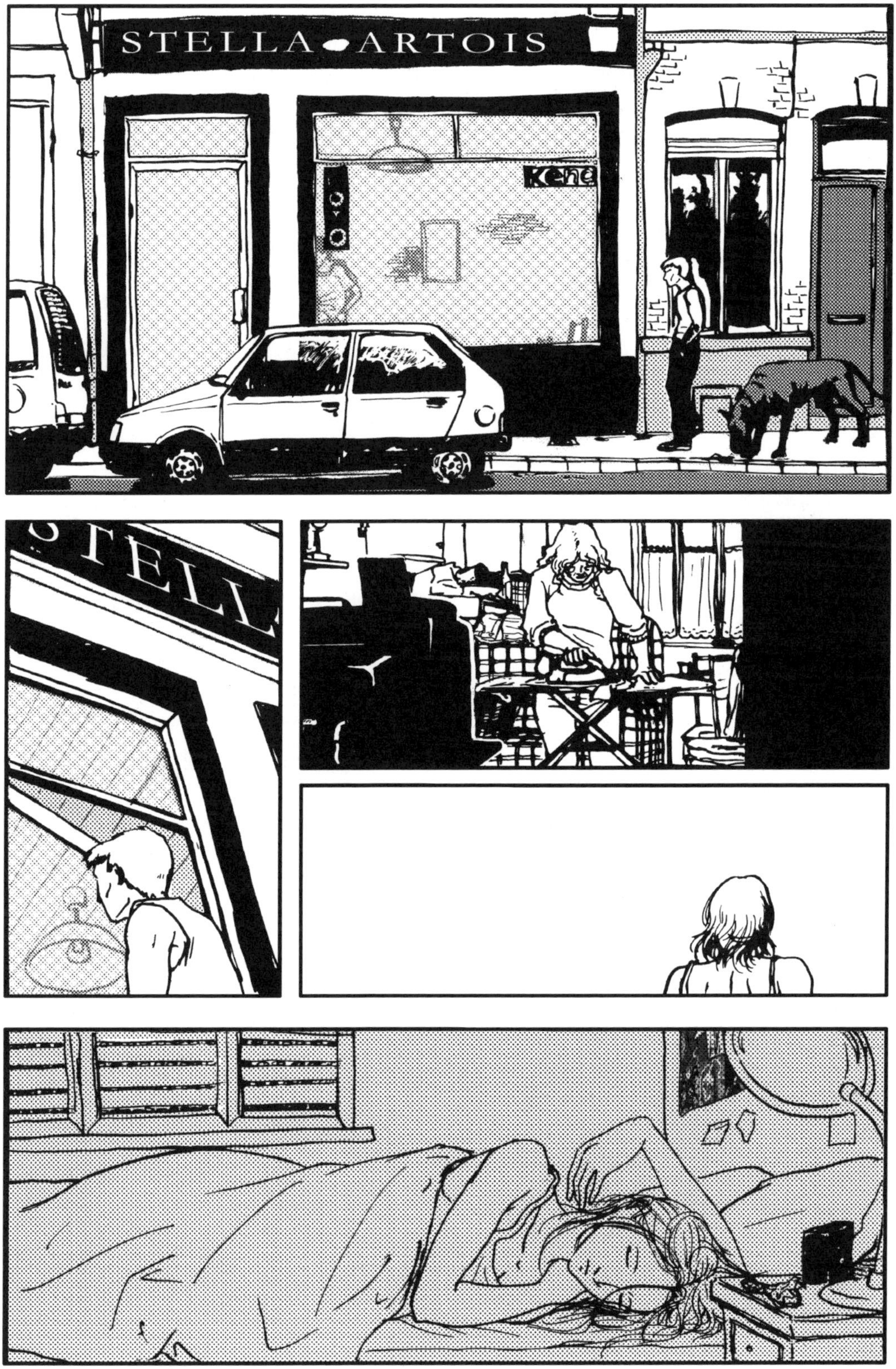
STELLA ARTOIS
STELL

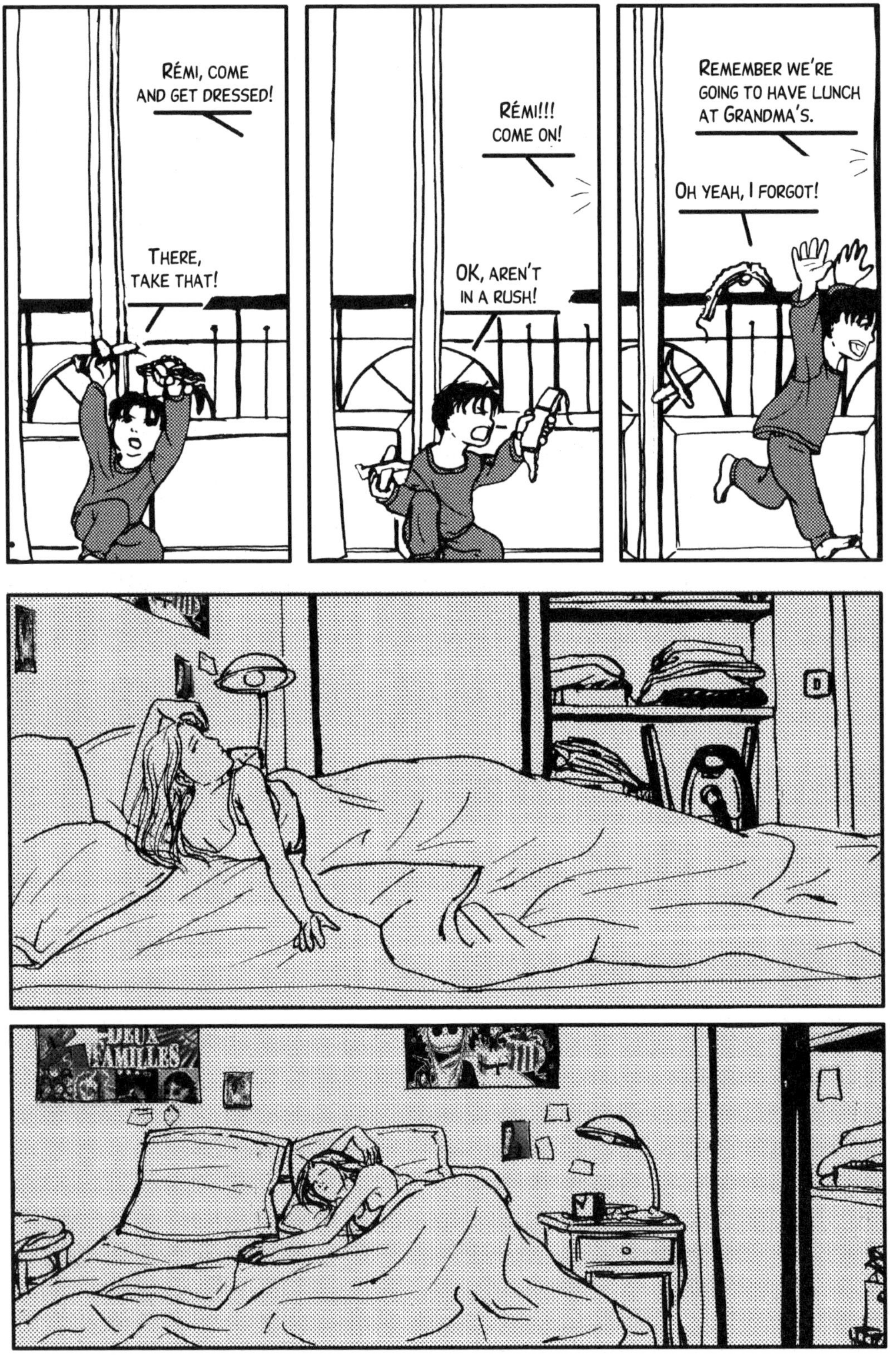
RÉMI, COME AND GET DRESSED!
THERE, TAKE THAT!
RÉMI!!! COME ON!
OK, AREN'T IN A RUSH!
REMEMBER WE'RE GOING TO HAVE LUNCH AT GRANDMA'S.
OH YEAH, I FORGOT!

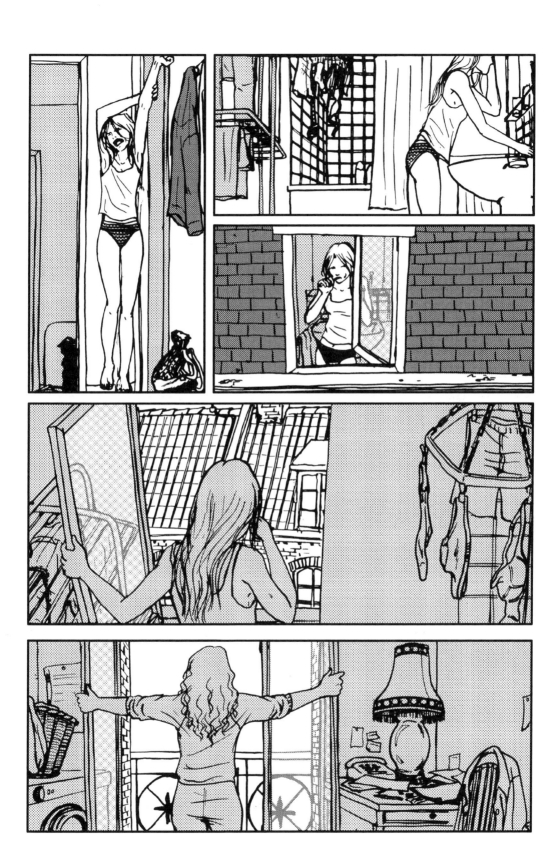

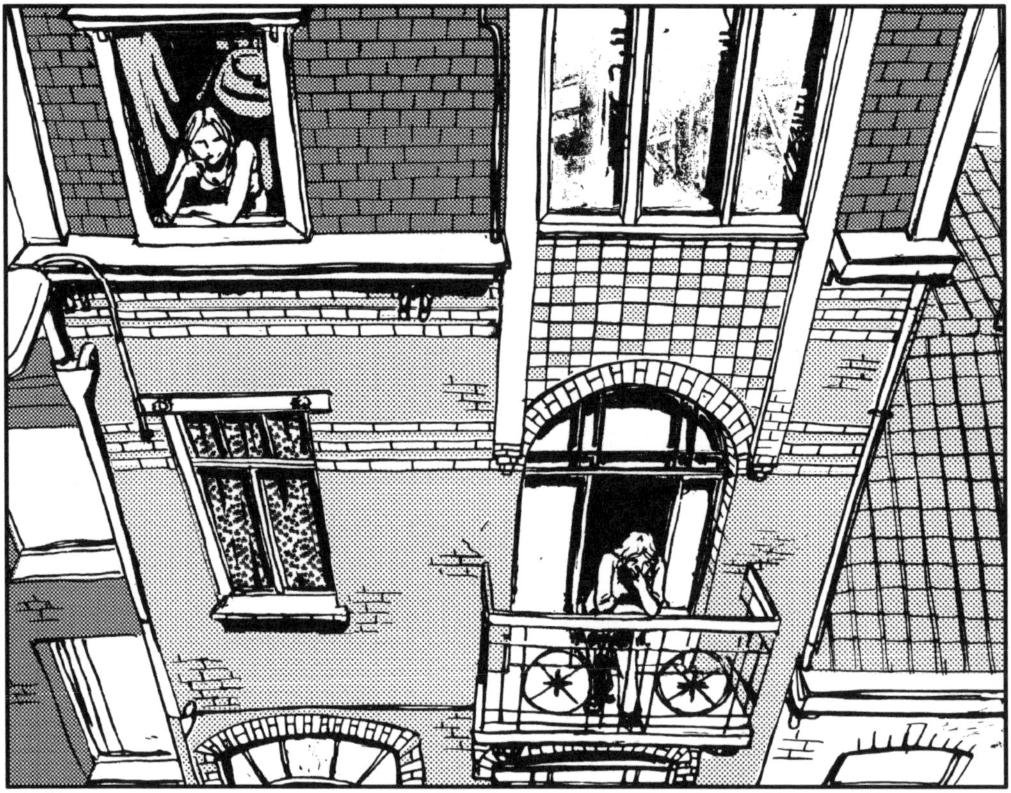

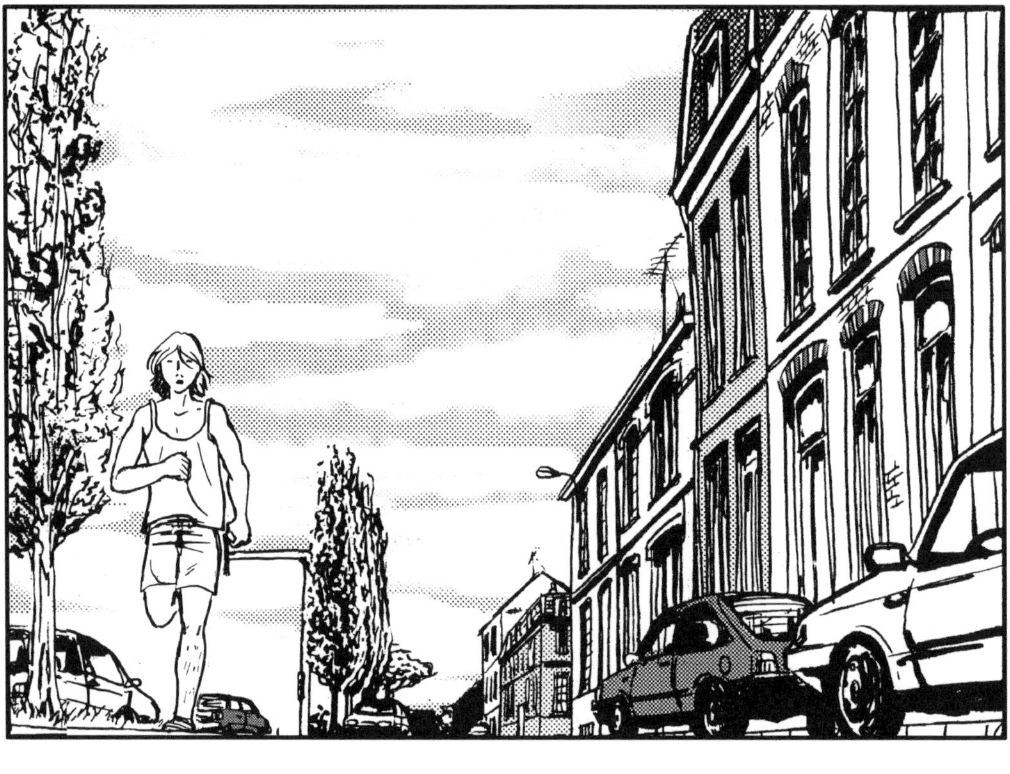

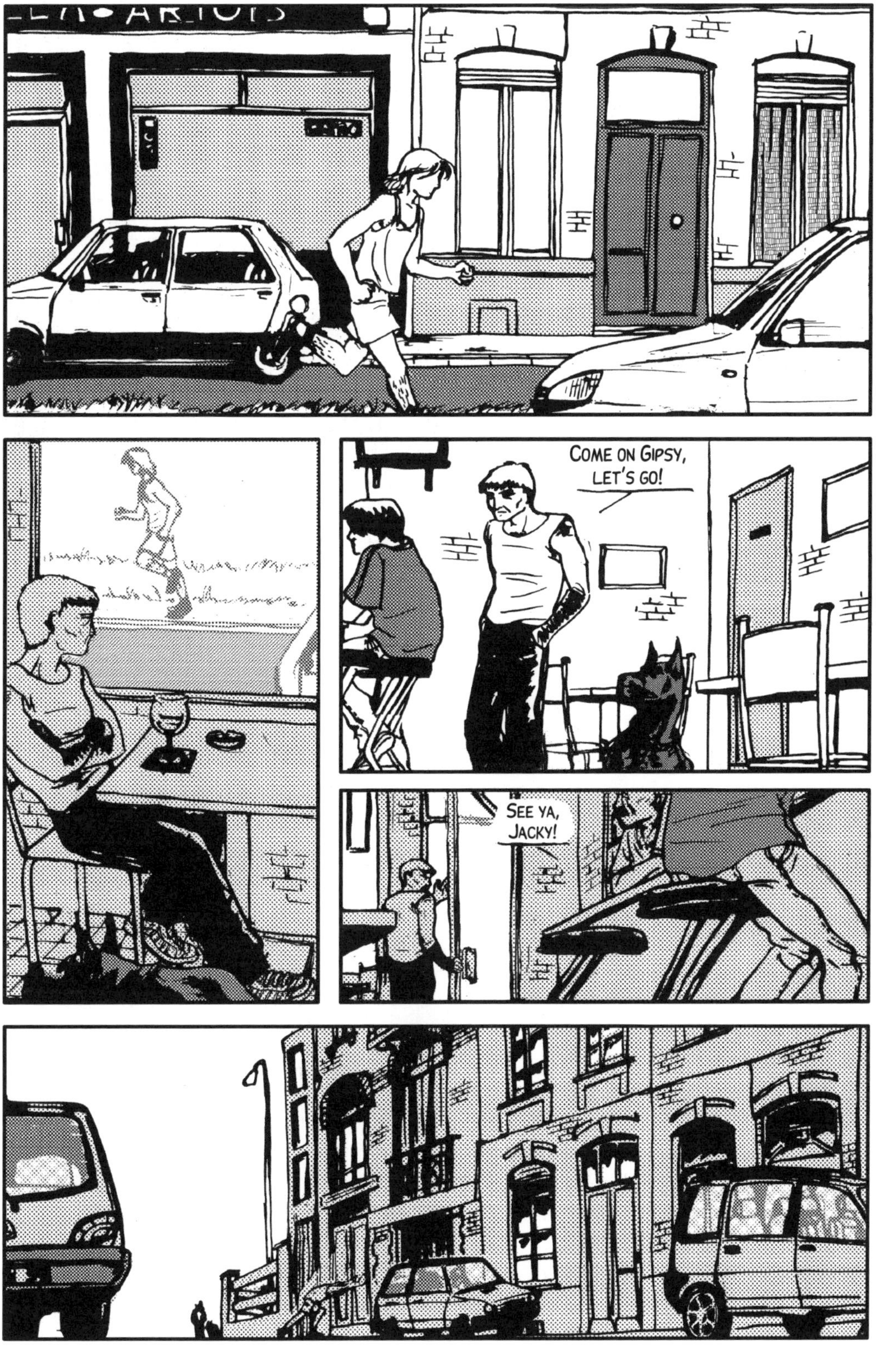

COME ON GIPSY, LET'S GO!
SEE YA, JACKY!

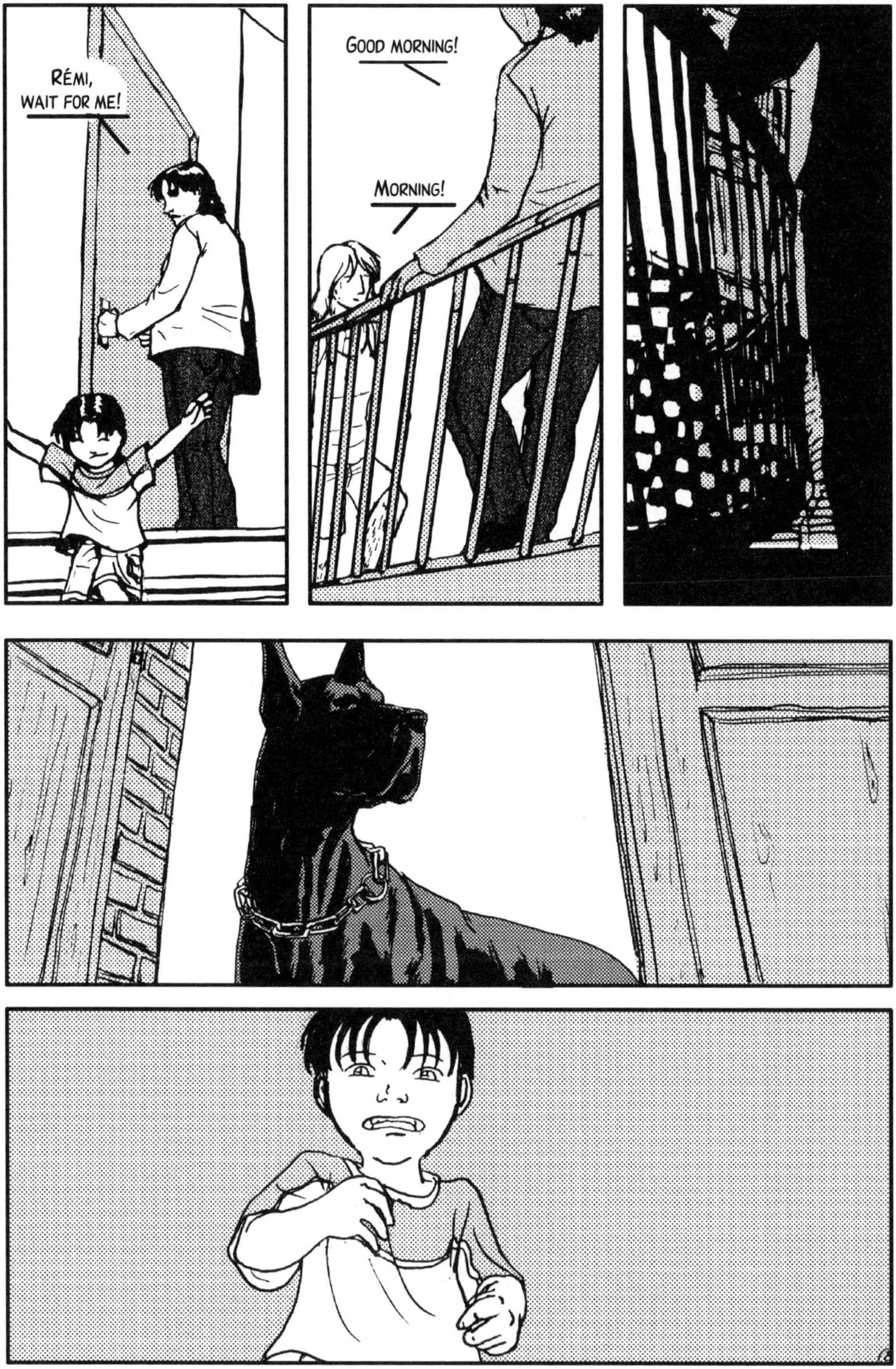
RÉMI,
WAIT FOR ME!
GOOD MORNING!
MORNING!

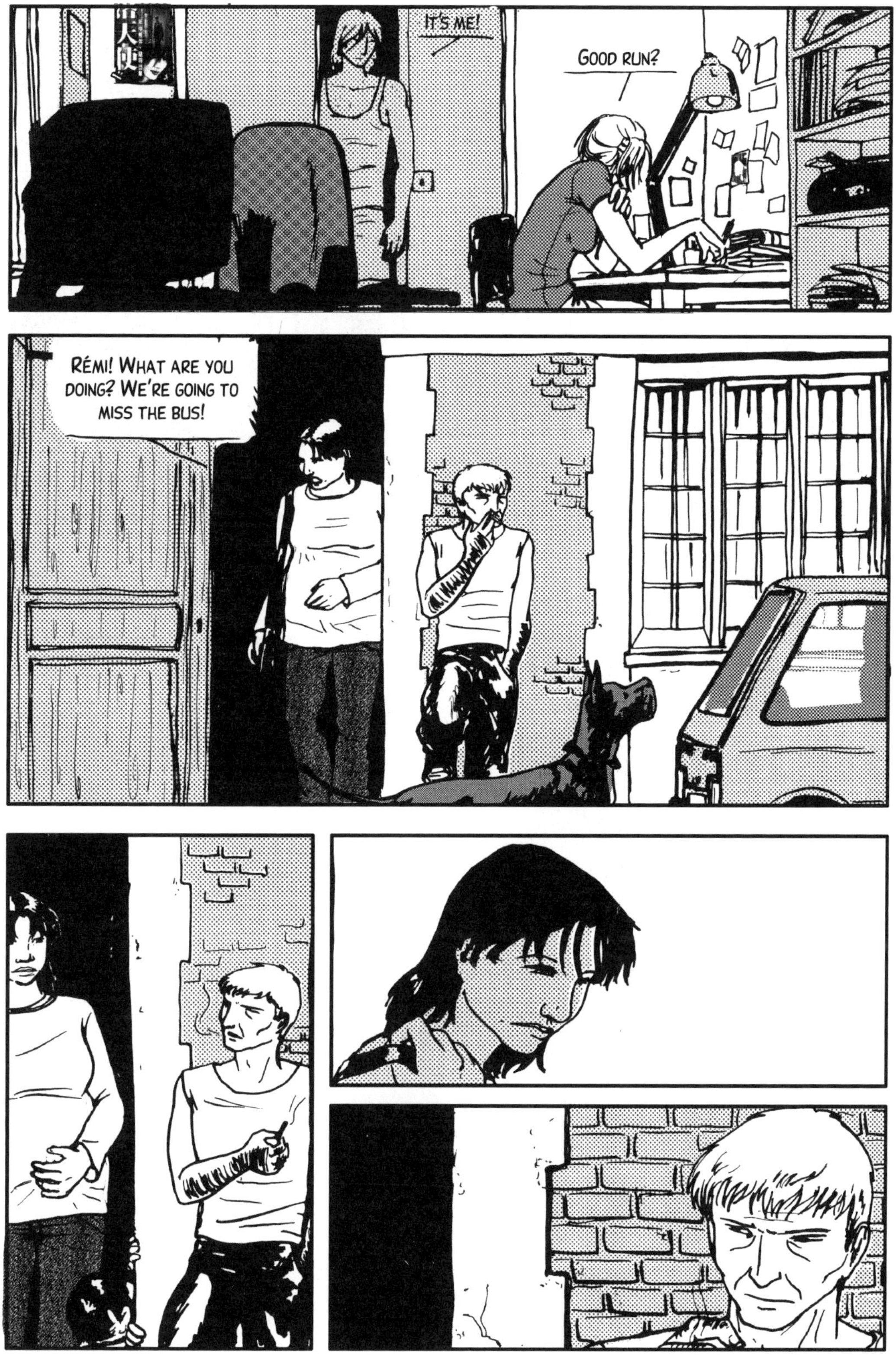
IT'S ME!
GOOD RUN?
RÉMI! WHAT ARE YOU DOING? WE'RE GOING TO MISS THE BUS!

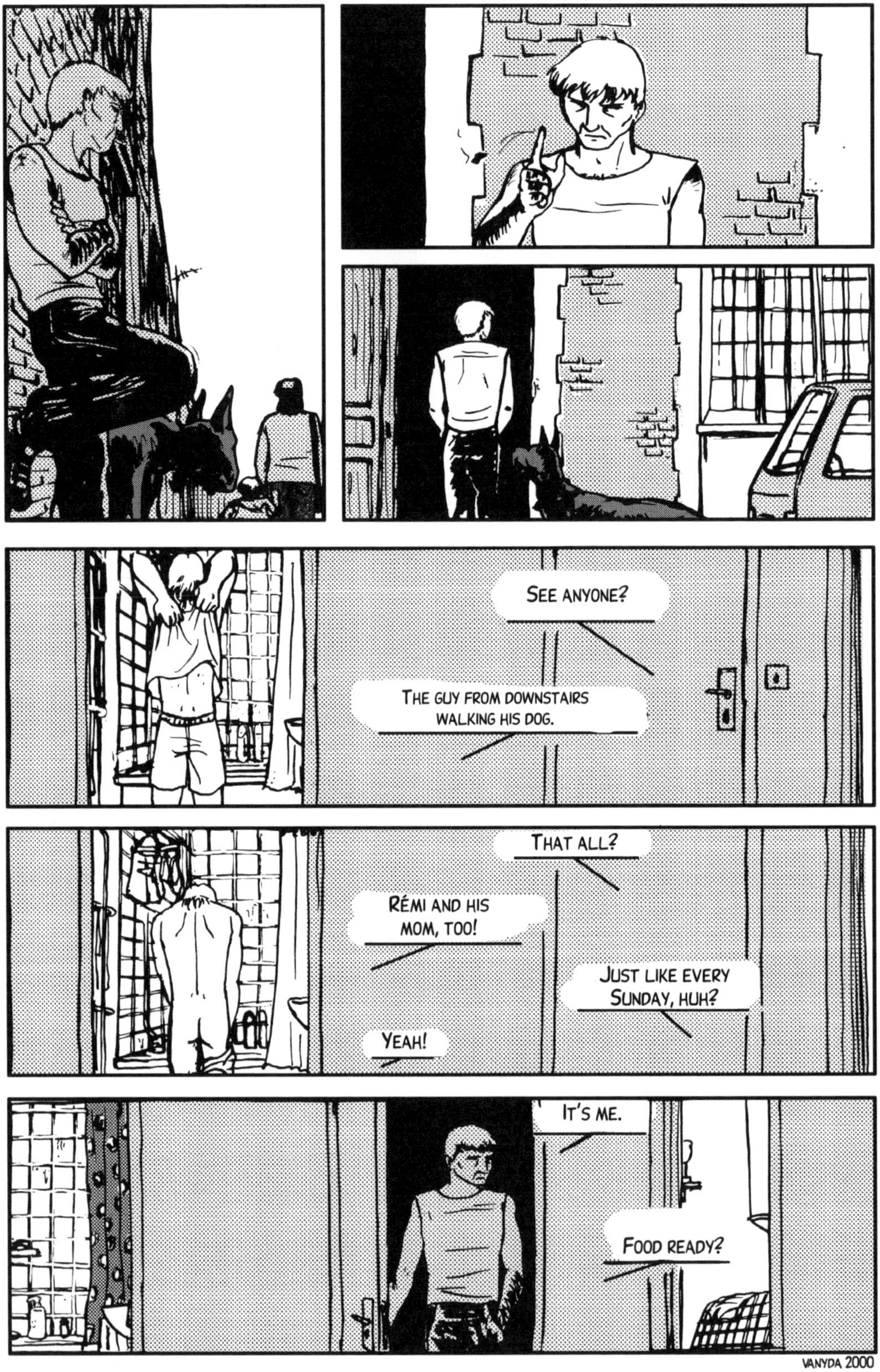
SEE ANYONE?
THE GUY FROM DOWNSTAIRS WALKING HIS DOG.
THAT ALL?
RÉMI AND HIS MOM, TOO!
JUST LIKE EVERY SUNDAY, HUH?
YEAH!
IT'S ME.
FOOD READY?
VANYDA 2000

Chapter 6
So what is she doing there?

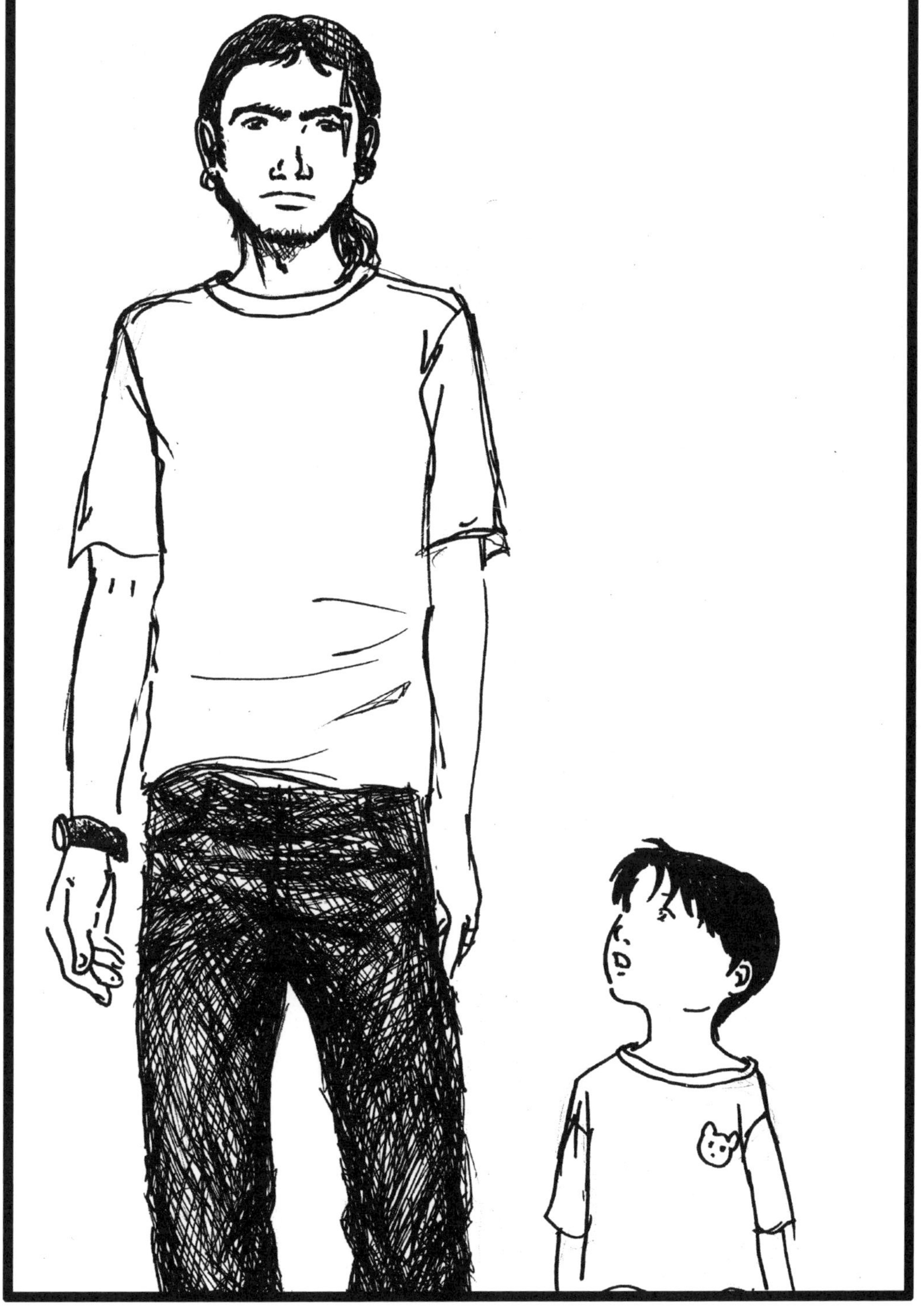

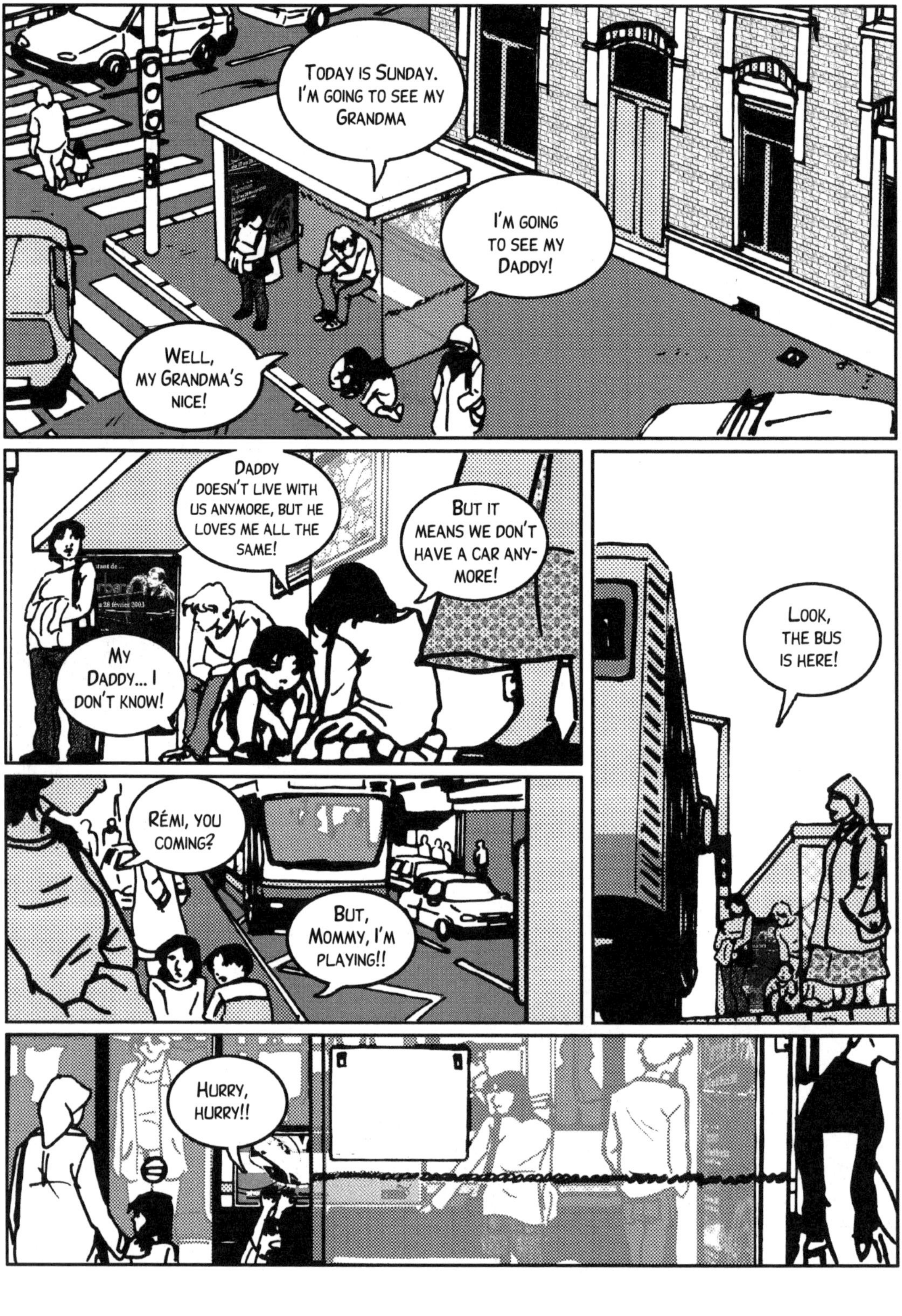
TODAY IS SUNDAY. I'M GOING TO SEE MY GRANDMA
I'M GOING TO SEE MY DADDY!
WELL, MY GRANDMA'S NICE!
DADDY DOESN'T LIVE WITH US ANYMORE, BUT HE LOVES ME ALL THE SAME!
BUT IT MEANS WE DON'T HAVE A CAR ANY-MORE!
MY DADDY... I DON'T KNOW!
RÉMI, YOU COMING?
BUT, MOMMY, I'M PLAYING!!
LOOK, THE BUS IS HERE!
HURRY, HURRY!!

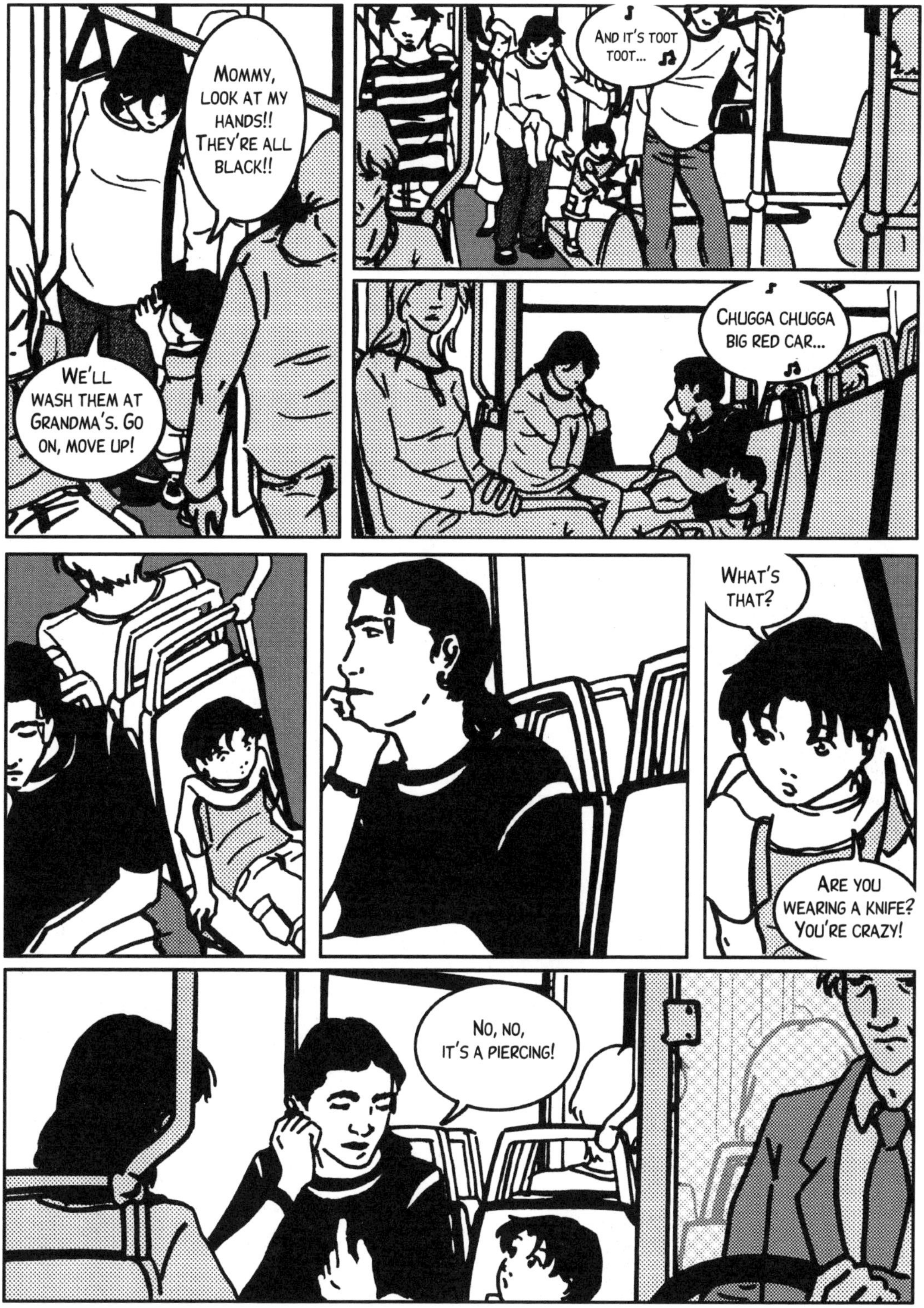
MOMMY, LOOK AT MY HANDS!! THEY'RE ALL BLACK!!
WE'LL WASH THEM AT GRANDMA'S. GO ON, MOVE UP!
AND IT'S TOOT TOOT...
CHUGGA CHUGGA BIG RED CAR...
WHAT'S THAT?
ARE YOU WEARING A KNIFE? YOU'RE CRAZY!
NO, NO, IT'S A PIERCING!

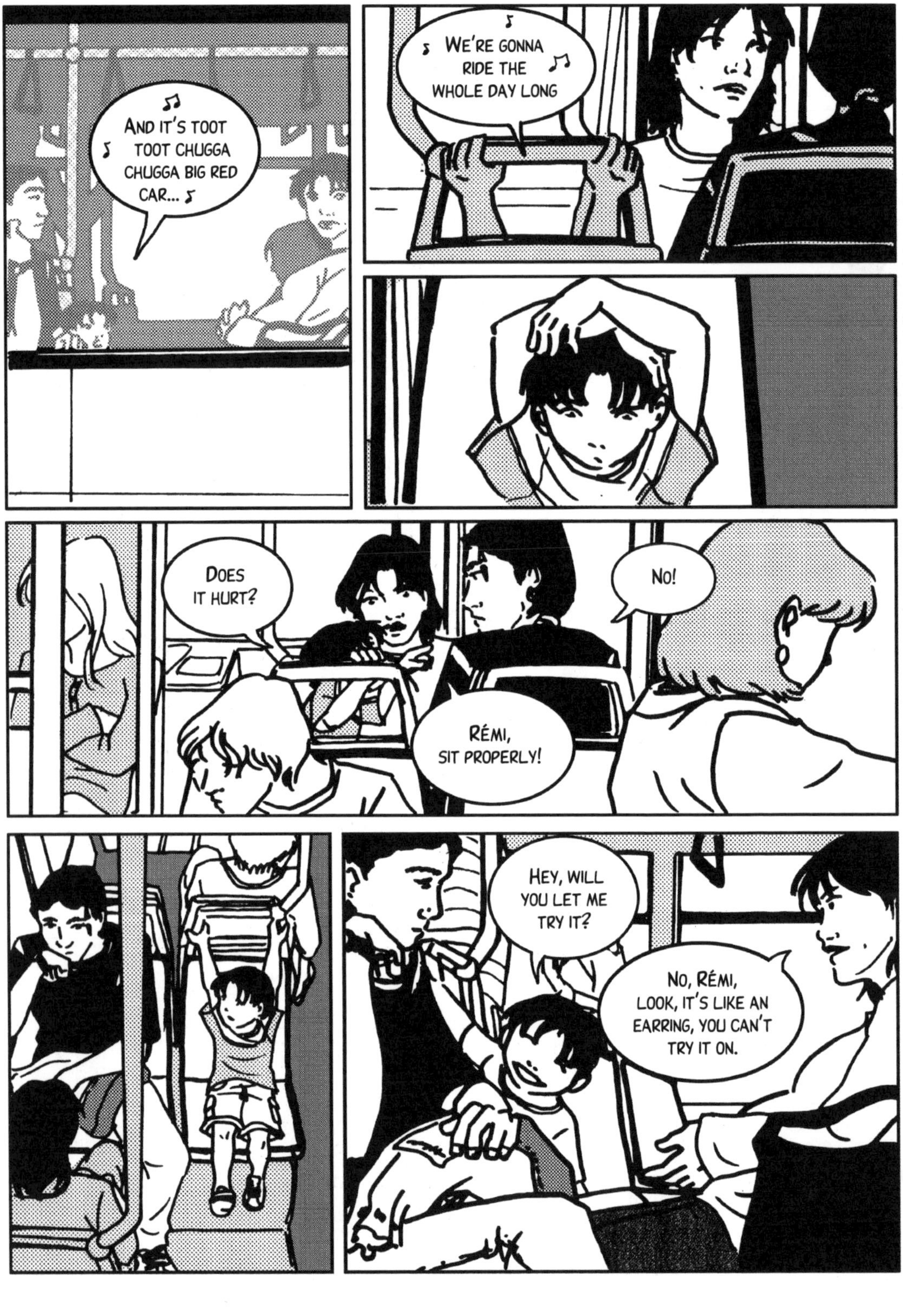
AND IT'S TOOT TOOT CHUGGA CHUGGA BIG RED CAR...
WE'RE GONNA RIDE THE WHOLE DAY LONG
DOES IT HURT?
NO!
RÉMI, SIT PROPERLY!
HEY, WILL YOU LET ME TRY IT?
NO, RÉMI, LOOK, IT'S LIKE AN EARRING, YOU CAN'T TRY IT ON.

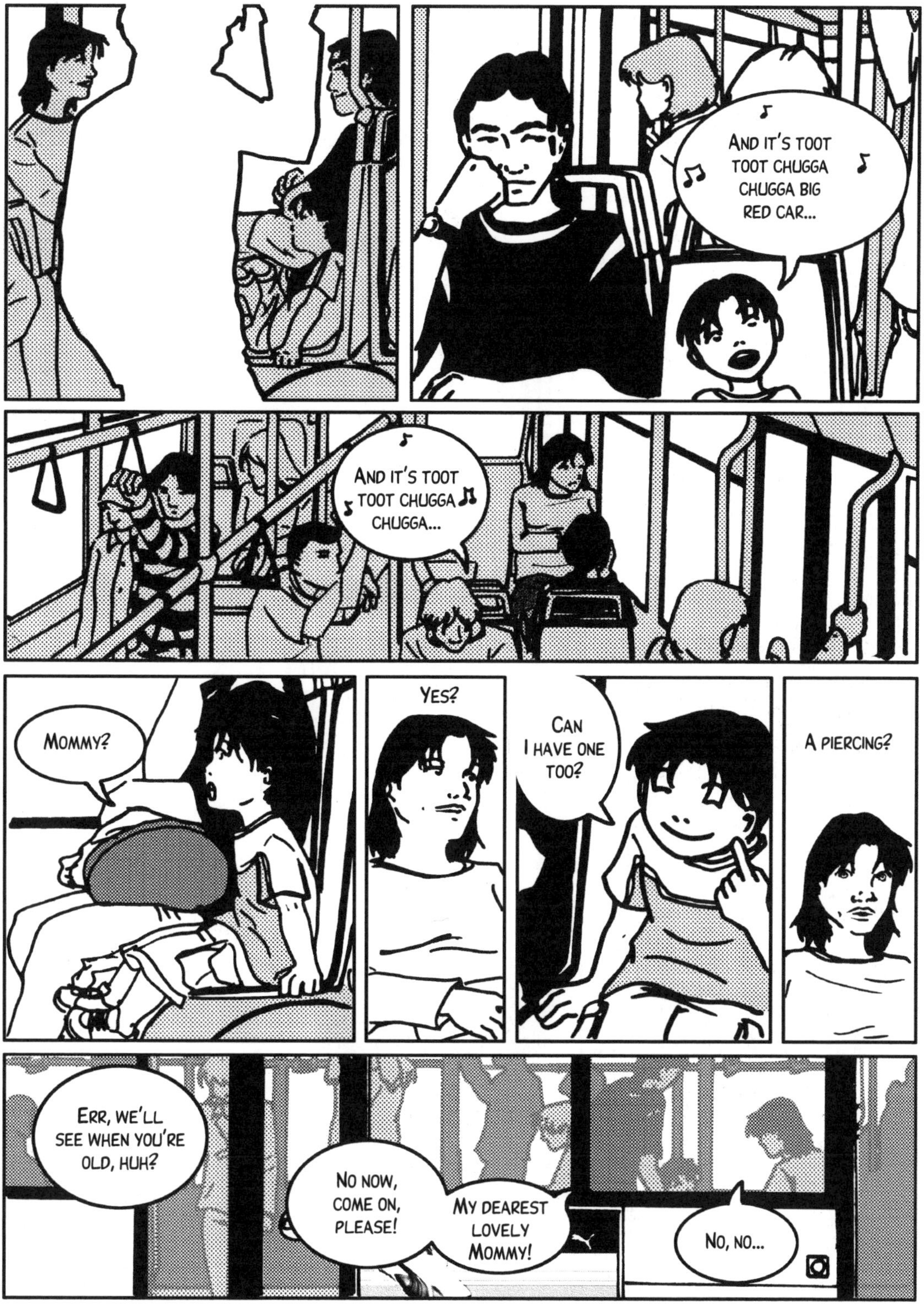
AND IT'S TOOT TOOT CHUGGA CHUGGA BIG RED CAR...
AND IT'S TOOT TOOT CHUGGA CHUGGA...
MOMMY?
YES?
CAN I HAVE ONE TOO?
A PIERCING?
ERR, WE'LL SEE WHEN YOU'RE OLD, HUH?
NO NOW, COME ON, PLEASE!
MY DEAREST LOVELY MOMMY!
NO, NO...

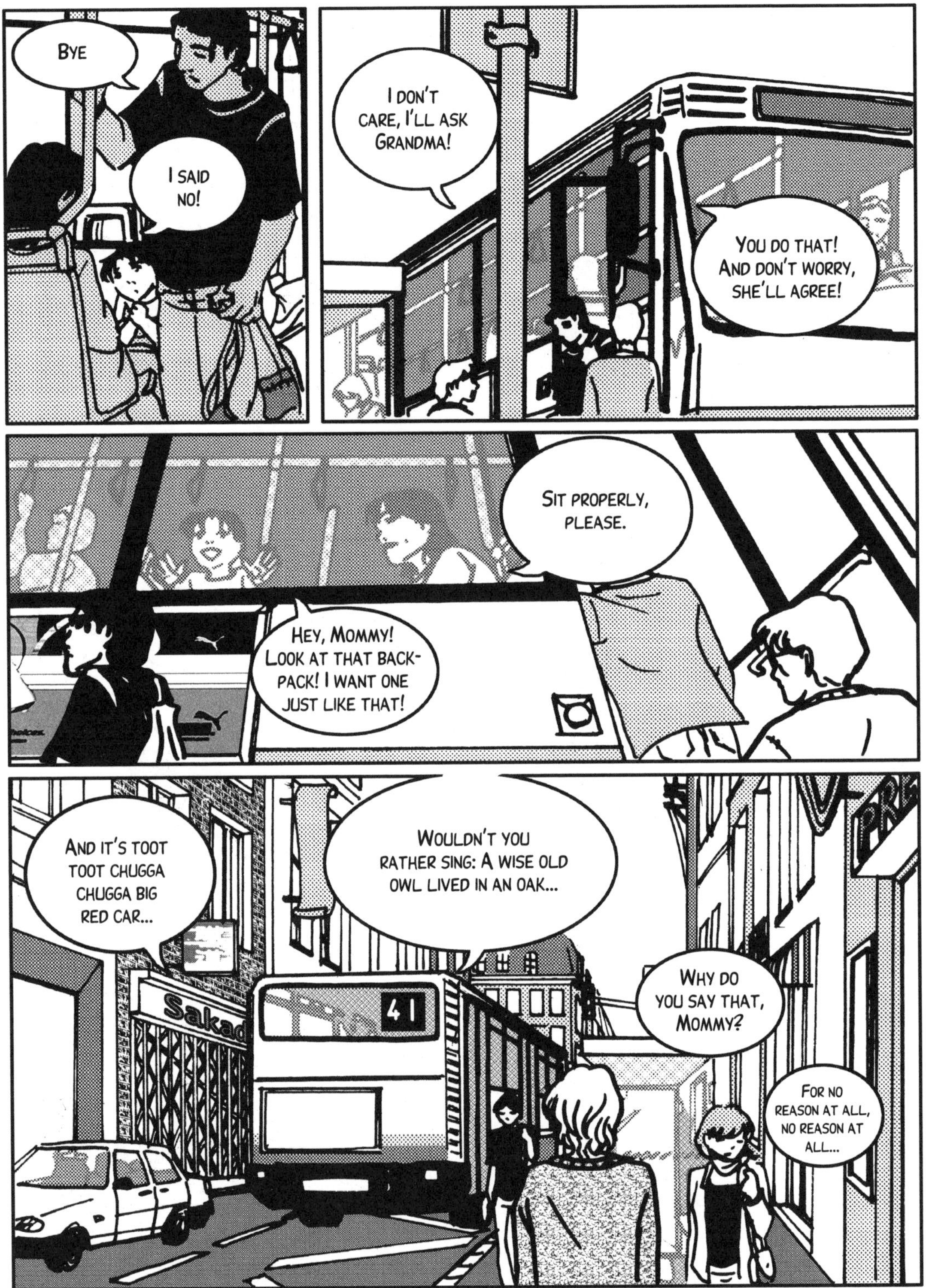

BYE
I SAID NO!
I DON'T CARE, I'LL ASK GRANDMA!
YOU DO THAT! AND DON'T WORRY, SHE'LL AGREE!
SIT PROPERLY, PLEASE.
HEY, MOMMY! LOOK AT THAT BACK-PACK! I WANT ONE JUST LIKE THAT!
AND IT'S TOOT TOOT CHUGGA CHUGGA BIG RED CAR...
WOULDN'T YOU RATHER SING: A WISE OLD OWL LIVED IN AN OAK...
41
WHY DO YOU SAY THAT, MOMMY?
FOR NO REASON AT ALL, NO REASON AT ALL...

VANYDA 2000

Fluoride Interlude

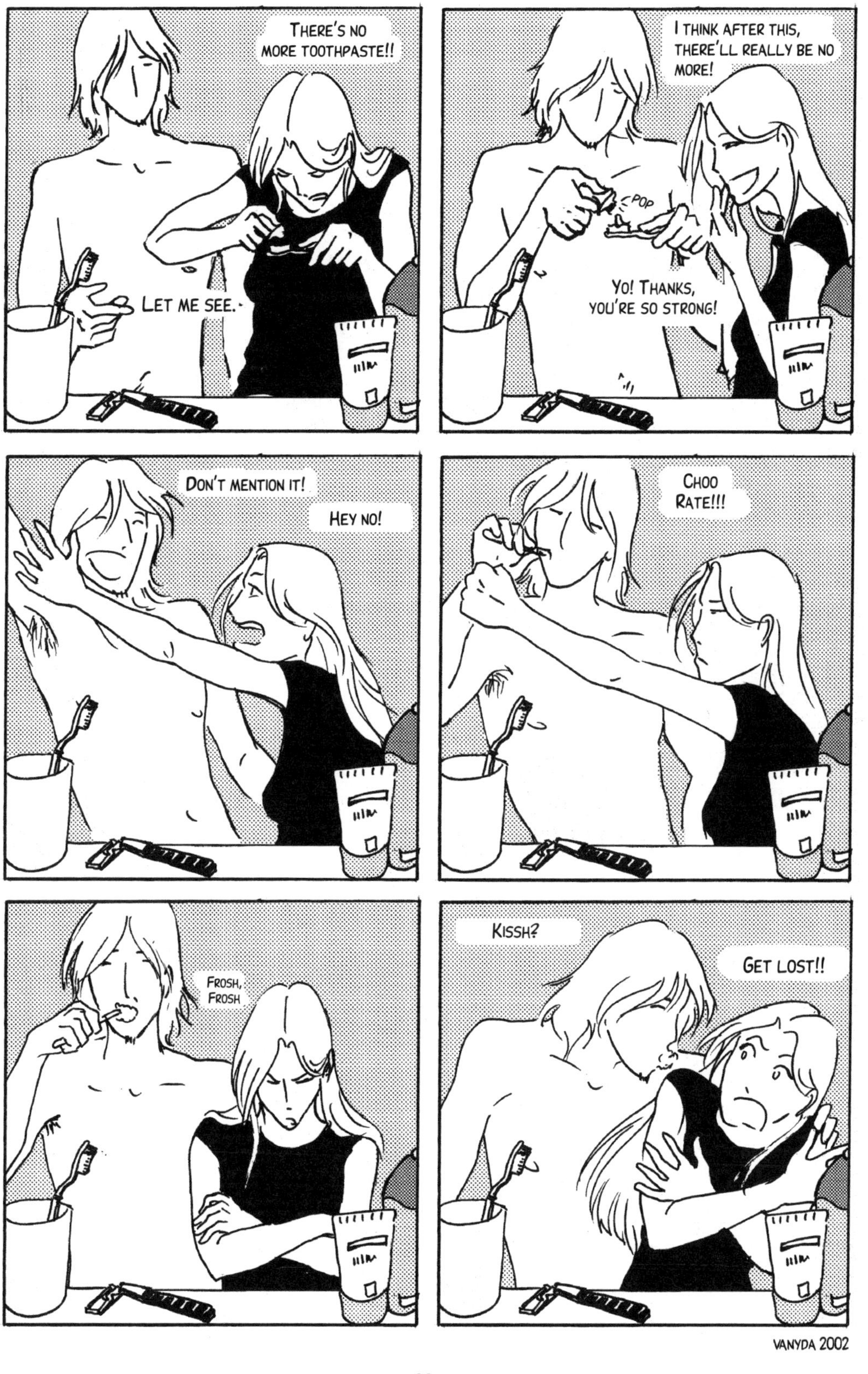

THERE'S NO MORE TOOTHPASTE!!
LET ME SEE.
I THINK AFTER THIS, THERE'LL REALLY BE NO MORE!
POP
YO! THANKS, YOU'RE SO STRONG!
DON'T MENTION IT!
HEY NO!
CHOO RATE!!!
FROSH, FROSH
KISSH?
GET LOST!!

VANYDA 2002

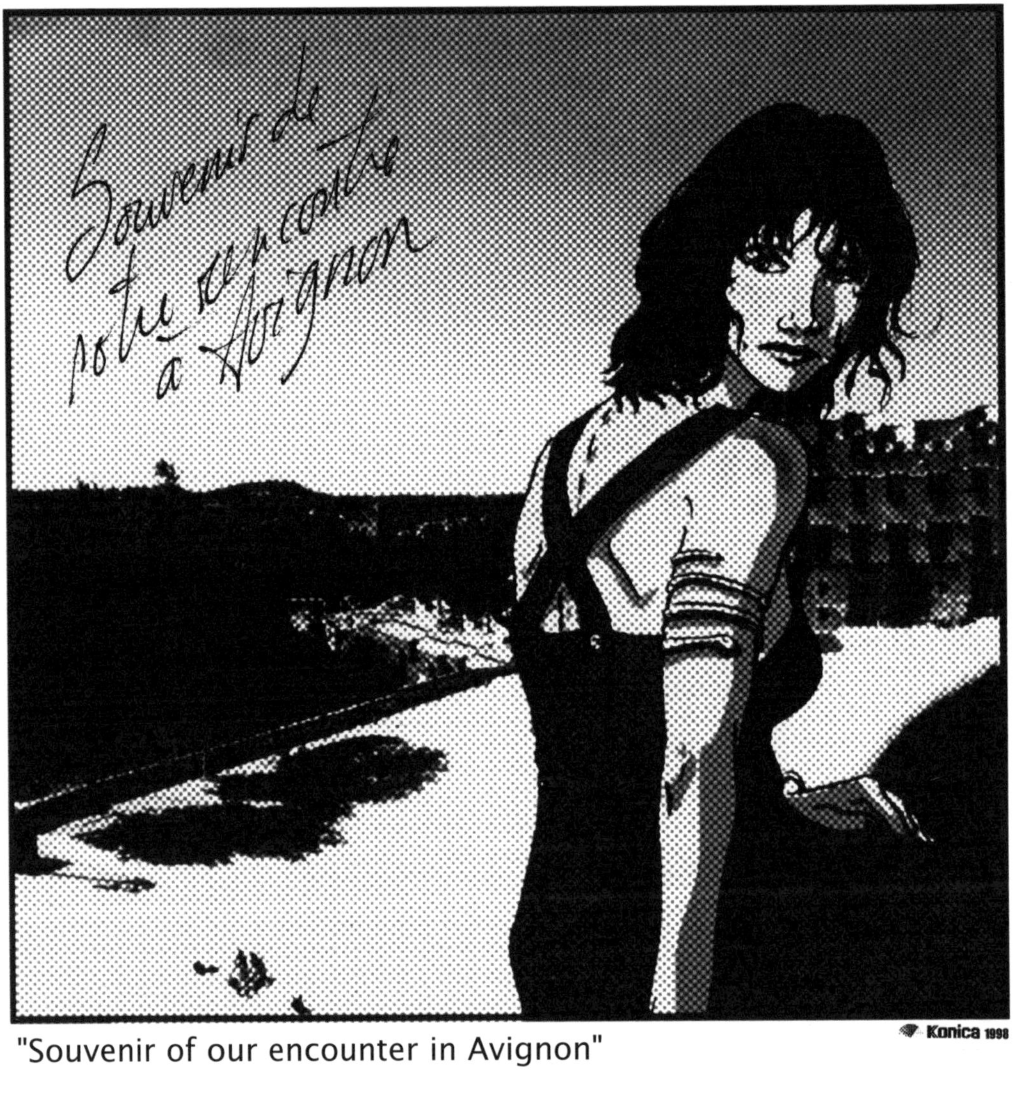
Souvenir de
notre rencontre
à Avignon

Konica 1998

"Souvenir of our encounter in Avignon"

Chapter 7

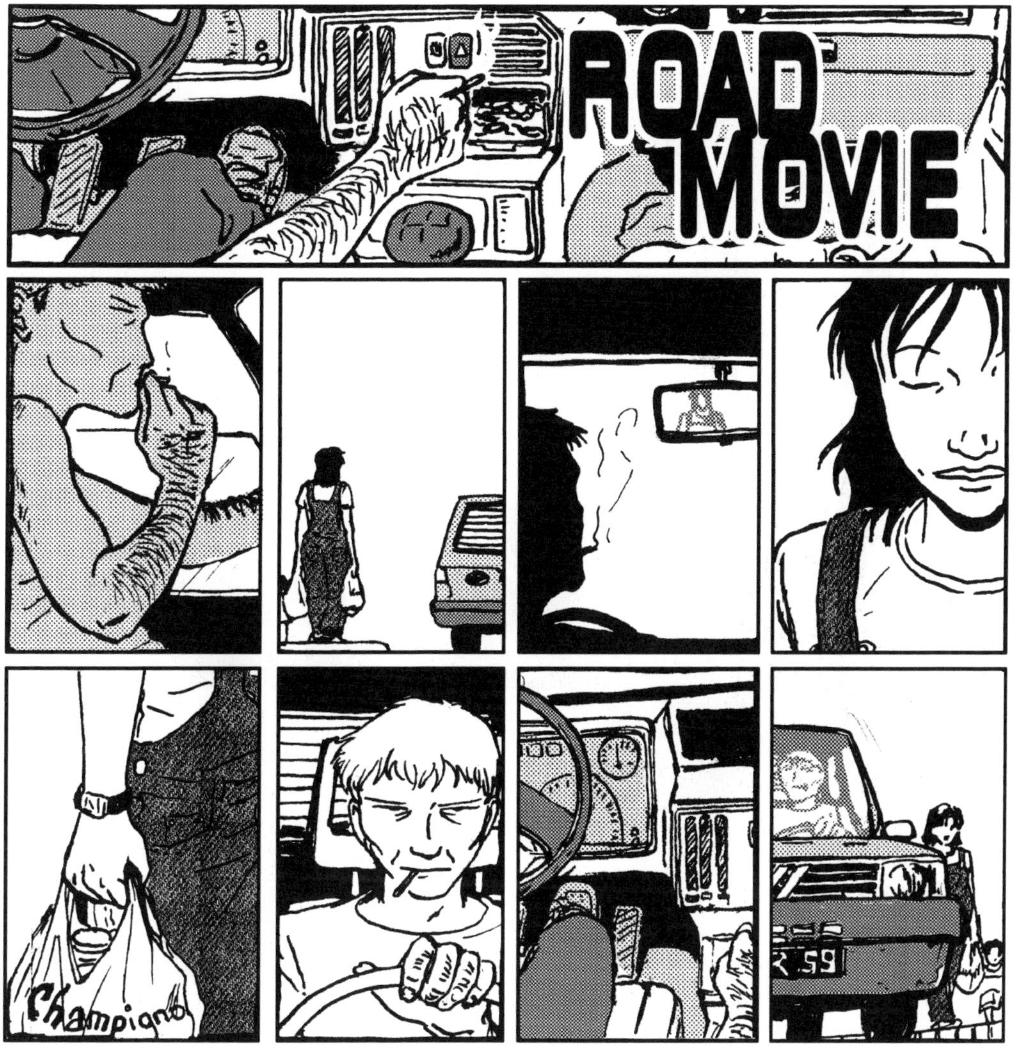
ROAD MOVIE
Champigno
59

HOP IN!

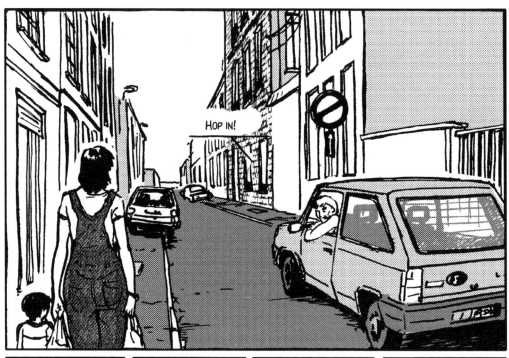

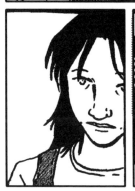

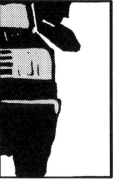

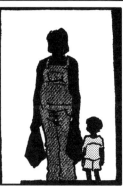

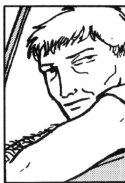

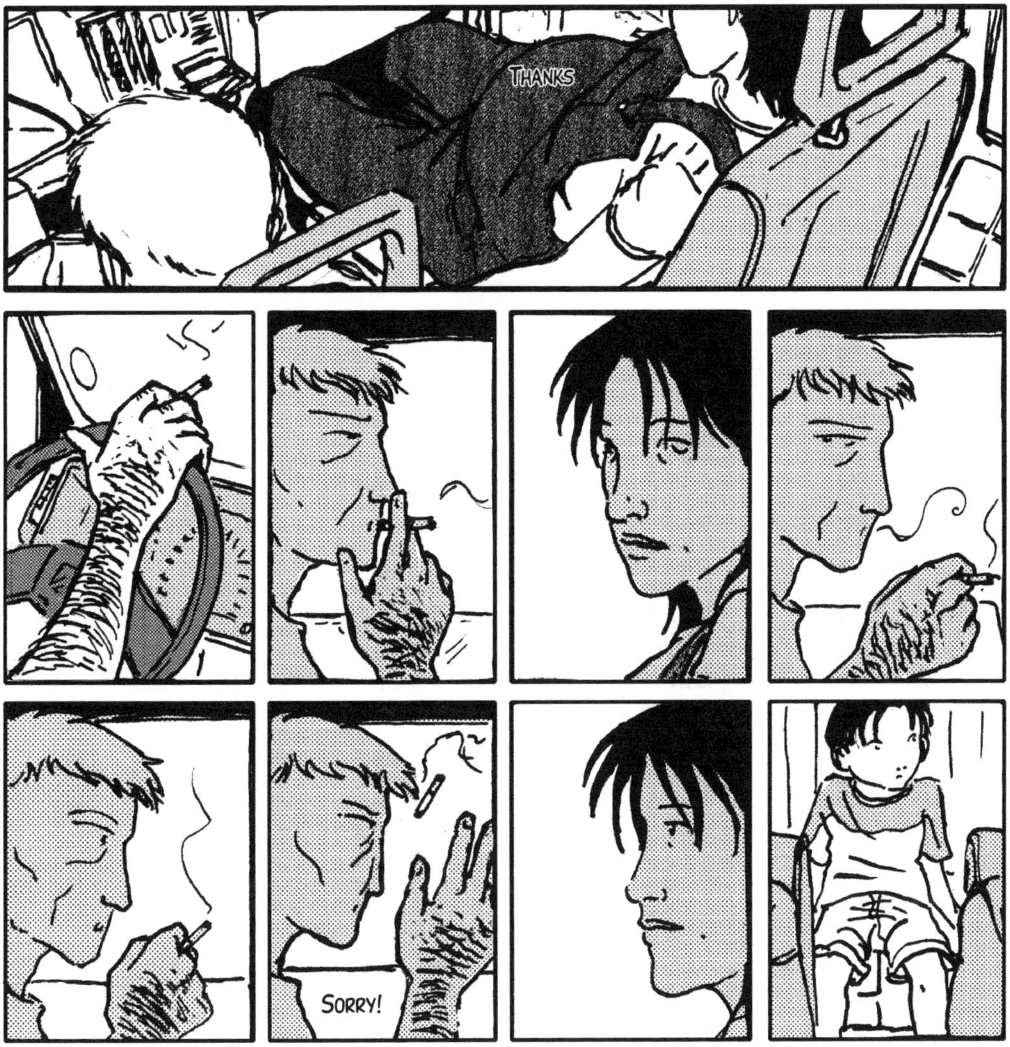
THANKS
SORRY!

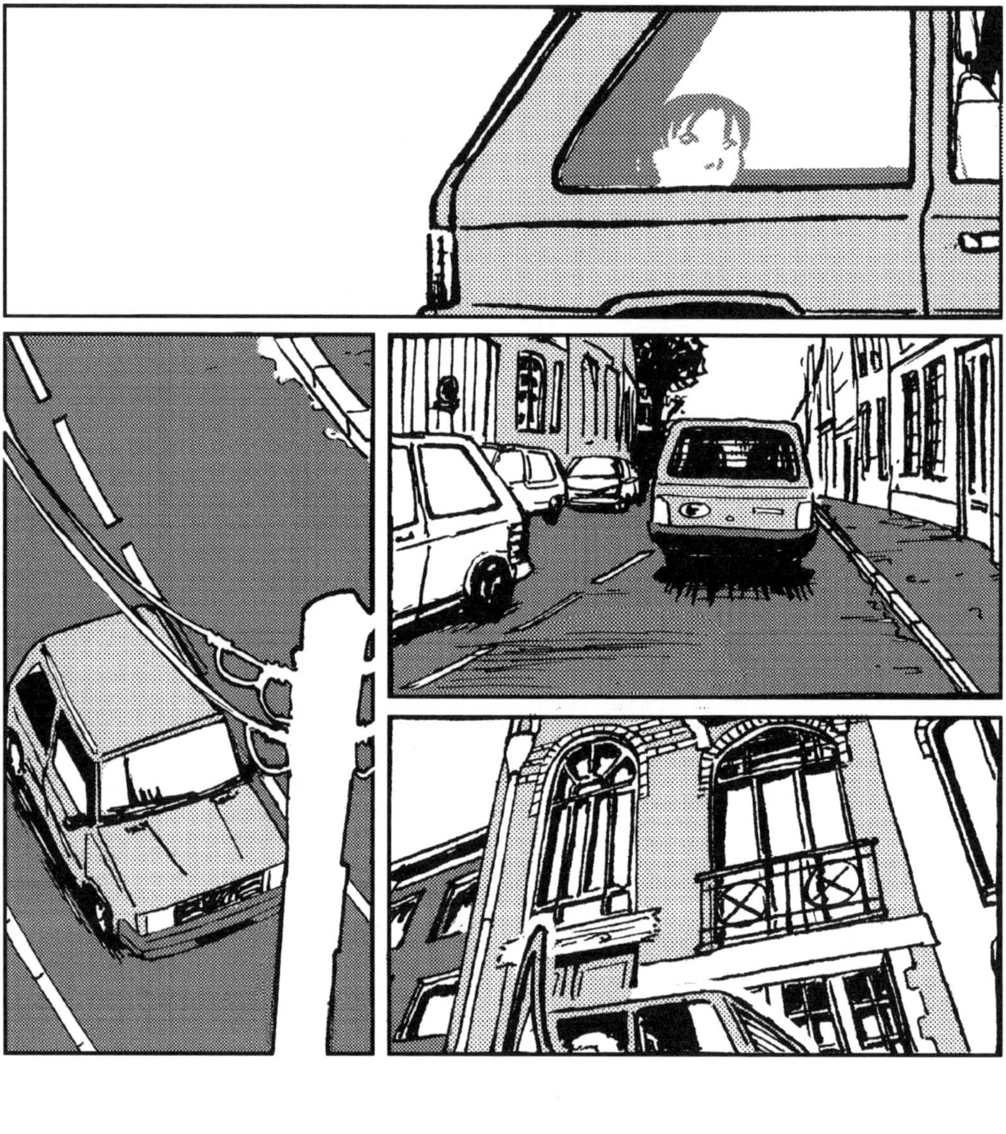

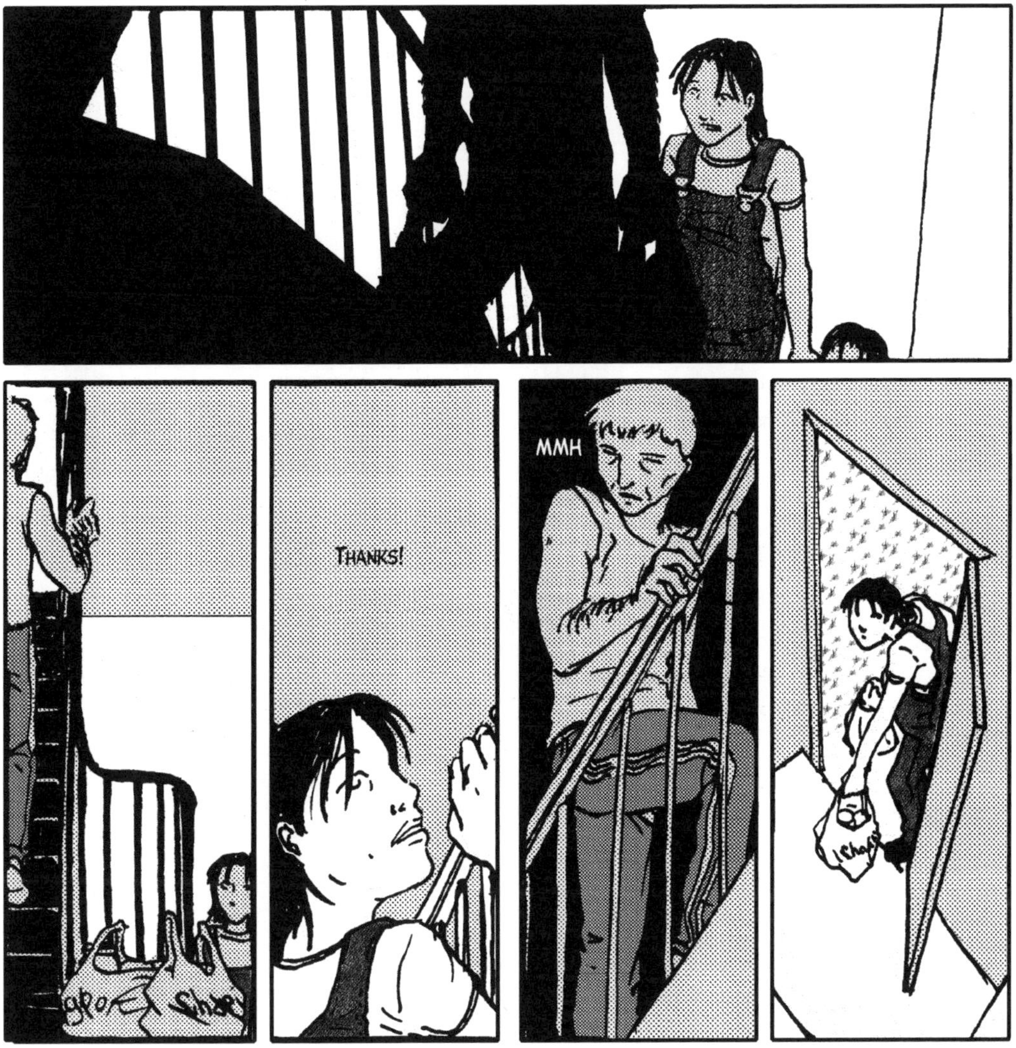
THANKS!
MMH

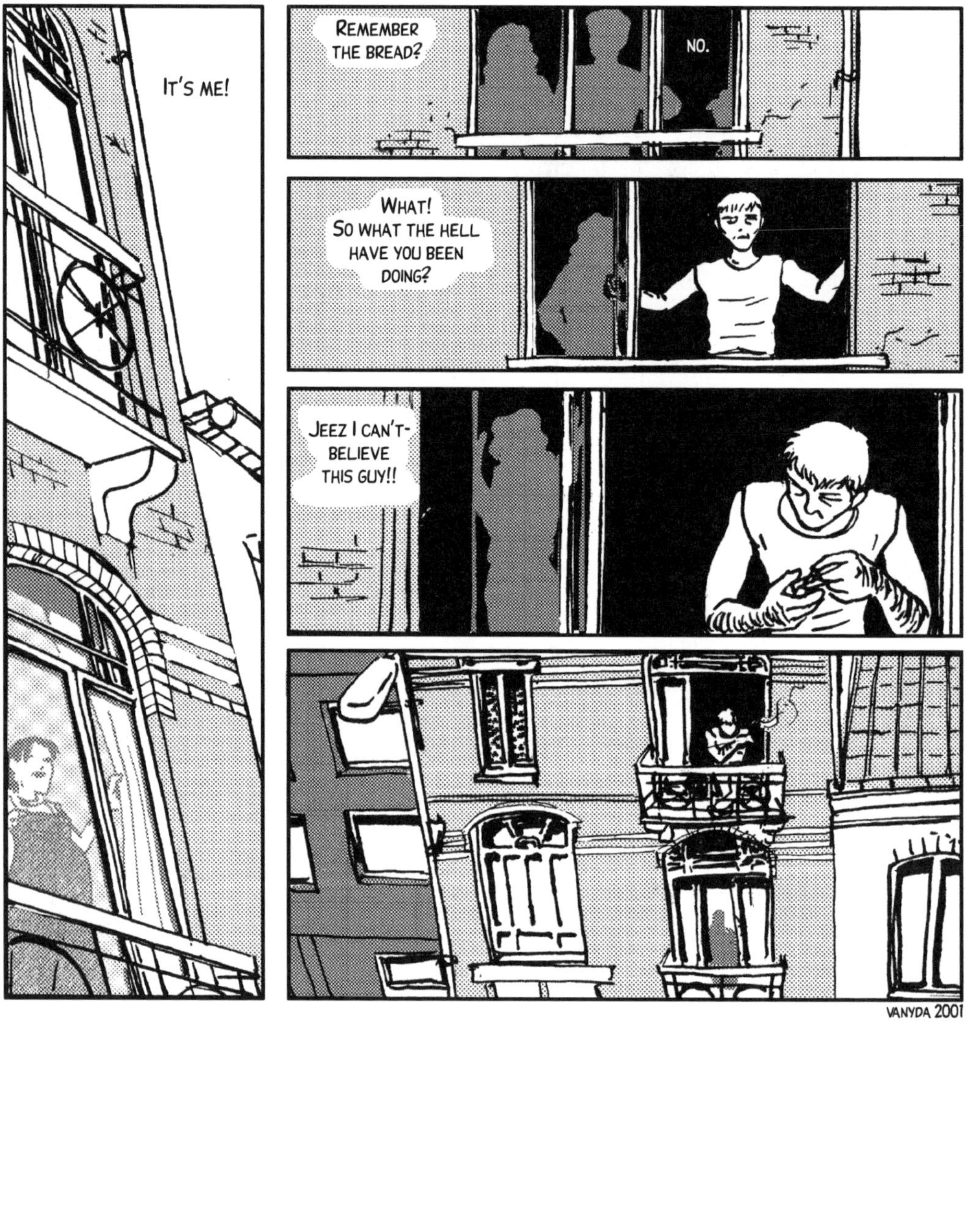
IT'S ME!
REMEMBER THE BREAD?
NO.
WHAT! SO WHAT THE HELL HAVE YOU BEEN DOING?
JEEZ I CAN'T-BELIEVE THIS GUY!!
VANYDA 2001

Chapter 8

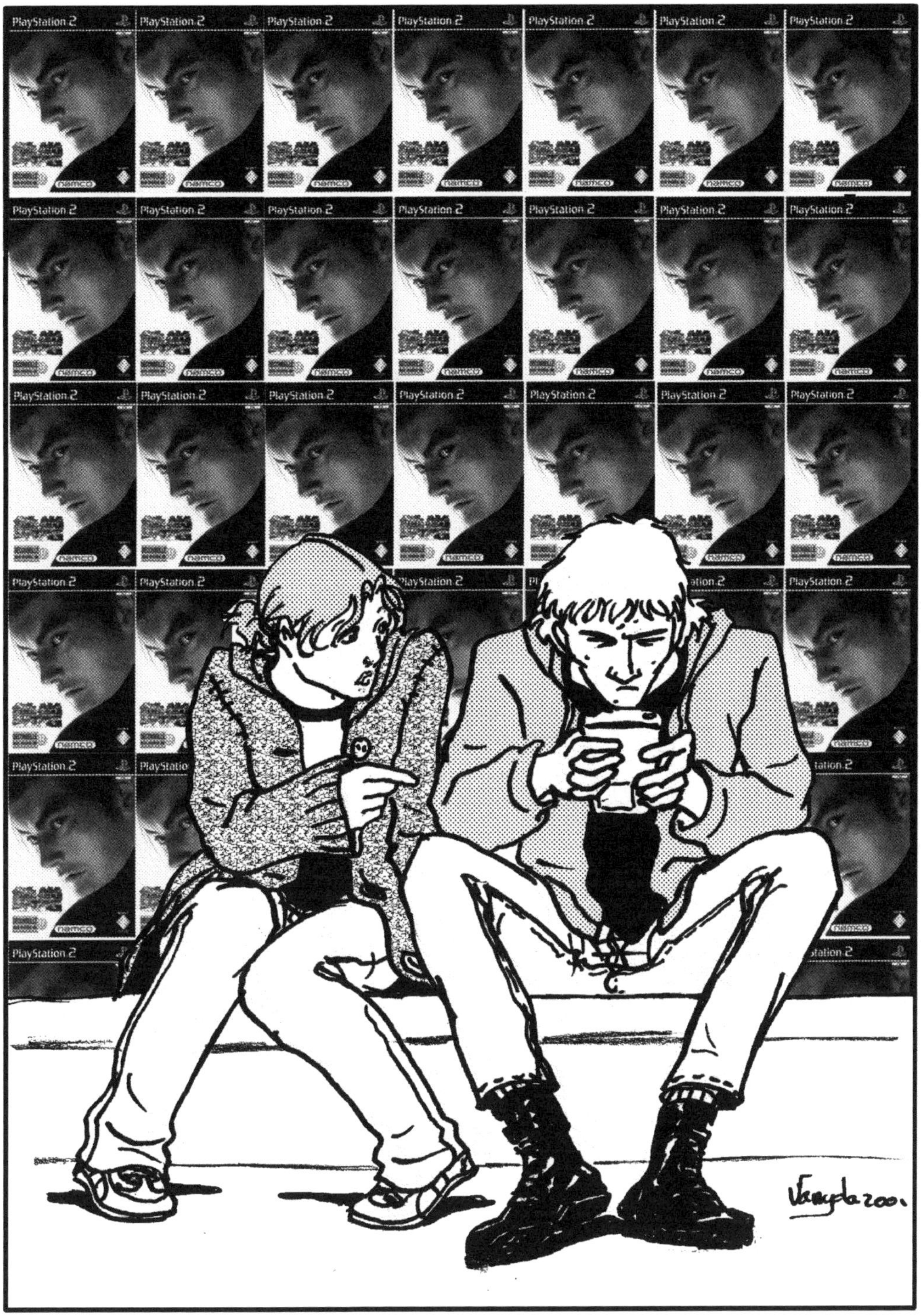
PlayStation 2
namco

GAME OVER

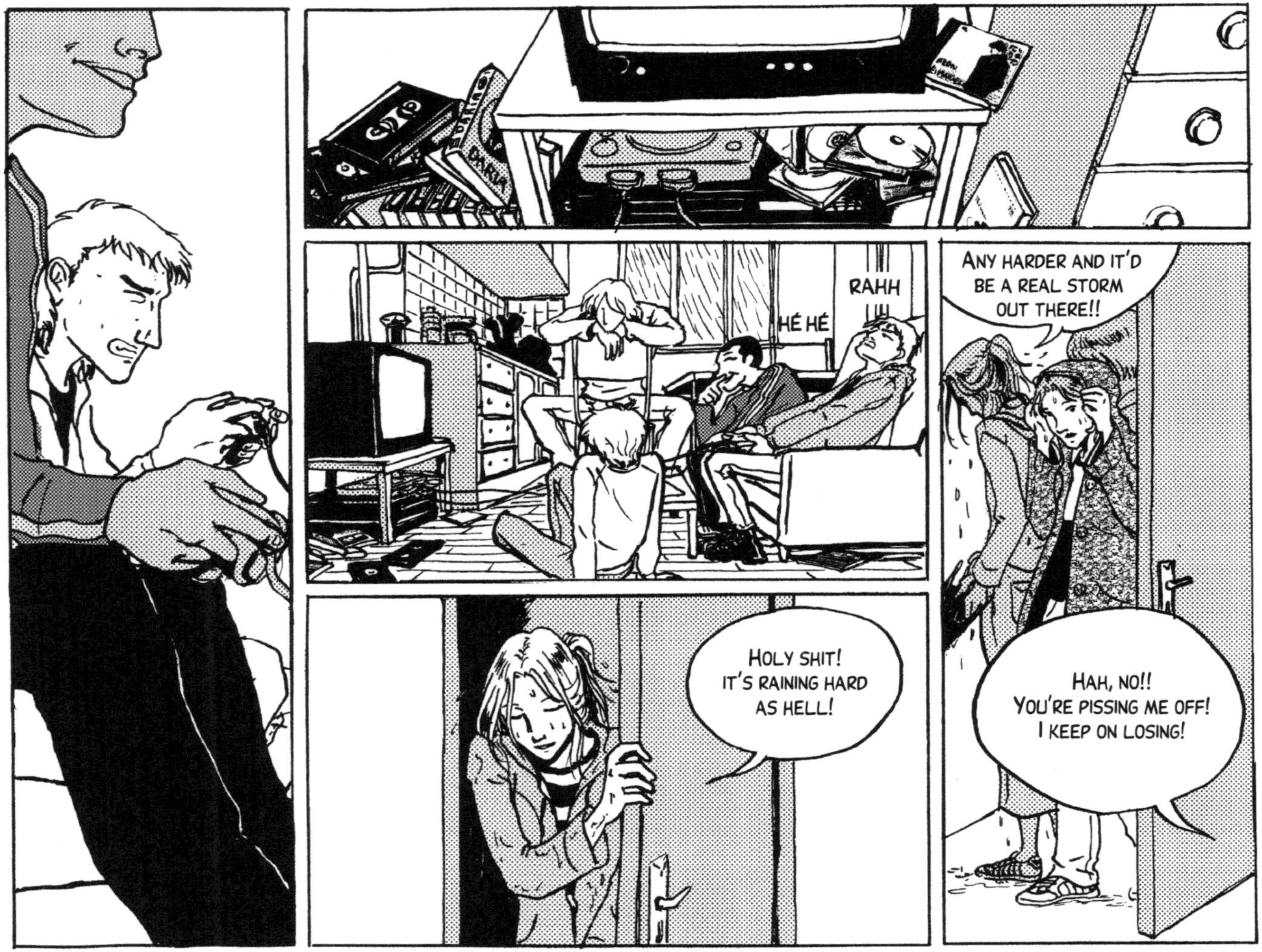
HÉ HÉ
RAHH
HOLY SHIT! IT'S RAINING HARD AS HELL!
ANY HARDER AND IT'D BE A REAL STORM OUT THERE!!
HAH, NO!! YOU'RE PISSING ME OFF! I KEEP ON LOSING!

Hi, Guys!!
What's this game?
Ha ha!! Someone's being hammered! Who's blue??
...
Great vibes!!

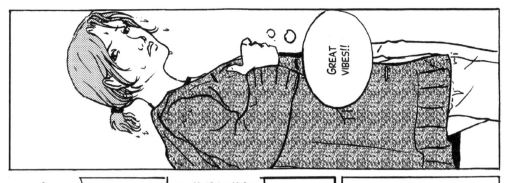

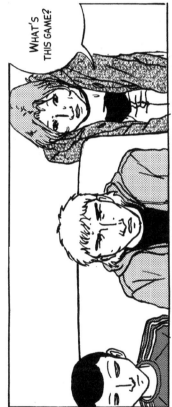

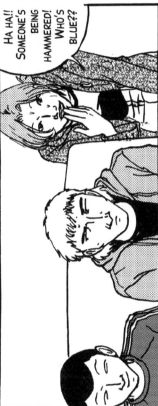

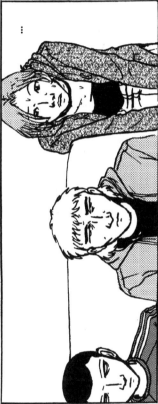

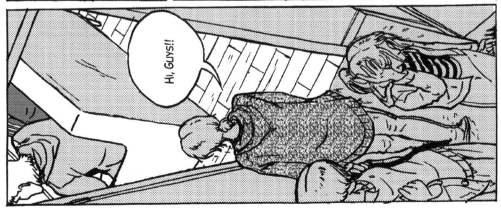

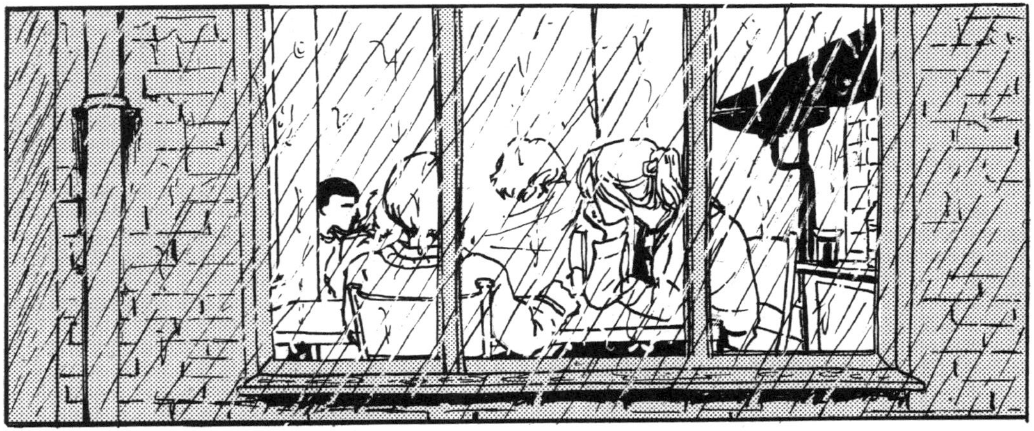

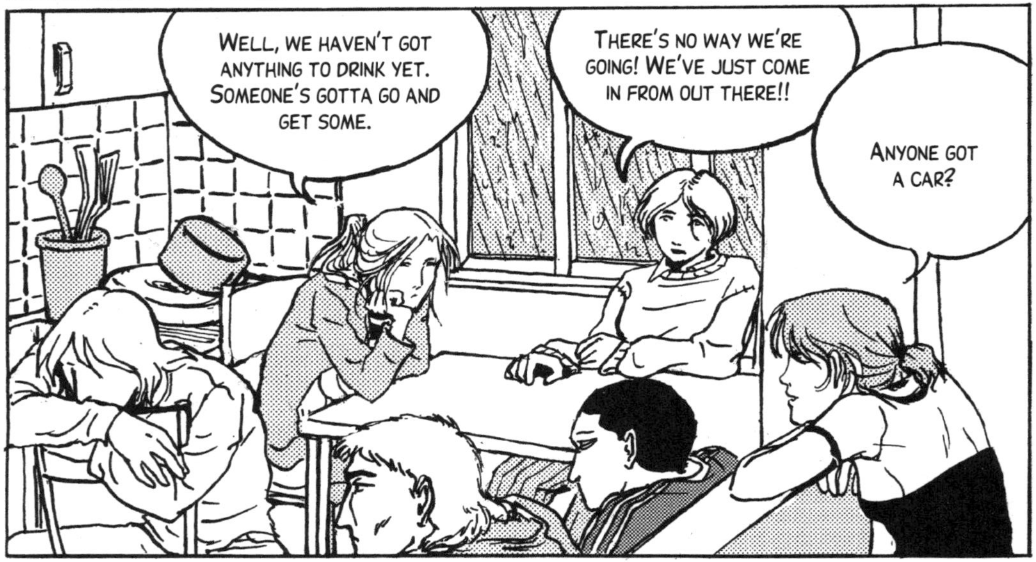
WELL, WE HAVEN'T GOT ANYTHING TO DRINK YET. SOMEONE'S GOTTA GO AND GET SOME.
THERE'S NO WAY WE'RE GOING! WE'VE JUST COME IN FROM OUT THERE!!
ANYONE GOT A CAR?

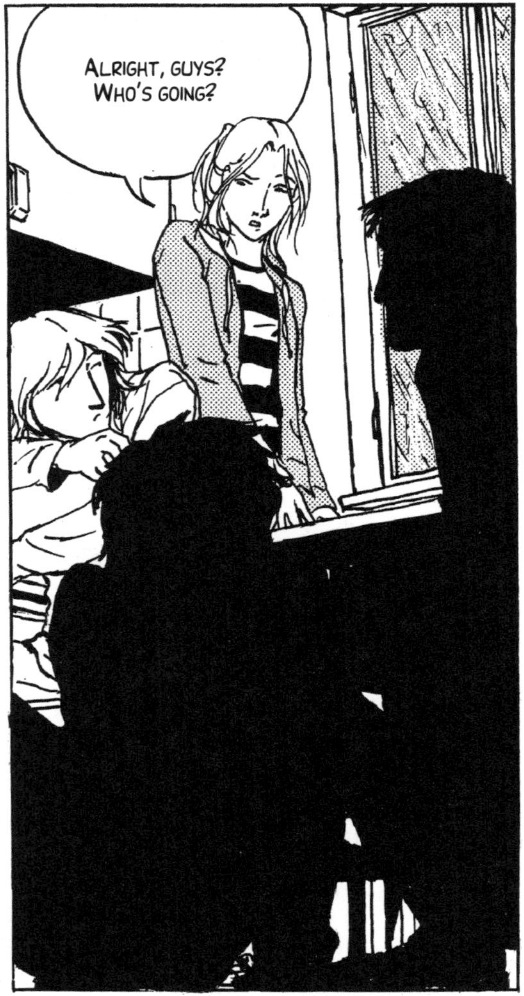
ALRIGHT, GUYS? WHO'S GOING?

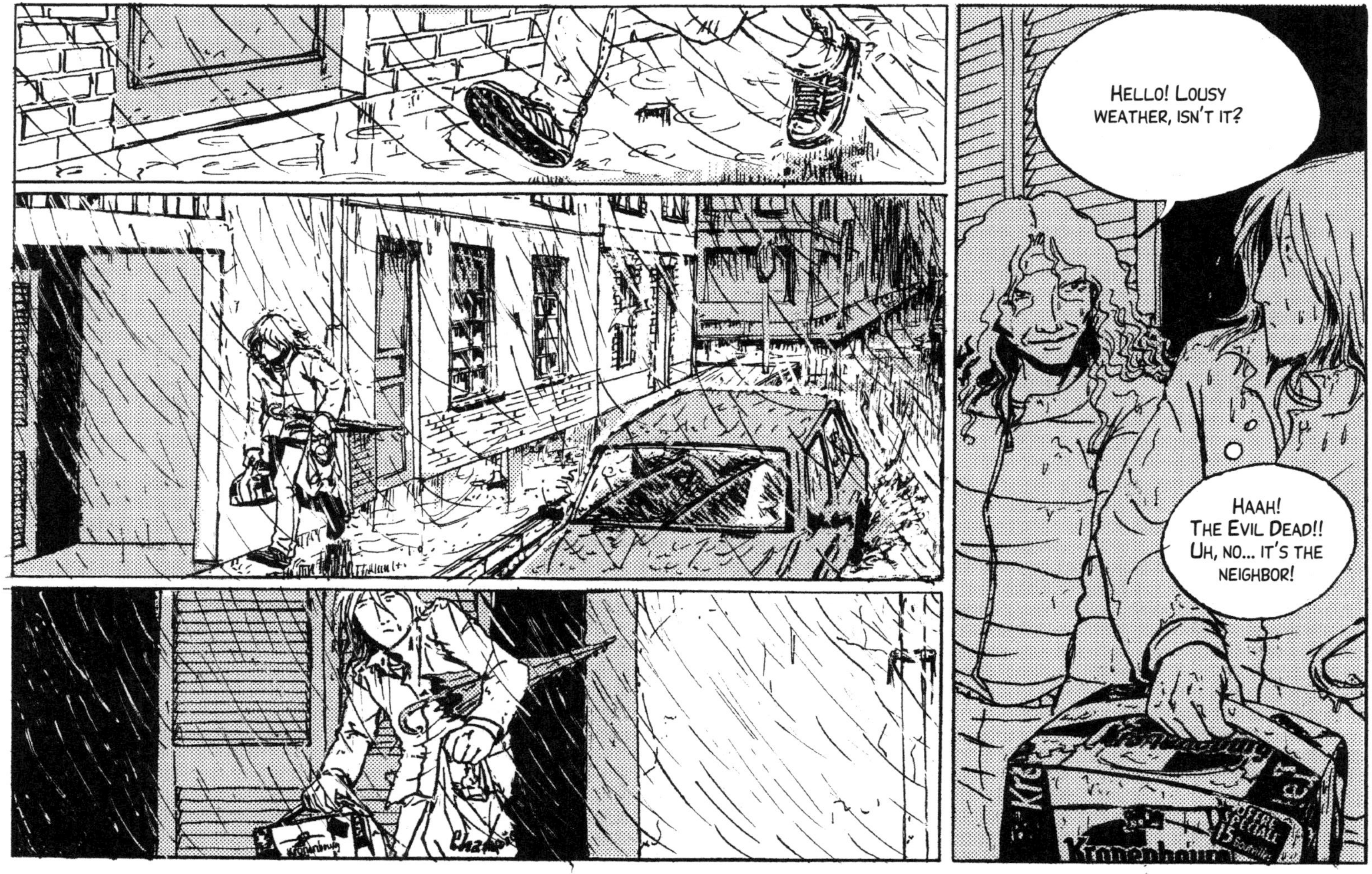
HELLO! LOUSY WEATHER, ISN'T IT?
HAAH! THE EVIL DEAD!! UH, NO... IT'S THE NEIGHBOR!

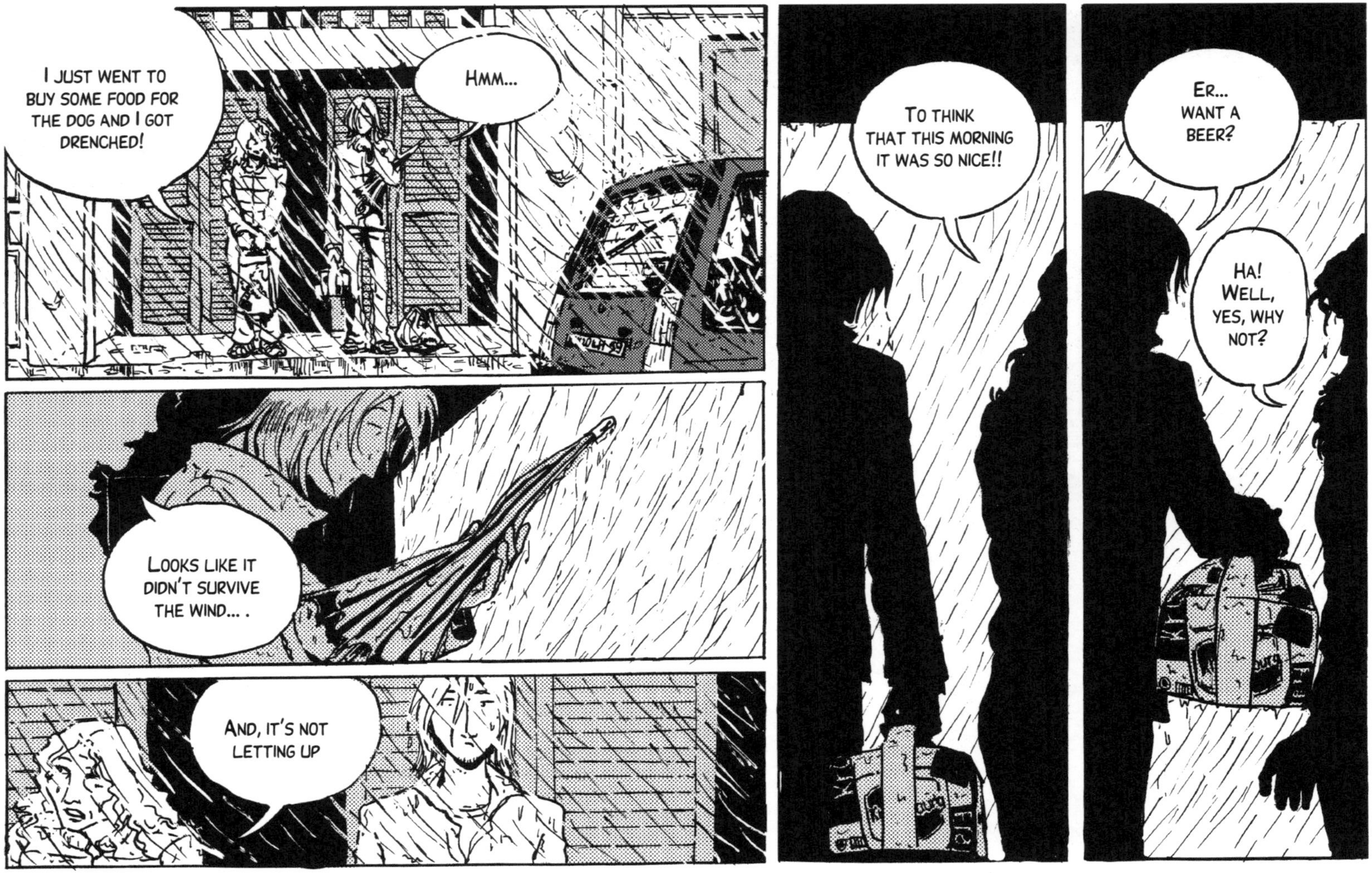
I JUST WENT TO BUY SOME FOOD FOR THE DOG AND I GOT DRENCHED!
HMM...
LOOKS LIKE IT DIDN'T SURVIVE THE WIND... .
AND, IT'S NOT LETTING UP
TO THINK THAT THIS MORNING IT WAS SO NICE!!
ER... WANT A BEER?
HA! WELL, YES, WHY NOT?

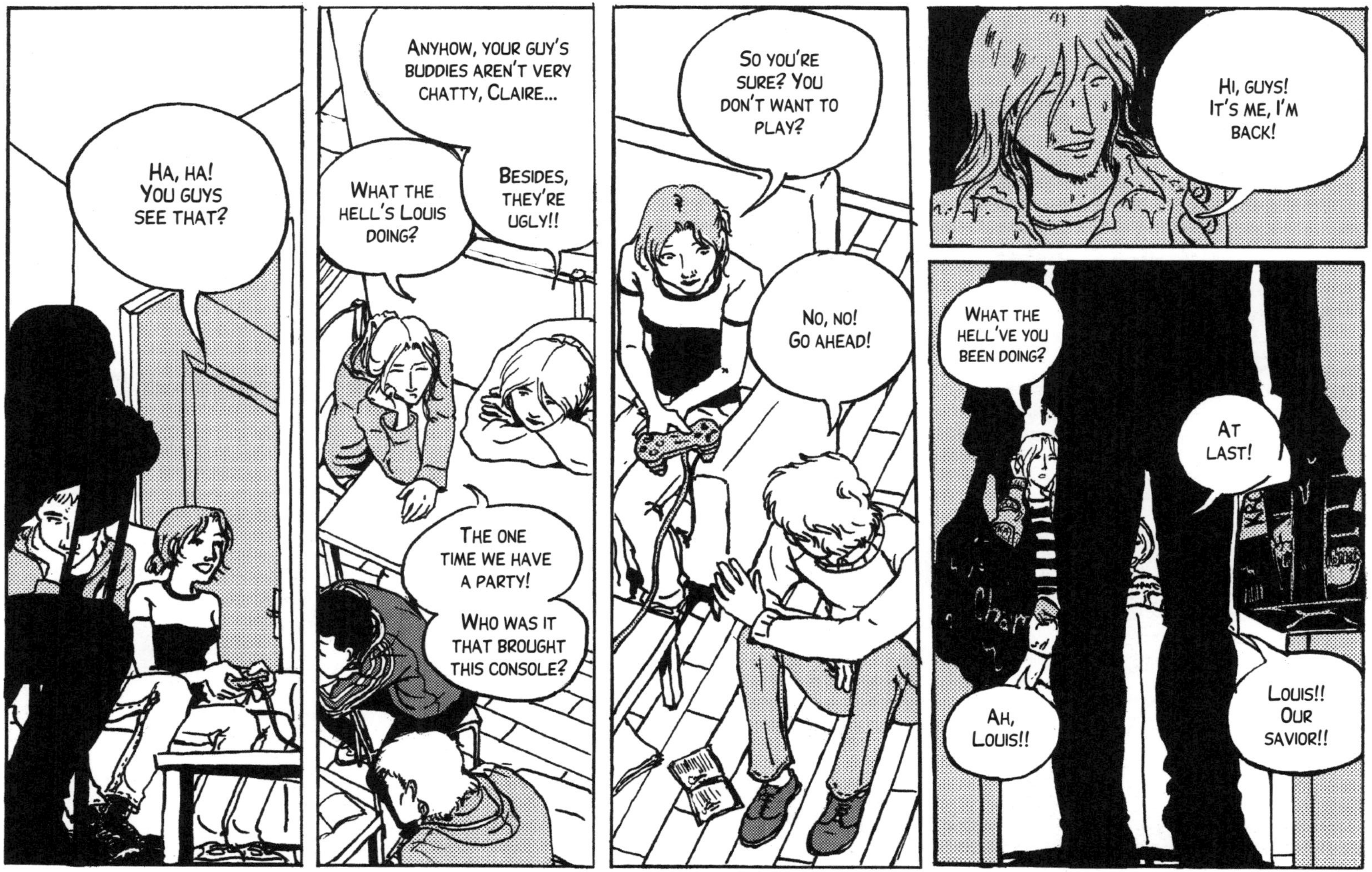
HA, HA! YOU GUYS SEE THAT?
ANYHOW, YOUR GUY'S BUDDIES AREN'T VERY CHATTY, CLAIRE...
WHAT THE HELL'S LOUIS DOING?
BESIDES, THEY'RE UGLY!!
THE ONE TIME WE HAVE A PARTY!
WHO WAS IT THAT BROUGHT THIS CONSOLE?
SO YOU'RE SURE? YOU DON'T WANT TO PLAY?
NO, NO! GO AHEAD!
HI, GUYS! IT'S ME, I'M BACK!
WHAT THE HELL'VE YOU BEEN DOING?
AT LAST!
AH, LOUIS!!
LOUIS!! OUR SAVIOR!!

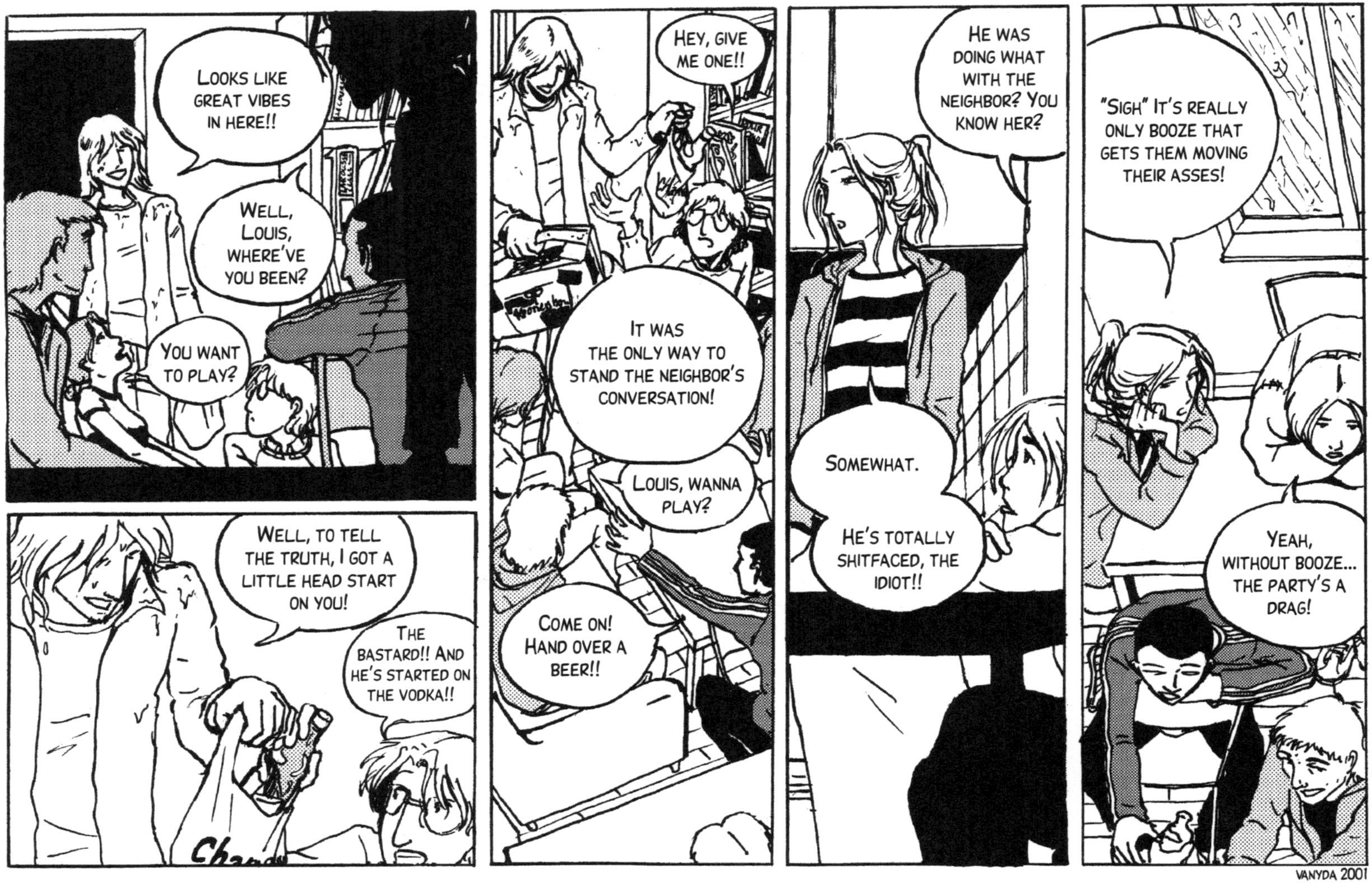
LOOKS LIKE GREAT VIBES IN HERE!!
WELL, LOUIS, WHERE'VE YOU BEEN?
YOU WANT TO PLAY?
WELL, TO TELL THE TRUTH, I GOT A LITTLE HEAD START ON YOU!
THE BASTARD!! AND HE'S STARTED ON THE VODKA!!
HEY, GIVE ME ONE!!
IT WAS THE ONLY WAY TO STAND THE NEIGHBOR'S CONVERSATION!
LOUIS, WANNA PLAY?
COME ON! HAND OVER A BEER!!
HE WAS DOING WHAT WITH THE NEIGHBOR? YOU KNOW HER?
SOMEWHAT.
HE'S TOTALLY SHITFACED, THE IDIOT!!
"SIGH" IT'S REALLY ONLY BOOZE THAT GETS THEM MOVING THEIR ASSES!
YEAH, WITHOUT BOOZE... THE PARTY'S A DRAG!
VANYDA 2001

Chapter 9
Neighbors,
Gossip, and so on...

SCENE 1:
(INTERIOR, LIVING-ROOM)

LOUIS

CLAIRE

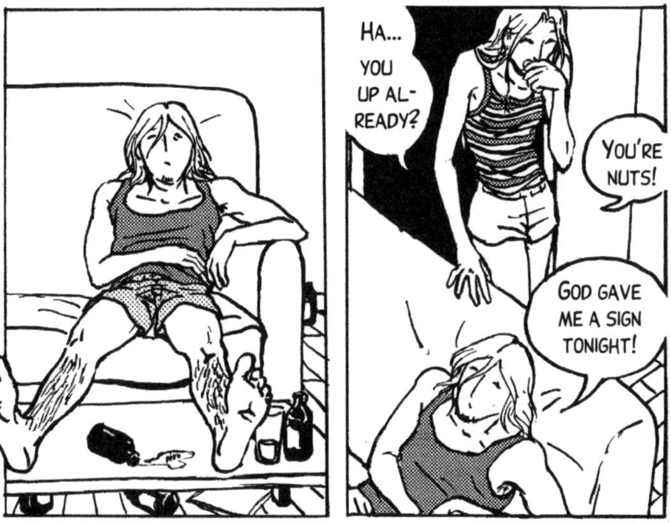
HA... YOU UP AL-READY?
YOU'RE NUTS!
GOD GAVE ME A SIGN TONIGHT!

SCENE 2:
(INTERIOR, KITCHEN)

JACKY

FABIENNE

GIPSY

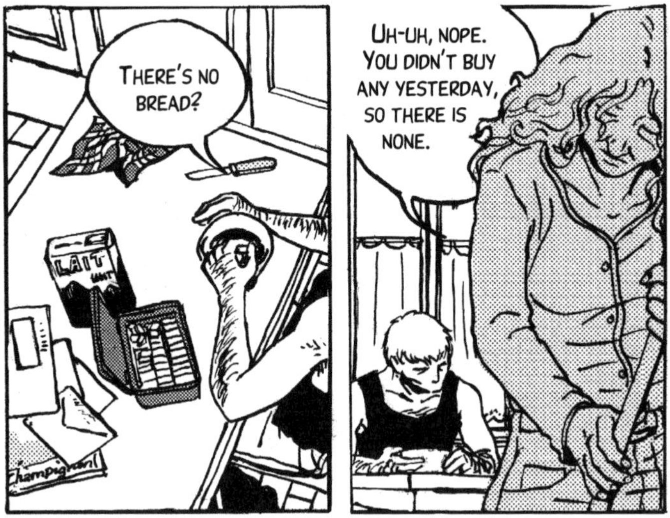
THERE'S NO BREAD?
LAIT
UH-UH, NOPE. YOU DIDN'T BUY ANY YESTERDAY, SO THERE IS NONE.

SCENE 3
(INTERIOR, BATHROOM)

RÉMI

BEATRICE

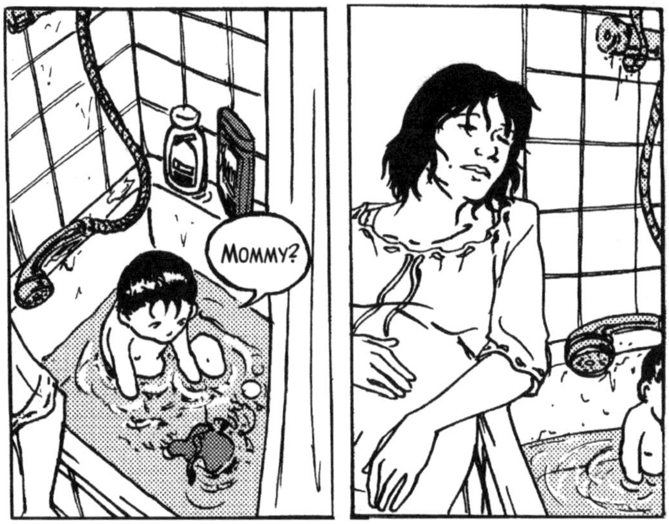
MOMMY?

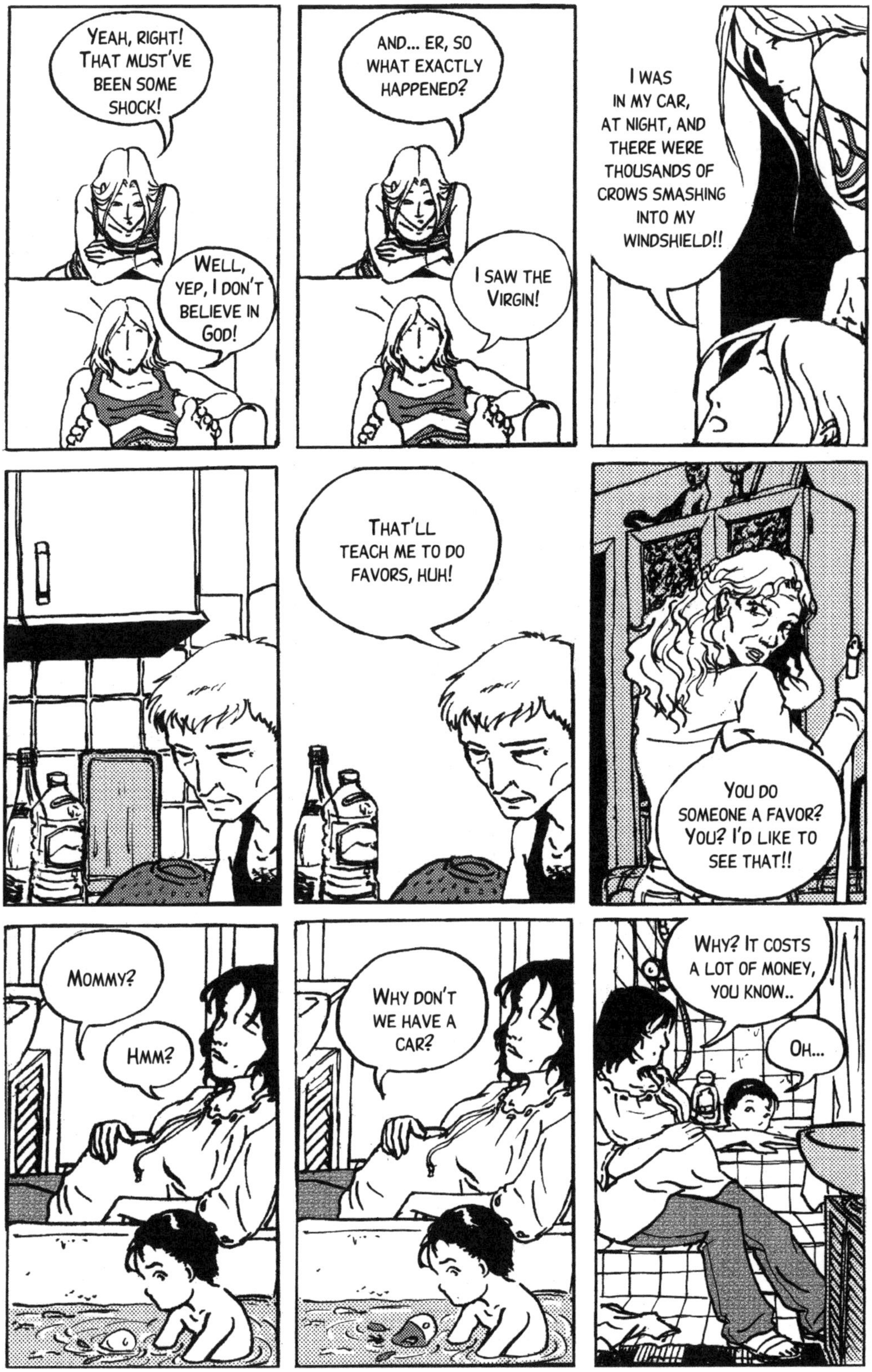
YEAH, RIGHT! THAT MUST'VE BEEN SOME SHOCK!
WELL, YEP, I DON'T BELIEVE IN GOD!
AND... ER, SO WHAT EXACTLY HAPPENED?
I SAW THE VIRGIN!
I WAS IN MY CAR, AT NIGHT, AND THERE WERE THOUSANDS OF CROWS SMASHING INTO MY WINDSHIELD!!
THAT'LL TEACH ME TO DO FAVORS, HUH!
YOU DO SOMEONE A FAVOR? YOU? I'D LIKE TO SEE THAT!!
MOMMY?
HMM?
WHY DON'T WE HAVE A CAR?
WHY? IT COSTS A LOT OF MONEY, YOU KNOW..
OH...

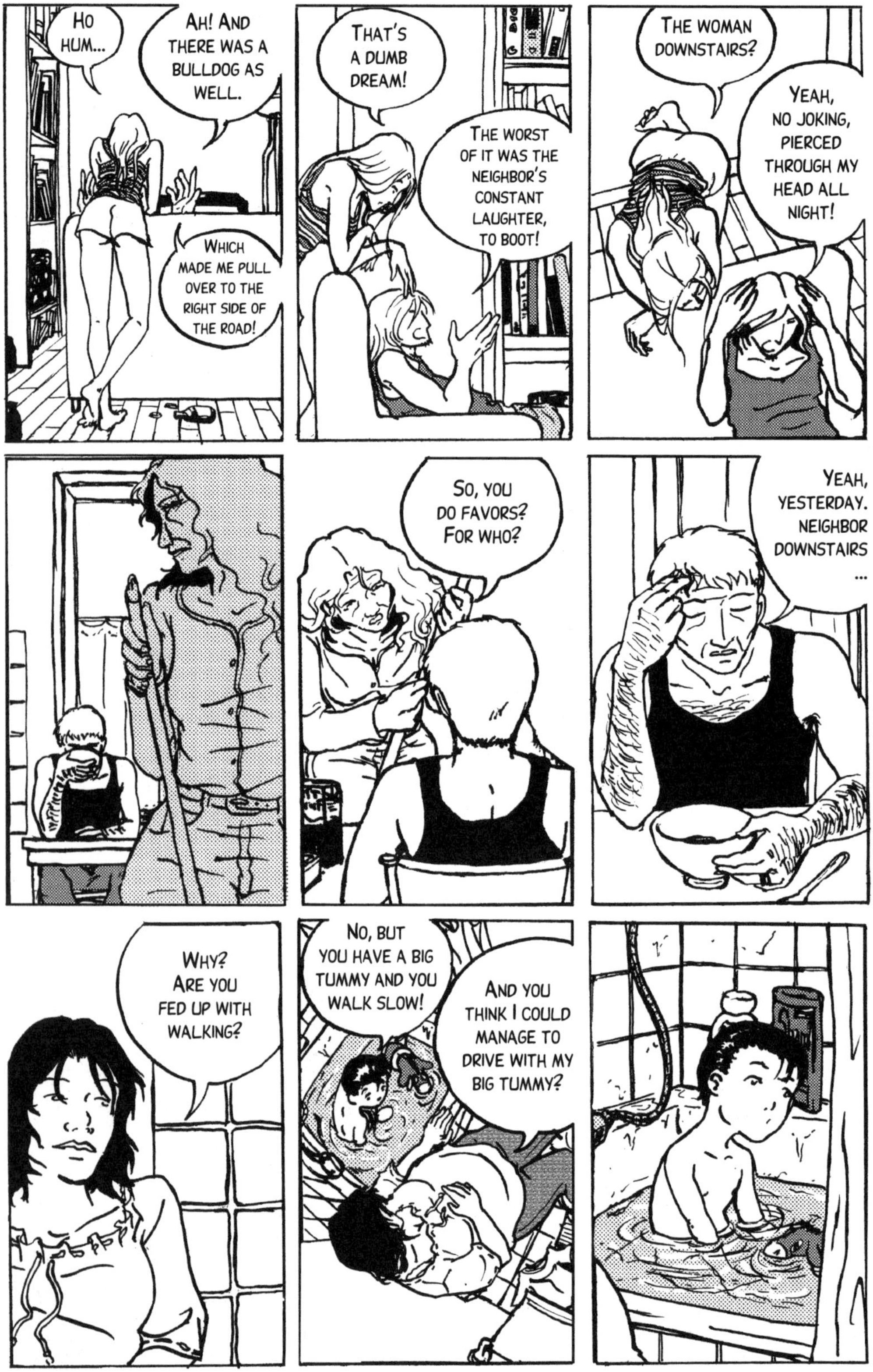
HO HUM...
AH! AND THERE WAS A BULLDOG AS WELL.
WHICH MADE ME PULL OVER TO THE RIGHT SIDE OF THE ROAD!
THAT'S A DUMB DREAM!
THE WORST OF IT WAS THE NEIGHBOR'S CONSTANT LAUGHTER, TO BOOT!
THE WOMAN DOWNSTAIRS?
YEAH, NO JOKING, PIERCED THROUGH MY HEAD ALL NIGHT!
SO, YOU DO FAVORS? FOR WHO?
YEAH, YESTERDAY. NEIGHBOR DOWNSTAIRS ...
WHY? ARE YOU FED UP WITH WALKING?
NO, BUT YOU HAVE A BIG TUMMY AND YOU WALK SLOW!
AND YOU THINK I COULD MANAGE TO DRIVE WITH MY BIG TUMMY?

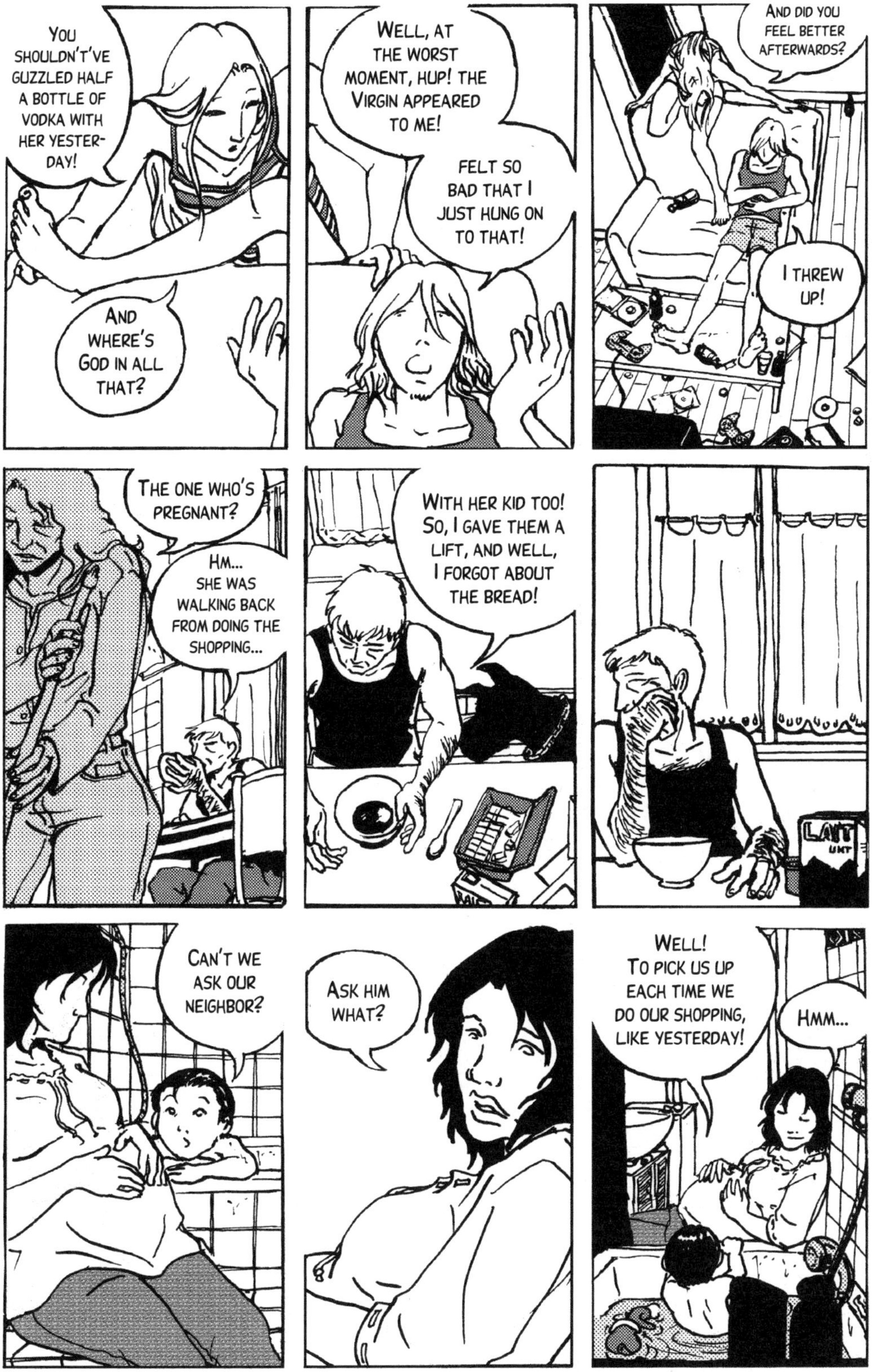
You shouldn't've guzzled half a bottle of vodka with her yester-day!
And where's God in all that?
Well, at the worst moment, hup! the Virgin appeared to me!
Felt so bad that I just hung on to that!
And did you feel better afterwards?
I threw up!
The one who's pregnant?
Hm... she was walking back from doing the shopping...
With her kid too! So, I gave them a lift, and well, I forgot about the bread!
Can't we ask our neighbor?
Ask him what?
Well! To pick us up each time we do our shopping, like yesterday!
Hmm...

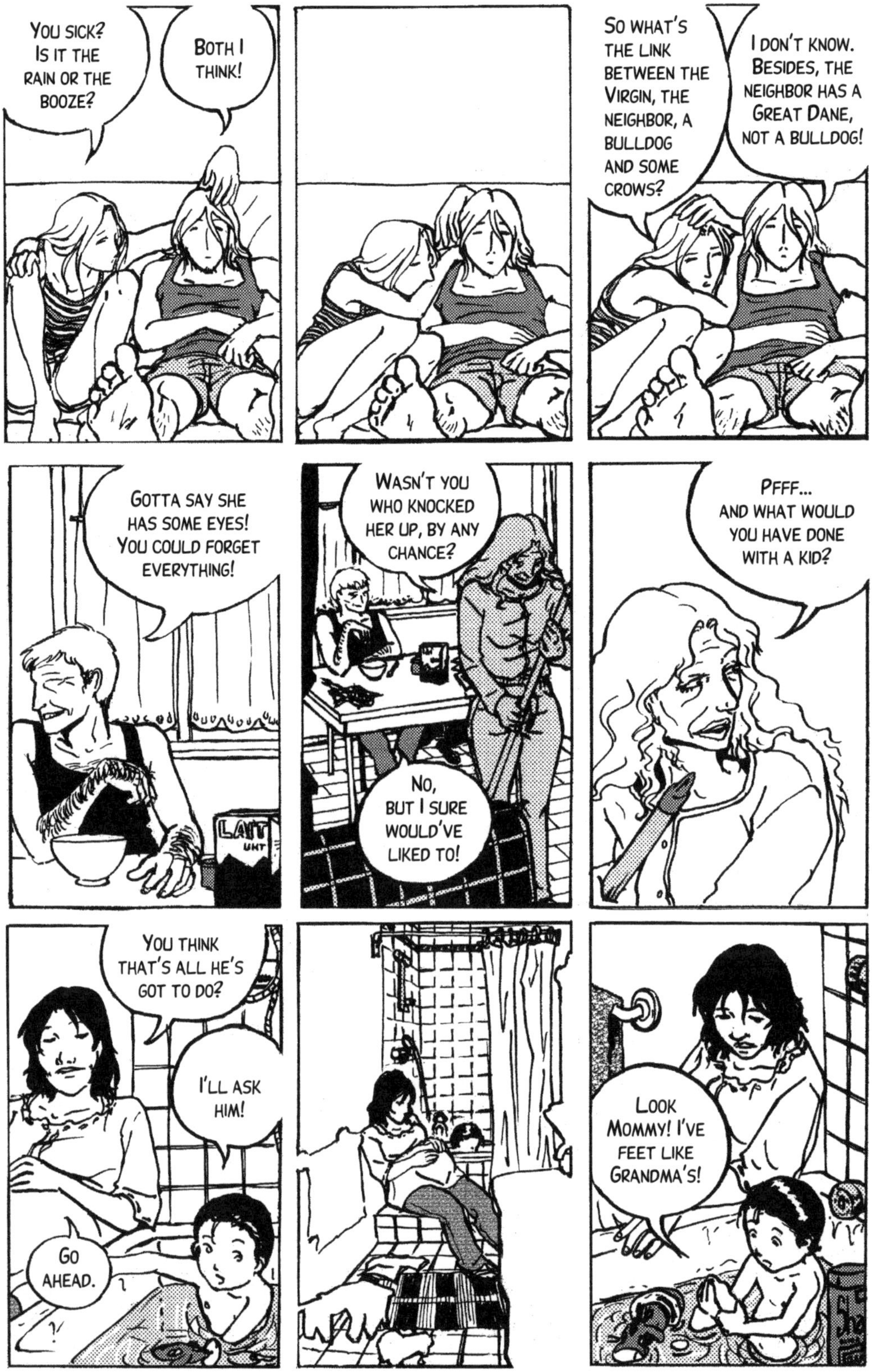
YOU SICK? IS IT THE RAIN OR THE BOOZE?
BOTH I THINK!
SO WHAT'S THE LINK BETWEEN THE VIRGIN, THE NEIGHBOR, A BULLDOG AND SOME CROWS?
I DON'T KNOW. BESIDES, THE NEIGHBOR HAS A GREAT DANE, NOT A BULLDOG!
GOTTA SAY SHE HAS SOME EYES! YOU COULD FORGET EVERYTHING!
LAIT
UHT
WASN'T YOU WHO KNOCKED HER UP, BY ANY CHANCE?
NO, BUT I SURE WOULD'VE LIKED TO!
PFFF... AND WHAT WOULD YOU HAVE DONE WITH A KID?
YOU THINK THAT'S ALL HE'S GOT TO DO?
I'LL ASK HIM!
GO AHEAD.
LOOK MOMMY! I'VE FEET LIKE GRANDMA'S!

WOULDN'T YOU LIKE TO GO BACK TO BED FOR A CUDDLE?

MY MIND SAYS YES, BUT MY BODY STILL HURTS!

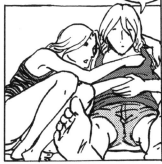

YOU CAN'T EVEN TRAIN YOUR OWN DOG!

YOU TALK CRAP! WATCH! GIPSY, HERE!

GIVE ME YOUR PAW...

GIVE ME YOUR PAW! C'MON, DON'T FUCK AROUND!

DON'T SAY THAT TO YOUR GRANDMA, OTHERWISE YOU'LL SEE THAT HER FACE WILL...

HEY, THIS IS COLD!

CRIKEY! HOW LONG HAVE YOU BEEN IN THERE?!

I DON'T KNOW!

GET OUT QUICK! YOU'LL CATCH A CHILL!

WHAT'S A CHILL?

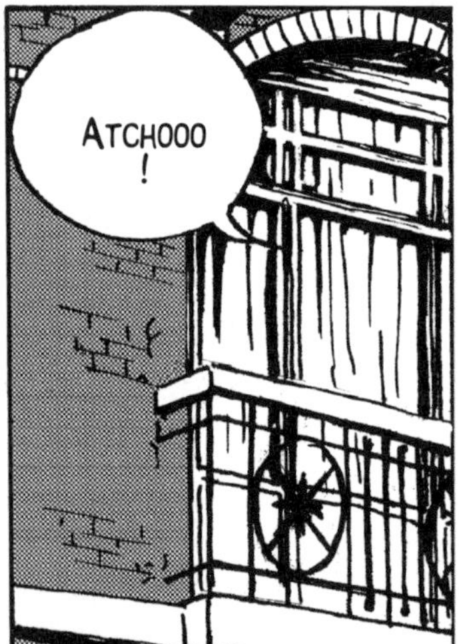
ATCHOOO
!
vanyda 2001

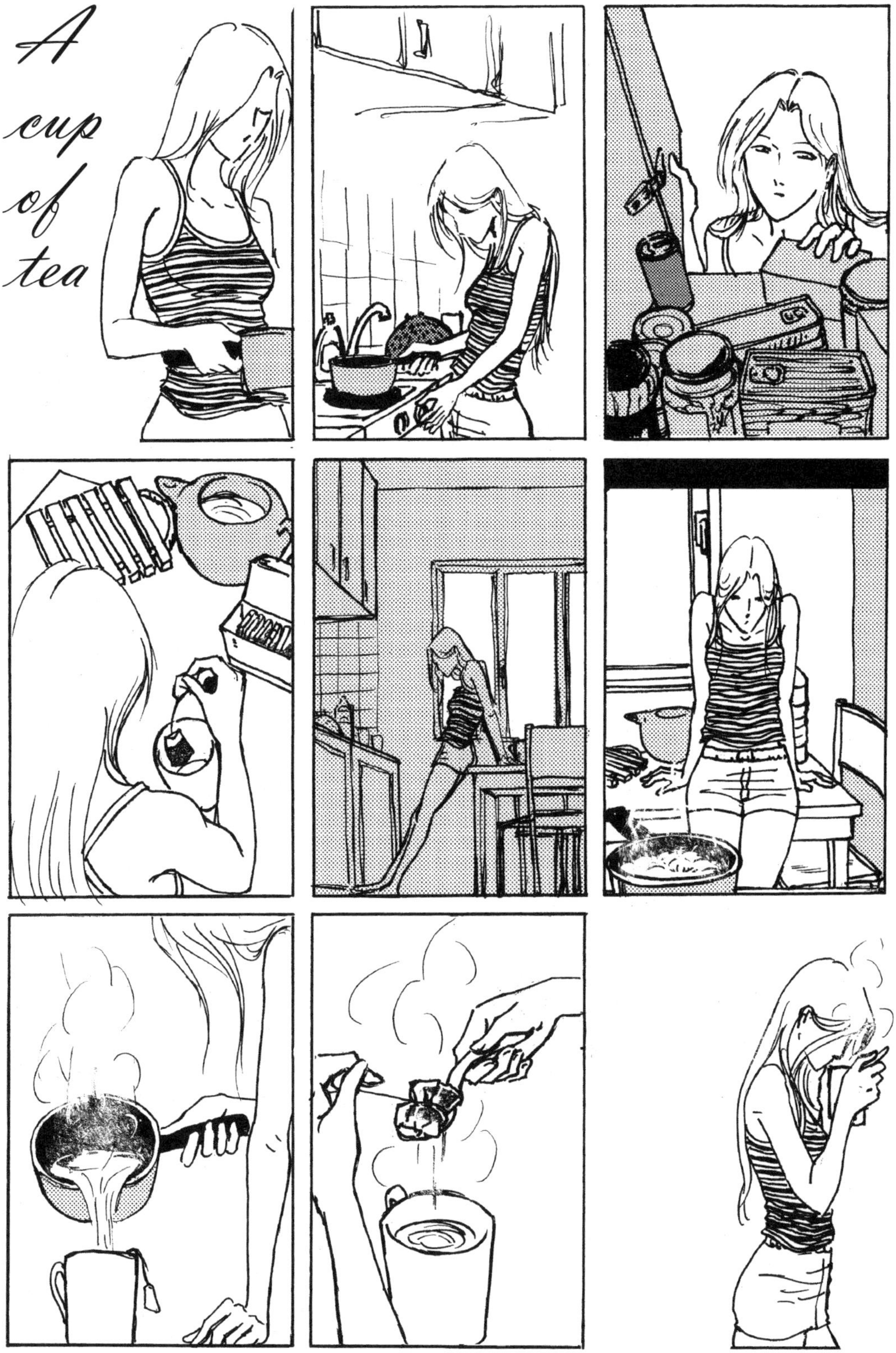
A cup of tea

Chapter 10

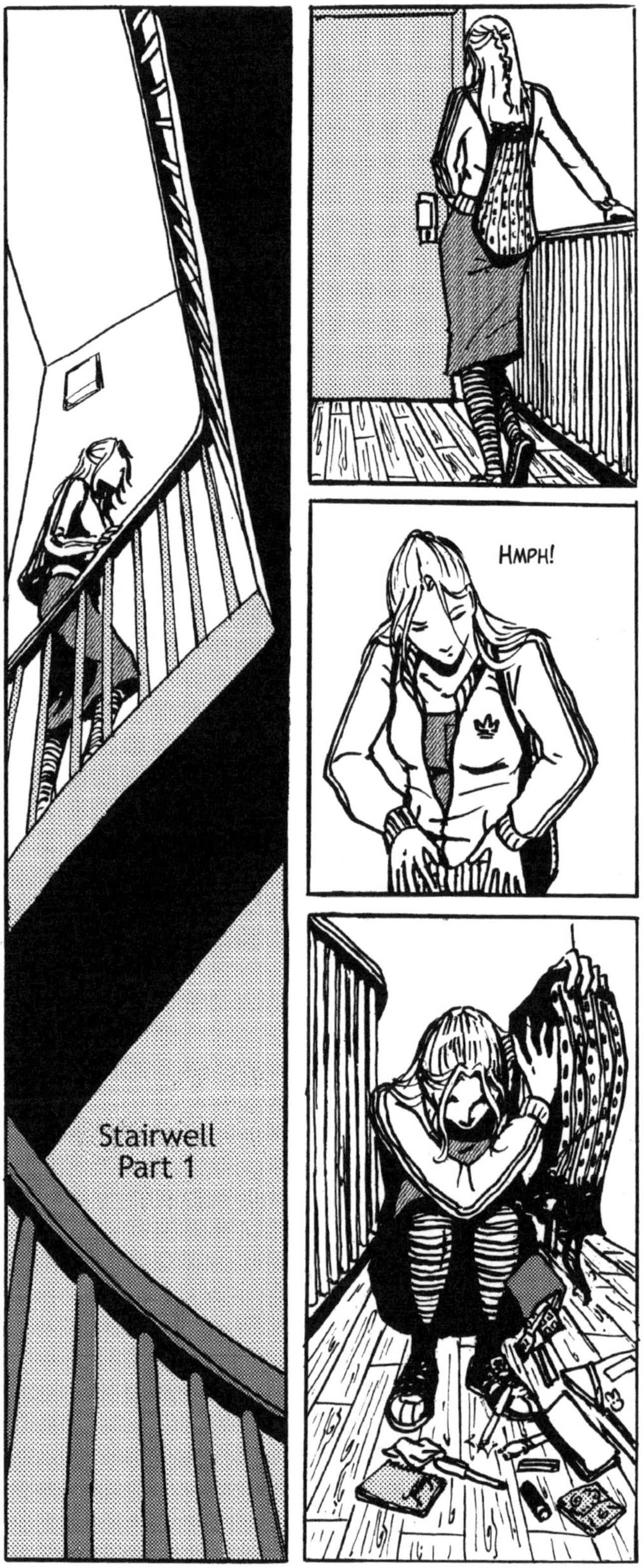
Stairwell
Part 1
HMPH!

Shit! Where are they?
Drrring
Drring
What?? The telephone??
Argh! Darn!

Shit, Shit
You have reached Claire and Louis after the... BEEP!!!
Not there, Not there!
Yes... Claire... Mom... to say...
Arh, I can't hear anything!
... Grandma... hospital... later...
Oh hell's bells...

GRANDMA... IN THE HOSPITAL
AND LOUIS'S NOT BACK FOR AN HOUR YET!!
WHAT COULD'VE HAPPENED TO HER...
I NEED A TELEPHONE!!

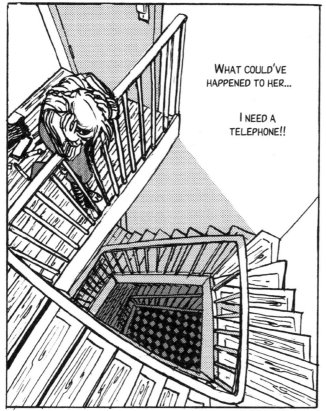

TO BE CONTINUED...

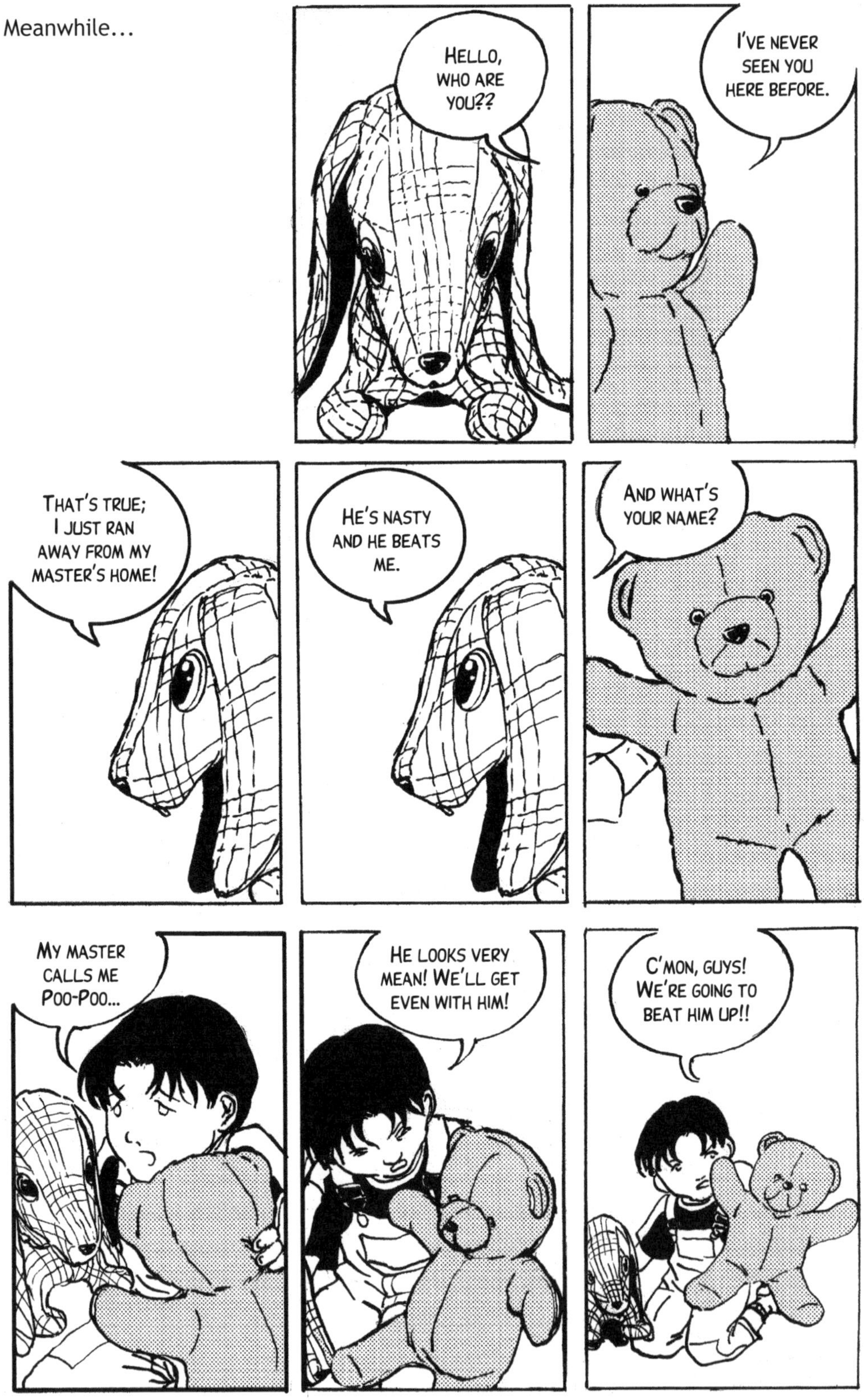
Meanwhile...
HELLO, WHO ARE YOU??
I'VE NEVER SEEN YOU HERE BEFORE.
THAT'S TRUE; I JUST RAN AWAY FROM MY MASTER'S HOME!
HE'S NASTY AND HE BEATS ME.
AND WHAT'S YOUR NAME?
MY MASTER CALLS ME POO-POO...
HE LOOKS VERY MEAN! WE'LL GET EVEN WITH HIM!
C'MON, GUYS! WE'RE GOING TO BEAT HIM UP!!

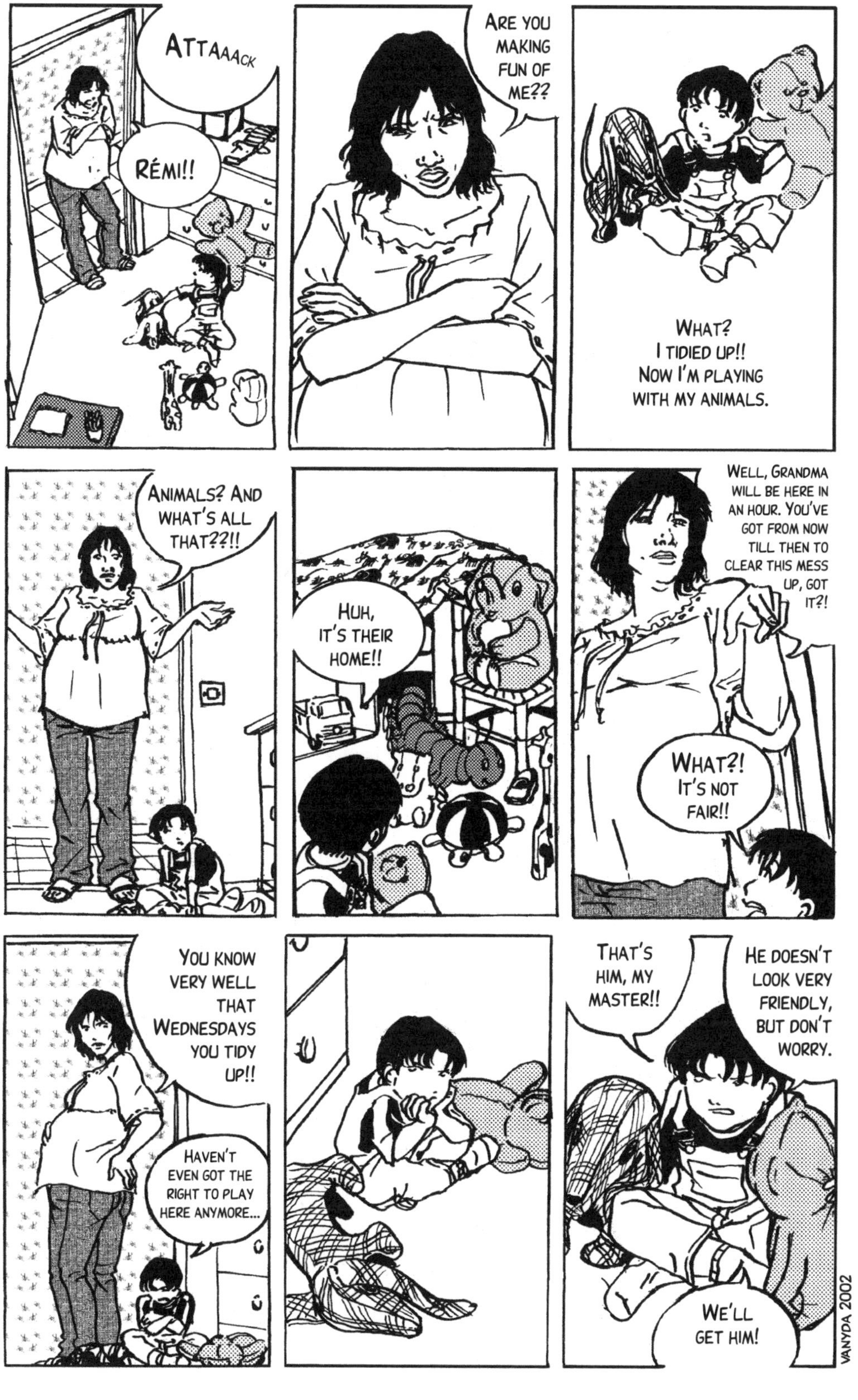
ATTAAACK
RÉMI!!
ARE YOU MAKING FUN OF ME??
WHAT? I TIDIED UP!! NOW I'M PLAYING WITH MY ANIMALS.
ANIMALS? AND WHAT'S ALL THAT??!!
HUH, IT'S THEIR HOME!!
WELL, GRANDMA WILL BE HERE IN AN HOUR. YOU'VE GOT FROM NOW TILL THEN TO CLEAR THIS MESS UP, GOT IT?!
WHAT?! IT'S NOT FAIR!!
YOU KNOW VERY WELL THAT WEDNESDAYS YOU TIDY UP!!
HAVEN'T EVEN GOT THE RIGHT TO PLAY HERE ANYMORE...
THAT'S HIM, MY MASTER!!
HE DOESN'T LOOK VERY FRIENDLY, BUT DON'T WORRY.
WE'LL GET HIM!
VANYDA 2002

Chapter 10
(encore)

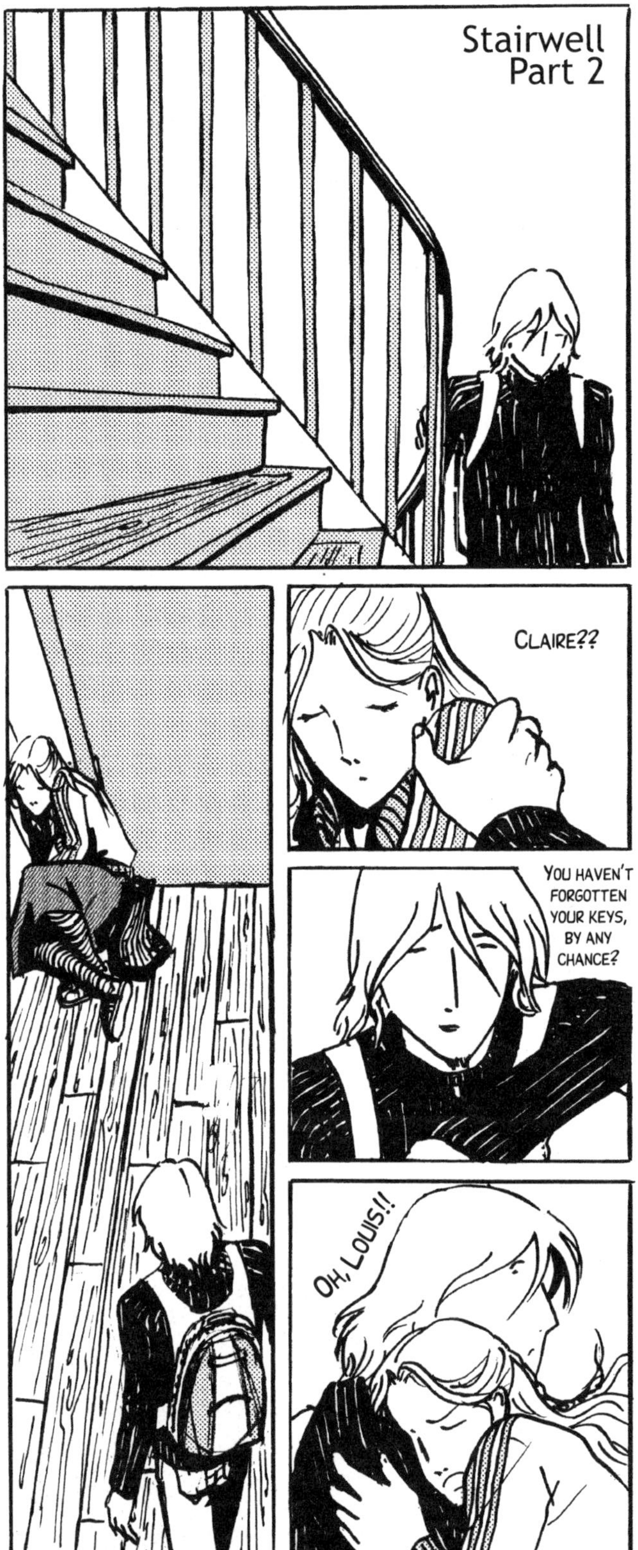
Stairwell
Part 2
CLAIRE??
YOU HAVEN'T FORGOTTEN YOUR KEYS, BY ANY CHANCE?
OH, LOUIS!!

I FORGOT MY KEYS!
IT'S NOT THE END OF THE WORLD!!
YES! MY GRANDMA IS IN THE HOSPITAL!!
WHAT?!
DON'T PANIC. WHAT'S WRONG WITH HER?
OH, I DON'T KNOW!! MY MOTHER CALLED WHEN I WAS STUCK OUTSIDE!
SHE LEFT A MESSAGE ON THE ANS-WERING MACHINE, BUT I DIDN'T CATCH ALL OF IT!!

SO? HAVE YOU TRIED CALLING HER BACK??

WELL, I WANTED TO GO CALL FROM SARAH'S, BUT THAT WOULD TAKE... AS LONG AS WAITING F... ...U, SO I SAID TO MYSE... ...AT IT'D BE BETTER ...ALL FROM A PAYPHO...

BUT OF COURSE, I DIDN'T HAVE A CARD... SO I WANTED TO BUY ONE AT ... KIOSK, BUT IT'S CL... ...DNESDAYS, SO I ... TO GO TO ANOT... ...FURTHER AWAY...

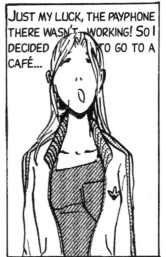

JUST MY LUCK, THE PAYPHONE THERE WASN'T WORKING! SO I DECIDED ... TO GO TO A CAFÉ...

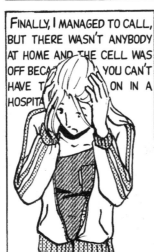

FINALLY, I MANAGED TO CALL, BUT THERE WASN'T ANYBODY AT HOME AND THE CELL WAS OFF BECA... ...YOU CAN'T HAVE T... ...ON IN A HOSPITA...

AFTER A WHOLE HOUR I STILL DON'T KNOW A THING!

IT WAS HORRIBLE!!

I fell asleep!!
Why didn't you try your voice mail?
I didn't think of that. Boohoo hoooo

Er, Louis? It turns out, Mom said that she needs to take my Grandma to the hospital on Saturday for her checkup so we won't be able to go over for lunch.
And that's it!
VANYDA 2002

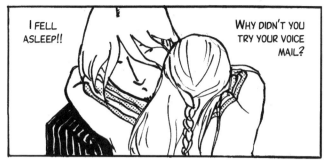

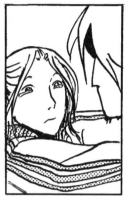

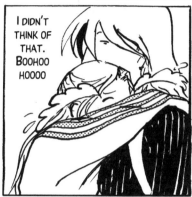

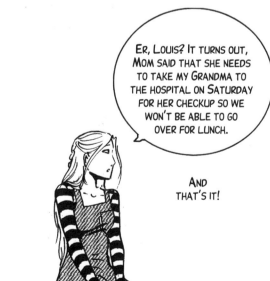

Chapter 11

ROAD MOVIE II

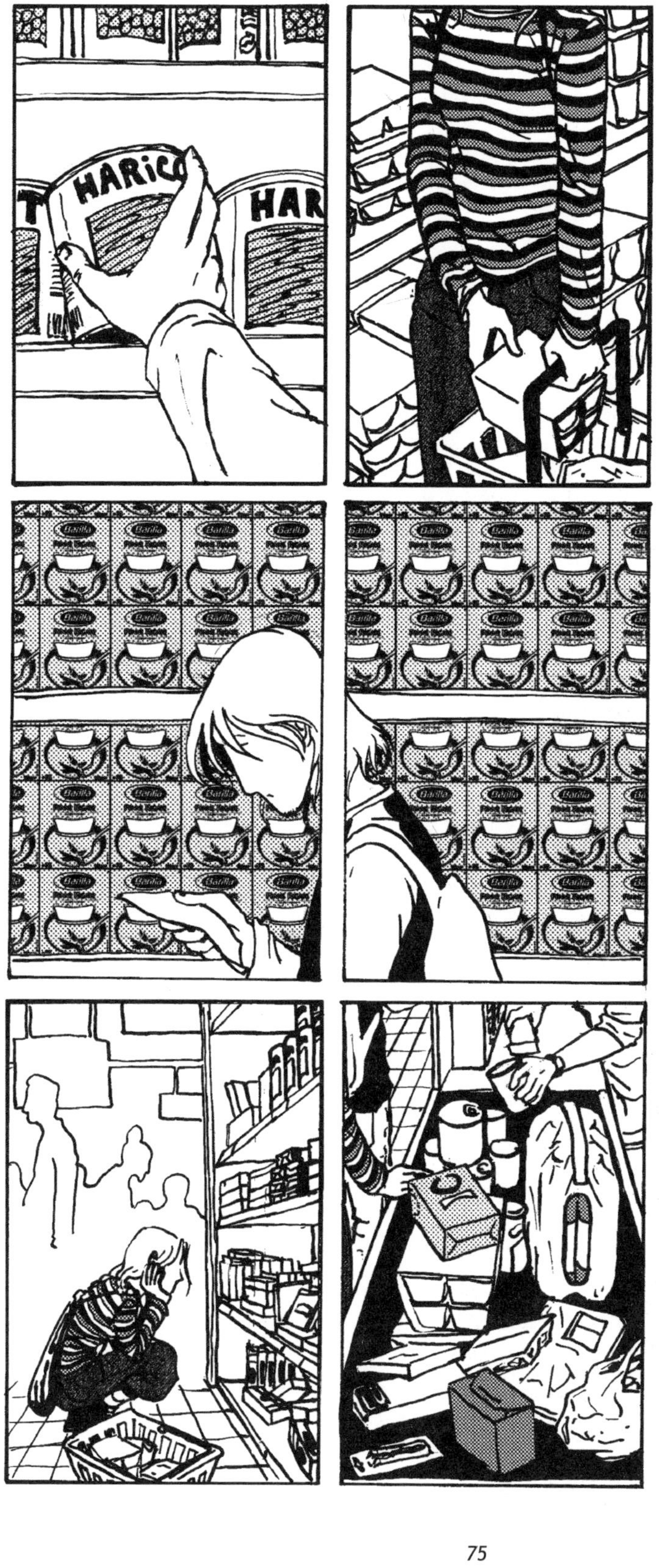
HARICO
HAR

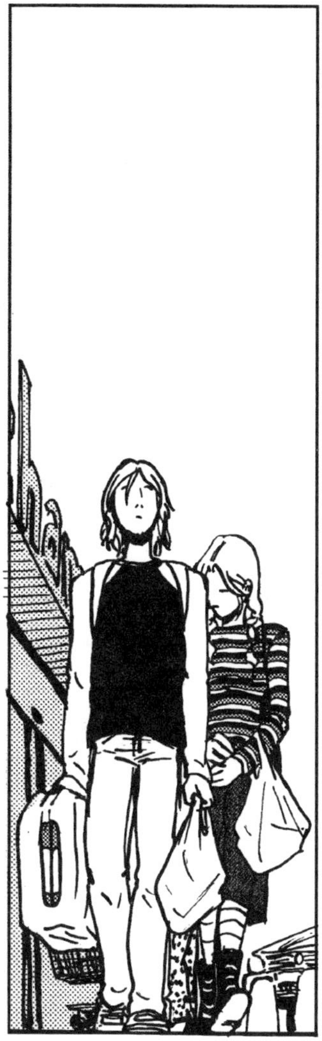

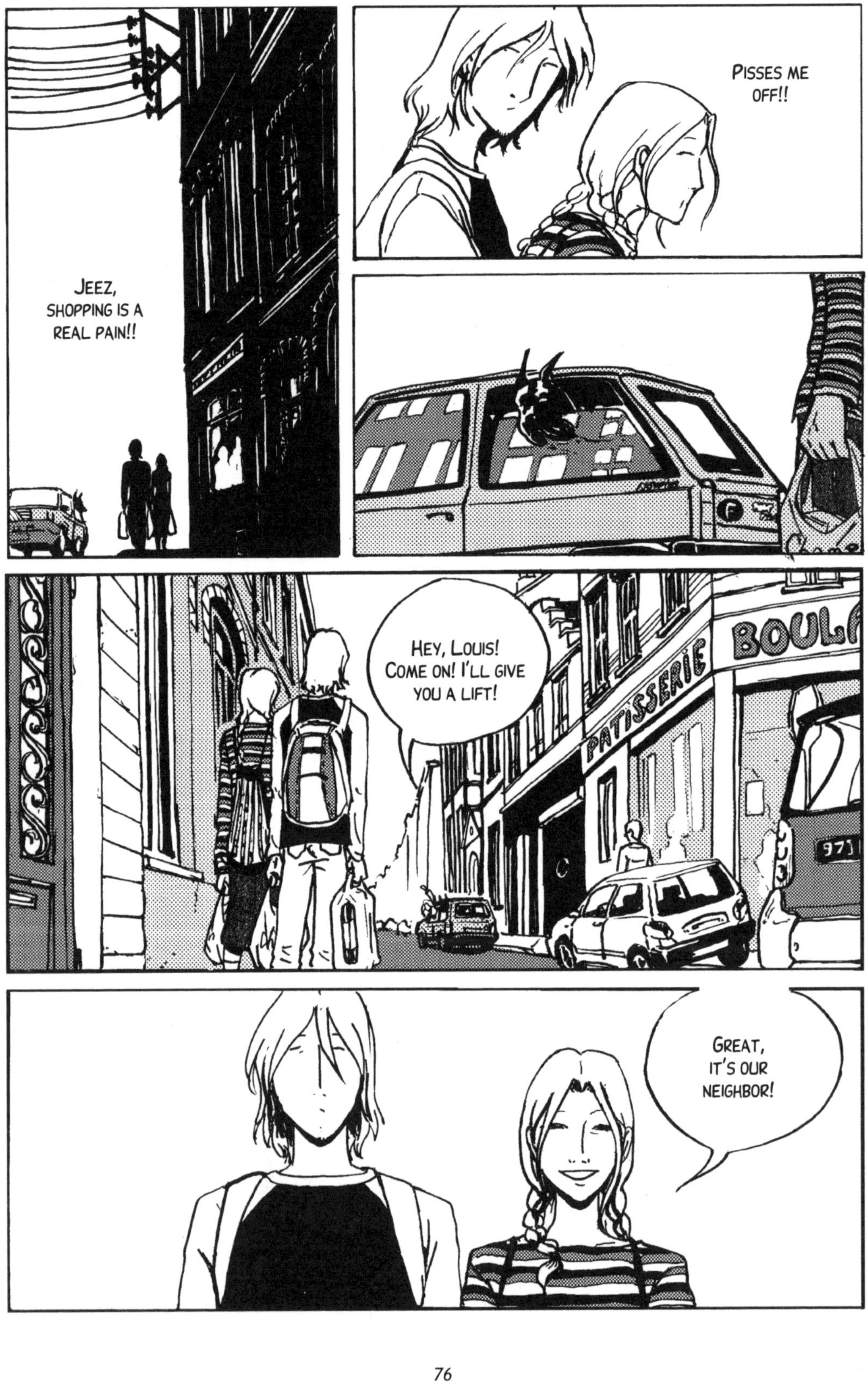
JEEZ, SHOPPING IS A REAL PAIN!!
PISSES ME OFF!!
HEY, LOUIS! COME ON! I'LL GIVE YOU A LIFT!
PATISSERIE
GREAT, IT'S OUR NEIGHBOR!

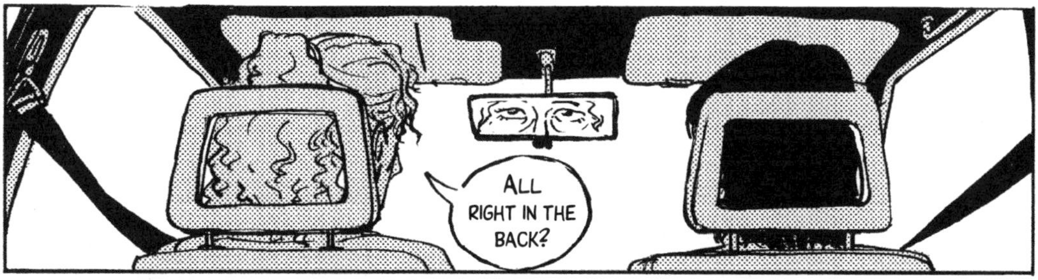
ALL RIGHT IN THE BACK?

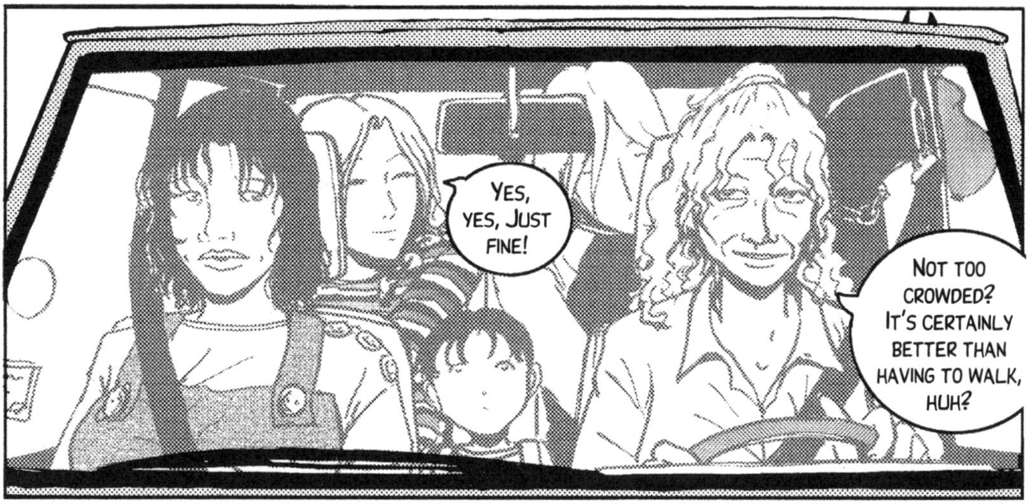
YES, YES, JUST FINE!
NOT TOO CROWDED? IT'S CERTAINLY BETTER THAN HAVING TO WALK, HUH?

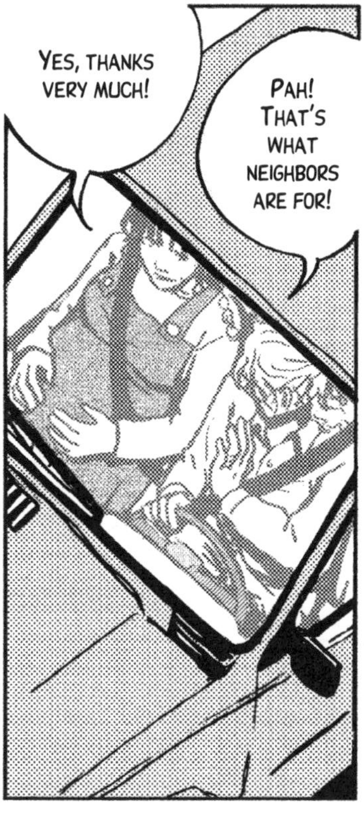
YES, THANKS VERY MUCH!
PAH! THAT'S WHAT NEIGHBORS ARE FOR!

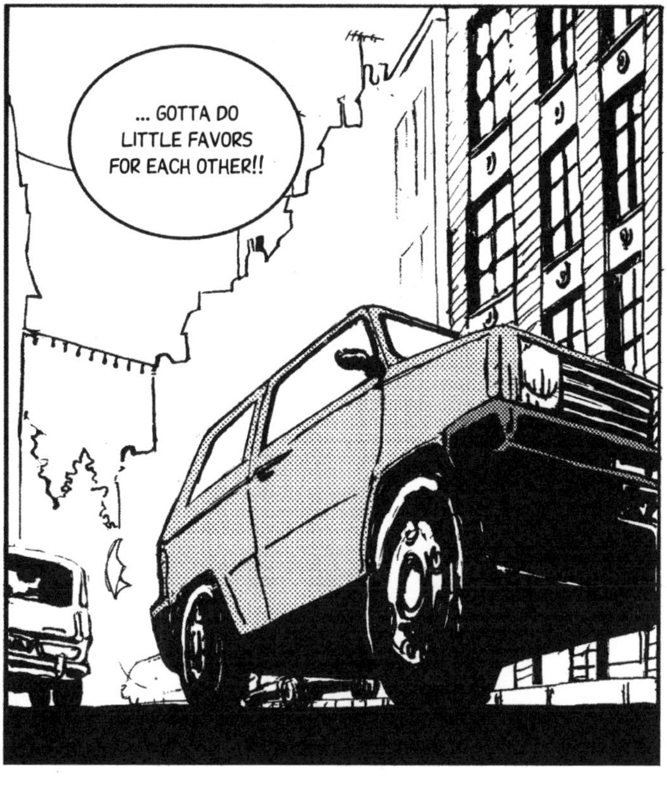
... GOTTA DO LITTLE FAVORS FOR EACH OTHER!!

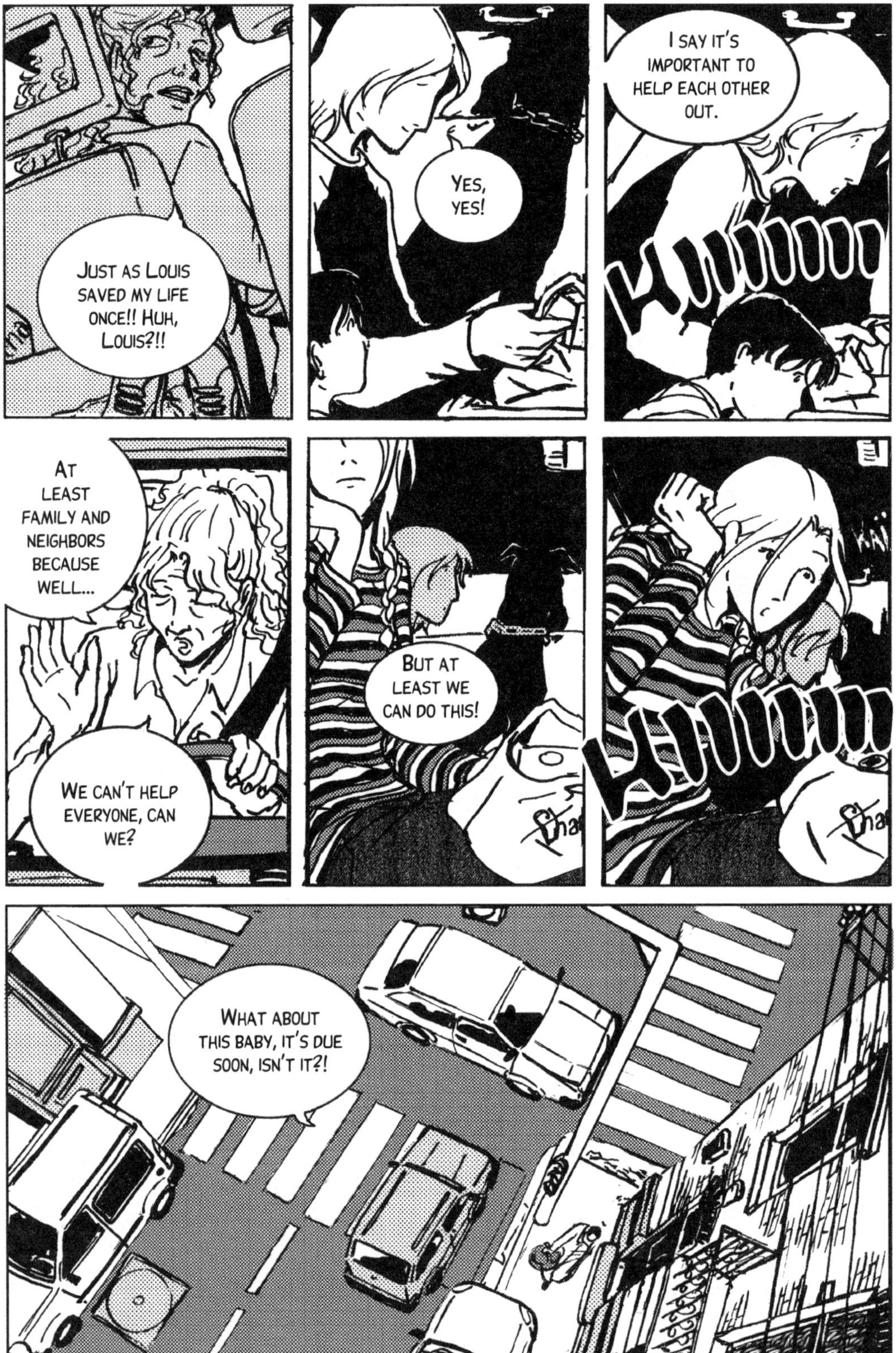
Just as Louis saved my life once!! Huh, Louis?!!
Yes, yes!
I say it's important to help each other out.
At least family and neighbors because well...
We can't help everyone, can we?
But at least we can do this!
What about this baby, it's due soon, isn't it?!

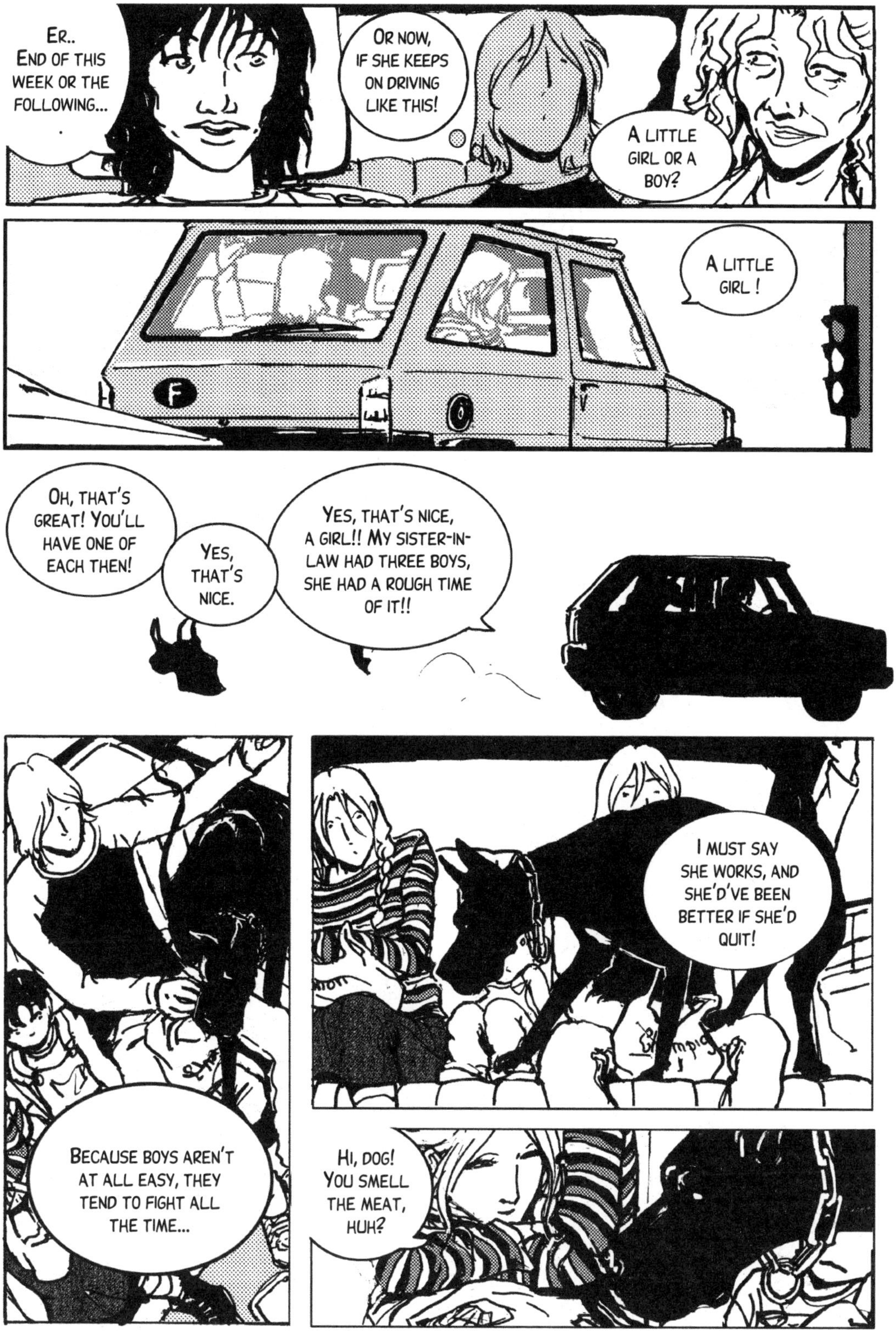
Er.. End of this week or the following...
Or now, if she keeps on driving like this!
A little girl or a boy?
A little girl !
Oh, that's great! You'll have one of each then!
Yes, that's nice.
Yes, that's nice, a girl!! My sister-in-law had three boys, she had a rough time of it!!
Because boys aren't at all easy, they tend to fight all the time...
I must say she works, and she'd've been better if she'd quit!
Hi, dog! You smell the meat, huh?

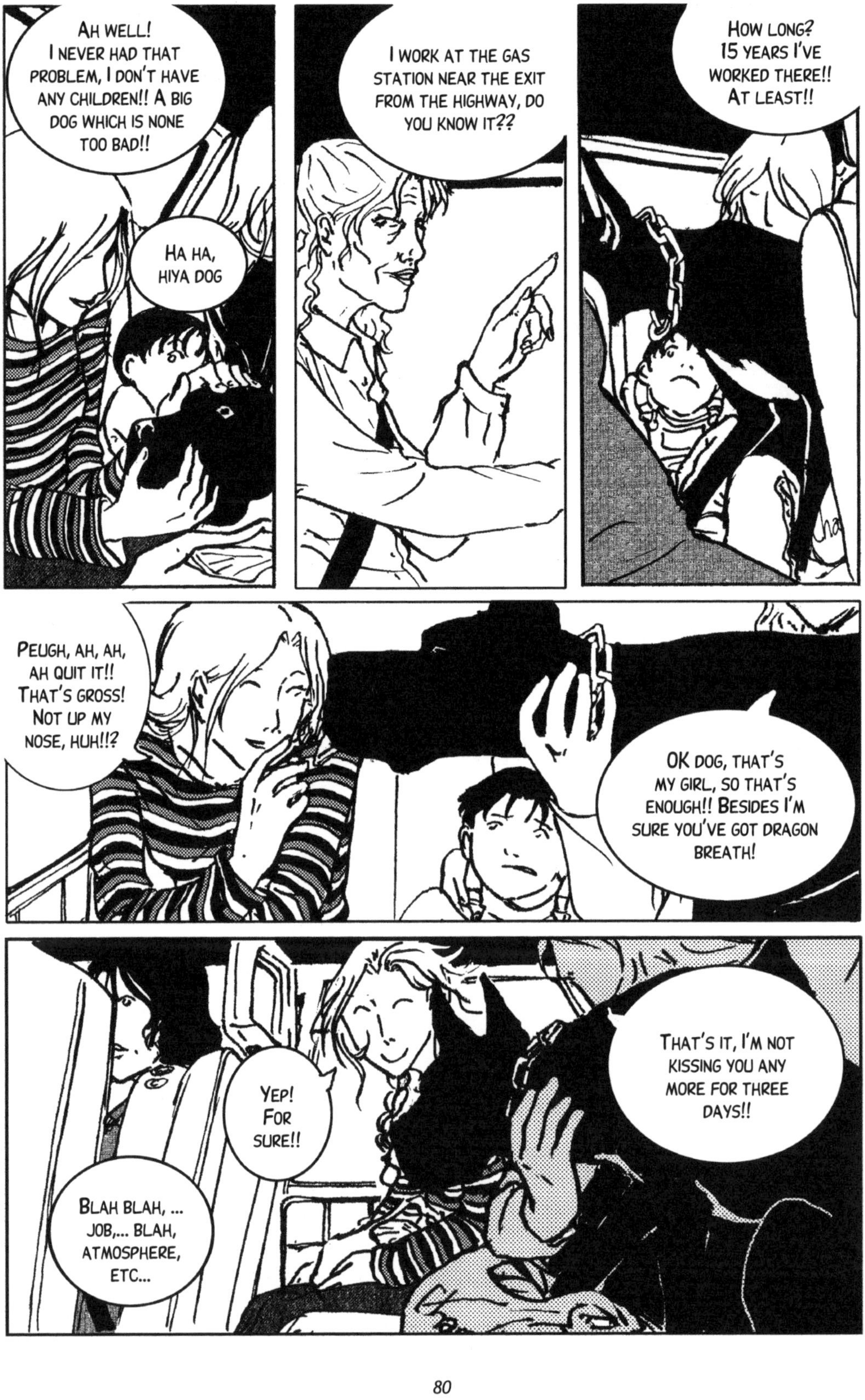
Ah well! I never had that problem, I don't have any children!! A big dog which is none too bad!!
Ha ha, hiya dog
I work at the gas station near the exit from the highway, do you know it??
How long? 15 years I've worked there!! At least!!
Peugh, ah, ah, ah quit it!! That's gross! Not up my nose, huh!!?
OK dog, that's my girl, so that's enough!! Besides I'm sure you've got dragon breath!
Yep! For sure!!
That's it, I'm not kissing you any more for three days!!
Blah blah, ... job,... blah, atmosphere, etc...

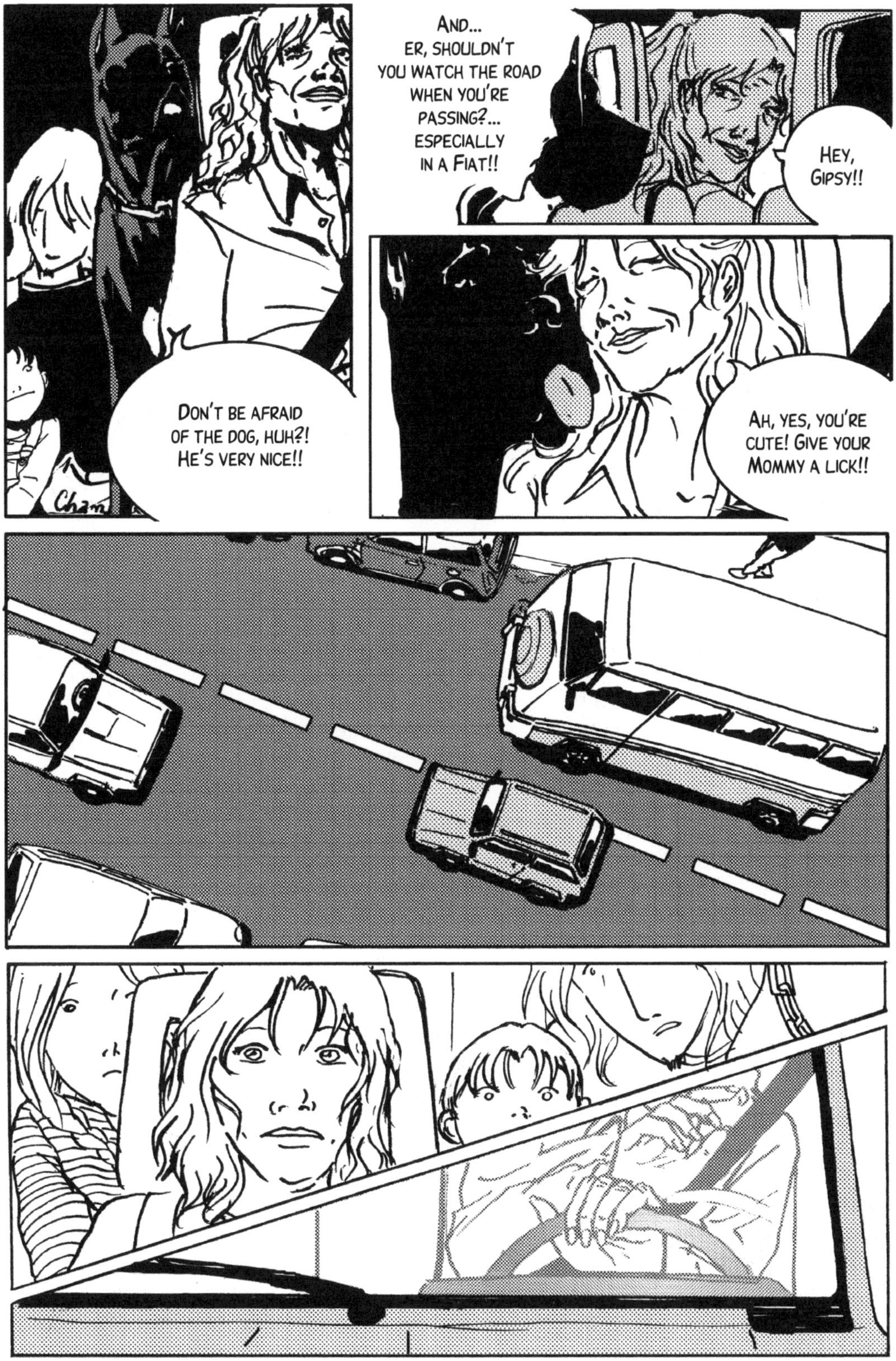
Don't be afraid of the dog, huh?! He's very nice!!
And... er, shouldn't you watch the road when you're passing?... especially in a Fiat!!
Hey, Gipsy!!
Ah, yes, you're cute! Give your Mommy a lick!!

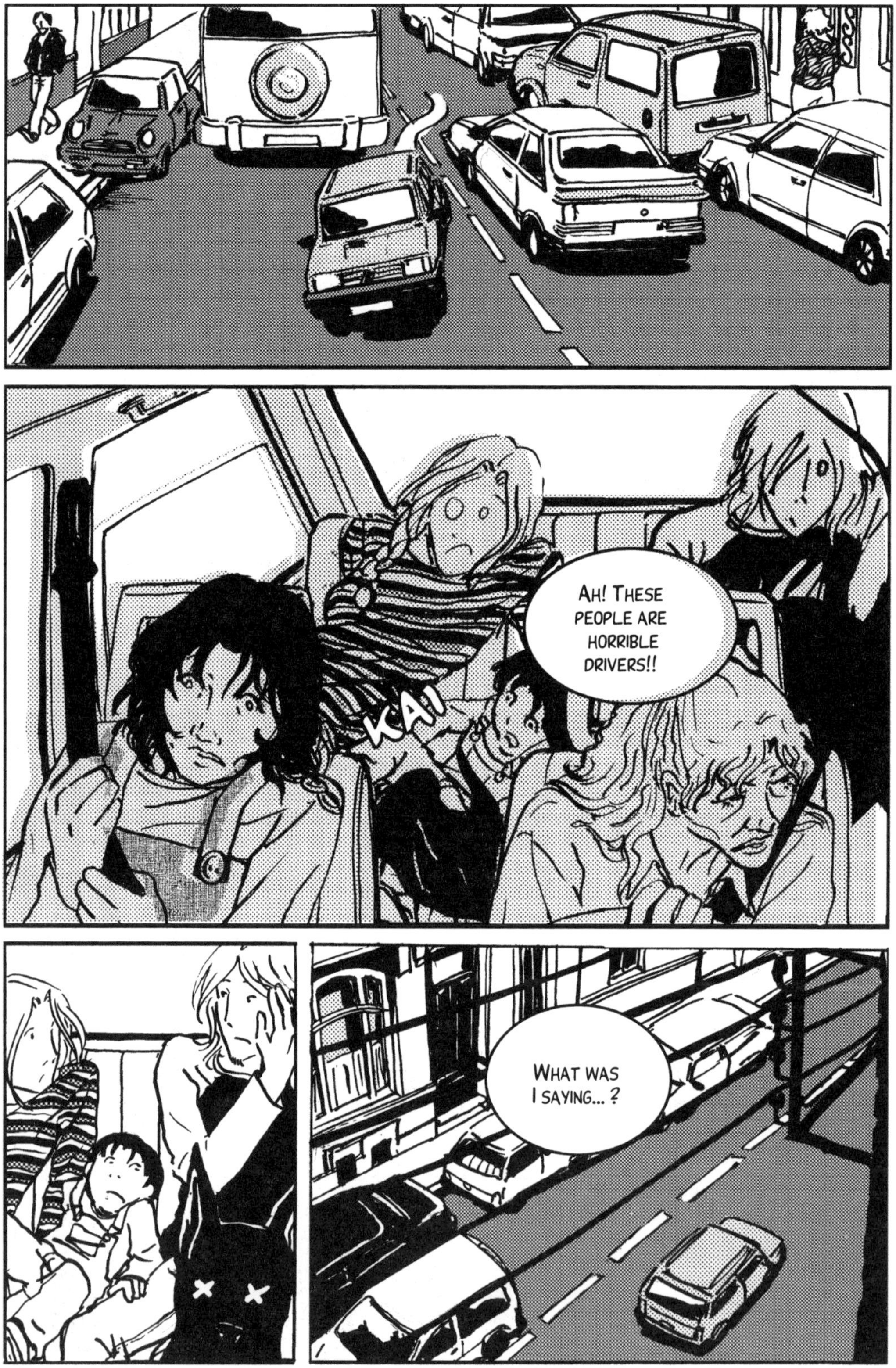
Ah! These people are horrible drivers!!
KAI
What was I saying... ?

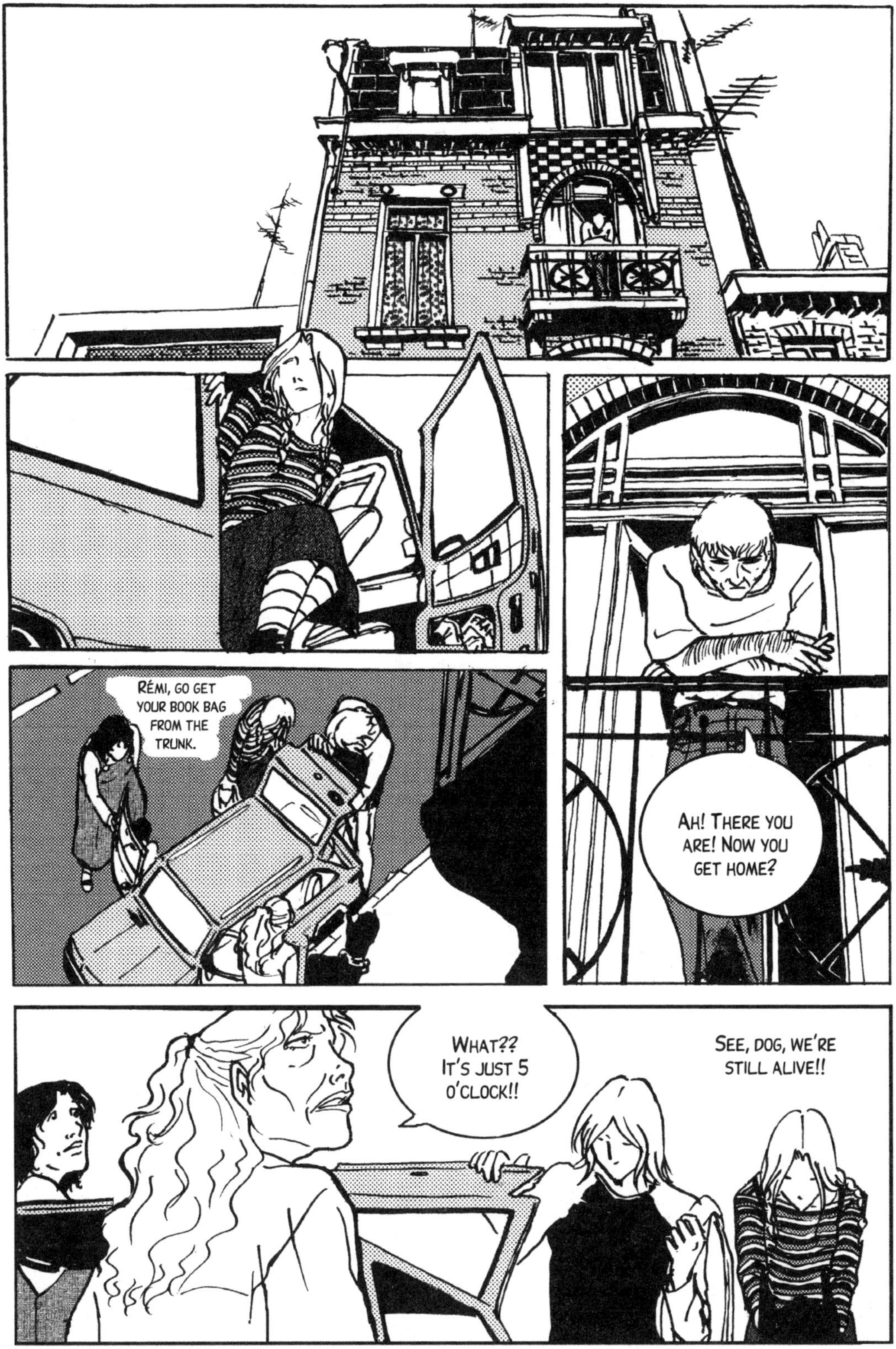
Rémi, go get your book bag from the trunk.
Ah! There you are! Now you get home?
What?? It's just 5 o'clock!!
See, dog, we're still alive!!

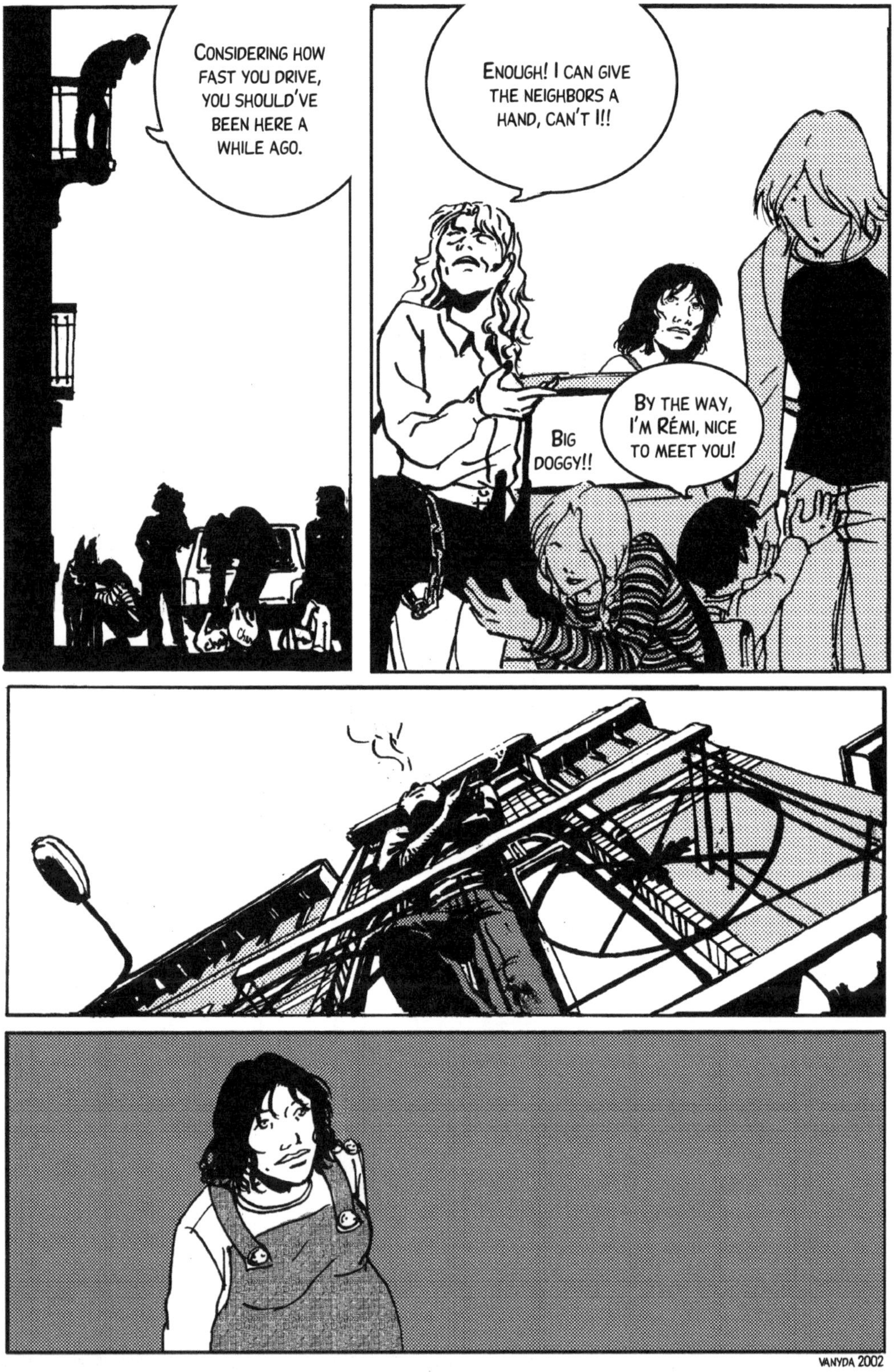
CONSIDERING HOW FAST YOU DRIVE, YOU SHOULD'VE BEEN HERE A WHILE AGO.
ENOUGH! I CAN GIVE THE NEIGHBORS A HAND, CAN'T I!!
BIG DOGGY!!
BY THE WAY, I'M RÉMI, NICE TO MEET YOU!
VANYDA 2002

OH, NO, NO! NO LICKING INSIDE MY MOUTH!!
ANYWAY, I JUST BLEW MY BOYFRIEND, SO... !
WHICH ONE OF US IS THE MOST DISGUSTED??
COMING, GIPSY?!
Vanyda 02

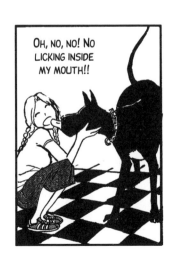

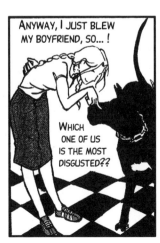

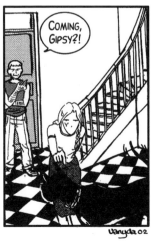

Chapter 12
(in)voluntary interruptions

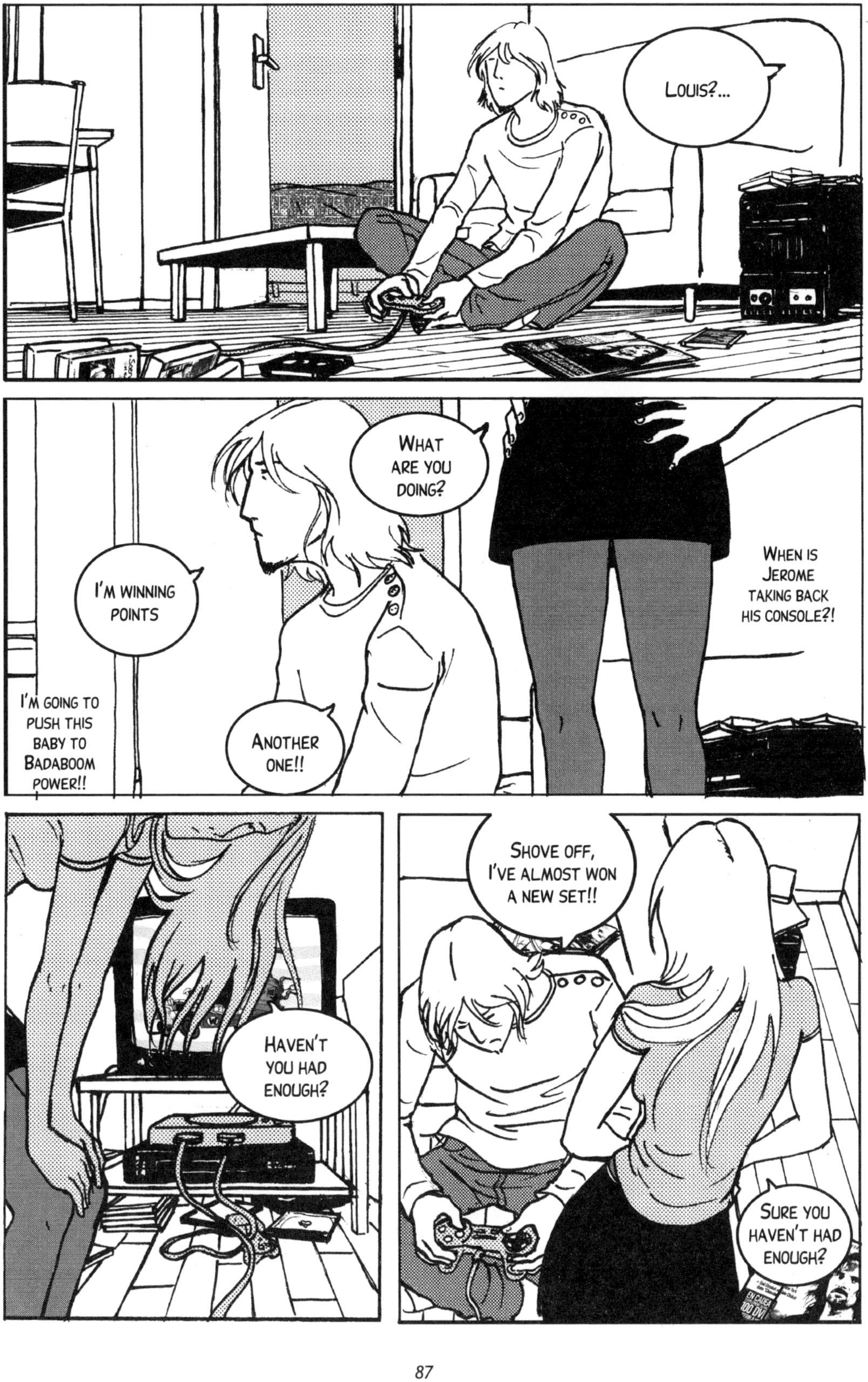
LOUIS?...
WHAT ARE YOU DOING?
I'M WINNING POINTS
WHEN IS JEROME TAKING BACK HIS CONSOLE?!
I'M GOING TO PUSH THIS BABY TO BADABOOM POWER!!
ANOTHER ONE!!
HAVEN'T YOU HAD ENOUGH?
SHOVE OFF, I'VE ALMOST WON A NEW SET!!
SURE YOU HAVEN'T HAD ENOUGH?

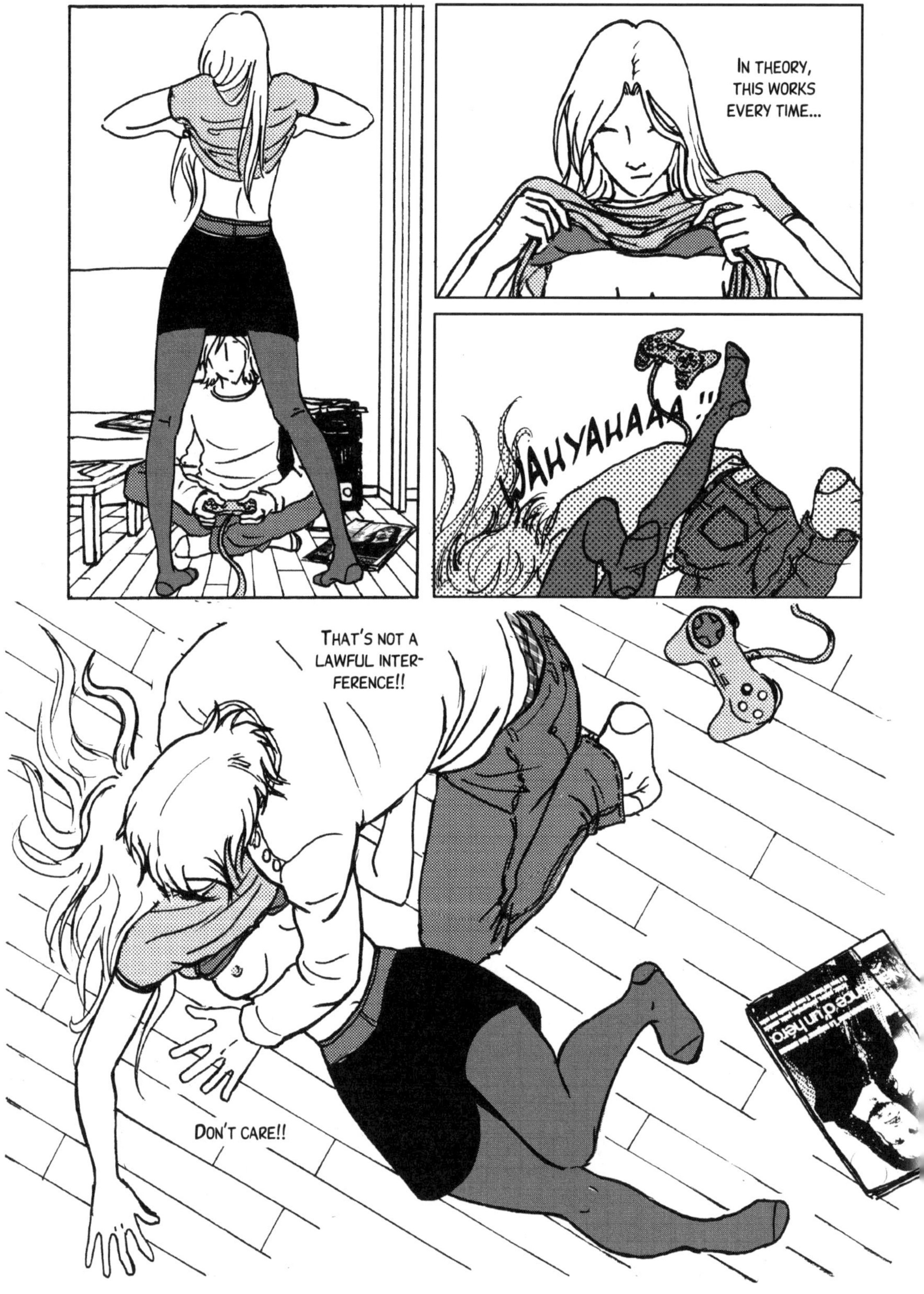
In theory, this works every time...
WAHYAHAAA!!
That's not a lawful inter-ference!!
Don't care!!

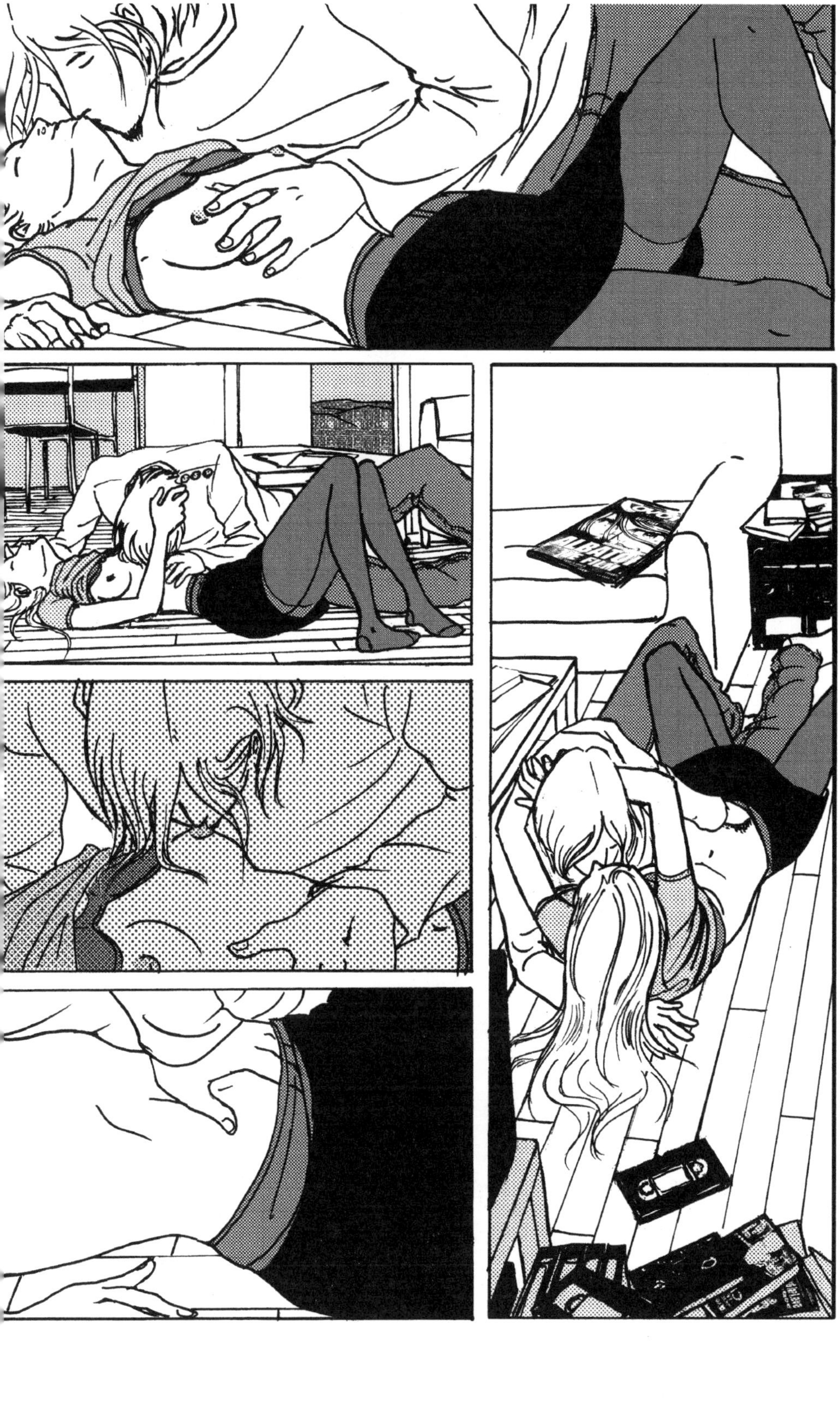
ALBATOR

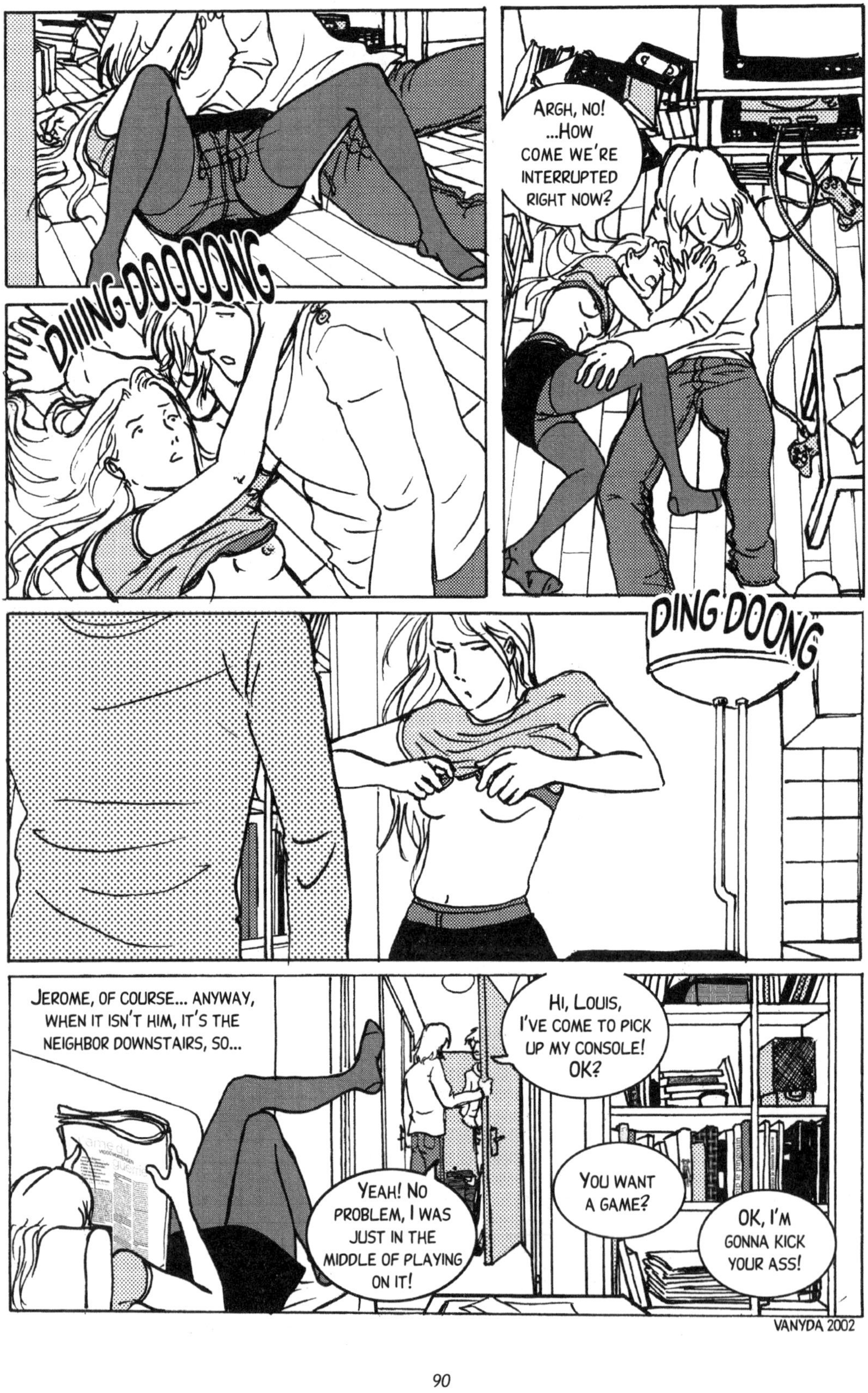
DIIING DOOOONG
ARGH, NO! ...HOW COME WE'RE INTERRUPTED RIGHT NOW?
DING DOONG
JEROME, OF COURSE... ANYWAY, WHEN IT ISN'T HIM, IT'S THE NEIGHBOR DOWNSTAIRS, SO...
HI, LOUIS, I'VE COME TO PICK UP MY CONSOLE! OK?
YEAH! NO PROBLEM, I WAS JUST IN THE MIDDLE OF PLAYING ON IT!
YOU WANT A GAME?
OK, I'M GONNA KICK YOUR ASS!

VANYDA 2002

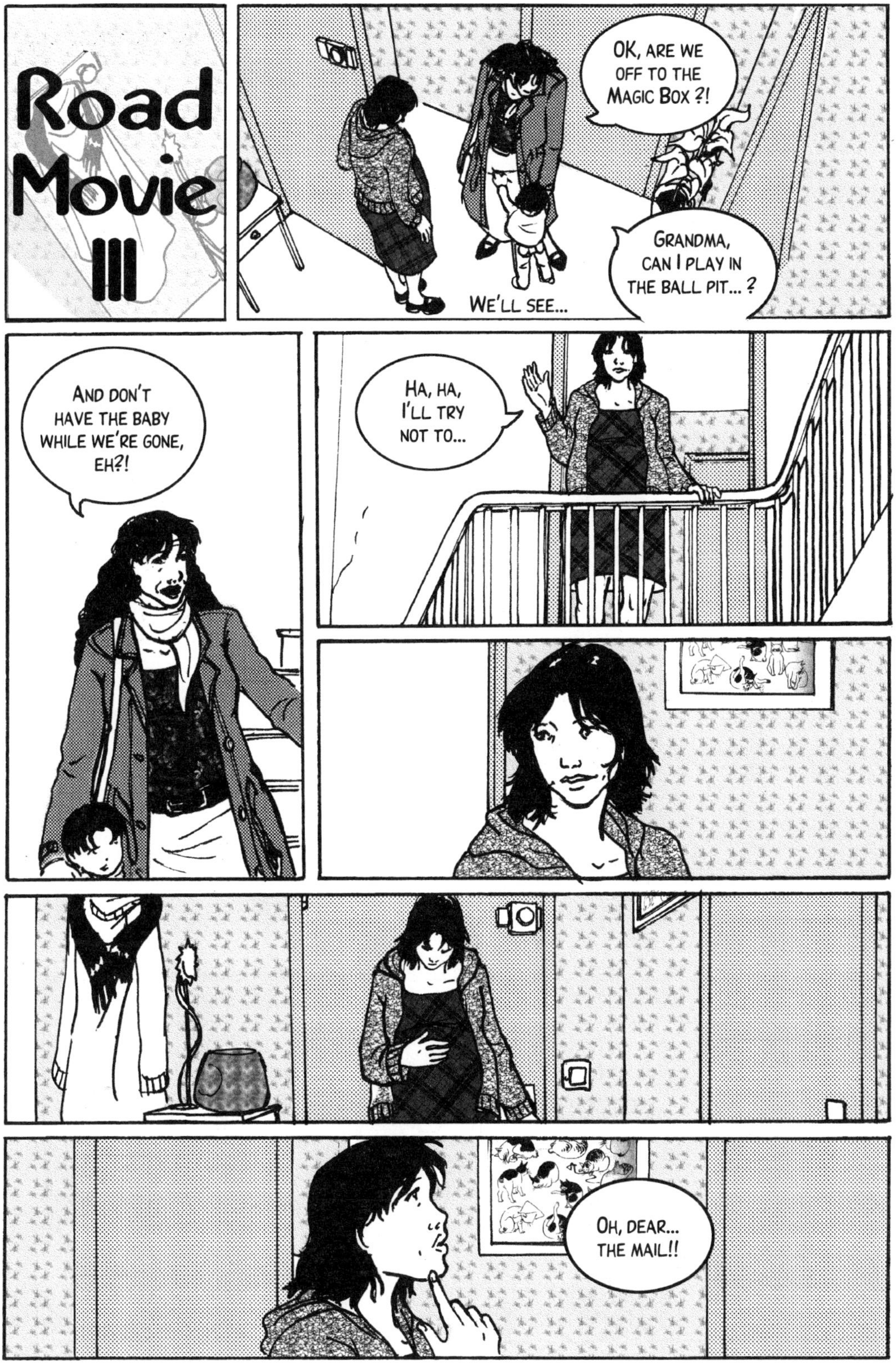
Road Movie III
OK, ARE WE OFF TO THE MAGIC BOX ?!
WE'LL SEE...
GRANDMA, CAN I PLAY IN THE BALL PIT... ?
AND DON'T HAVE THE BABY WHILE WE'RE GONE, EH?!
HA, HA, I'LL TRY NOT TO...
OH, DEAR... THE MAIL!!

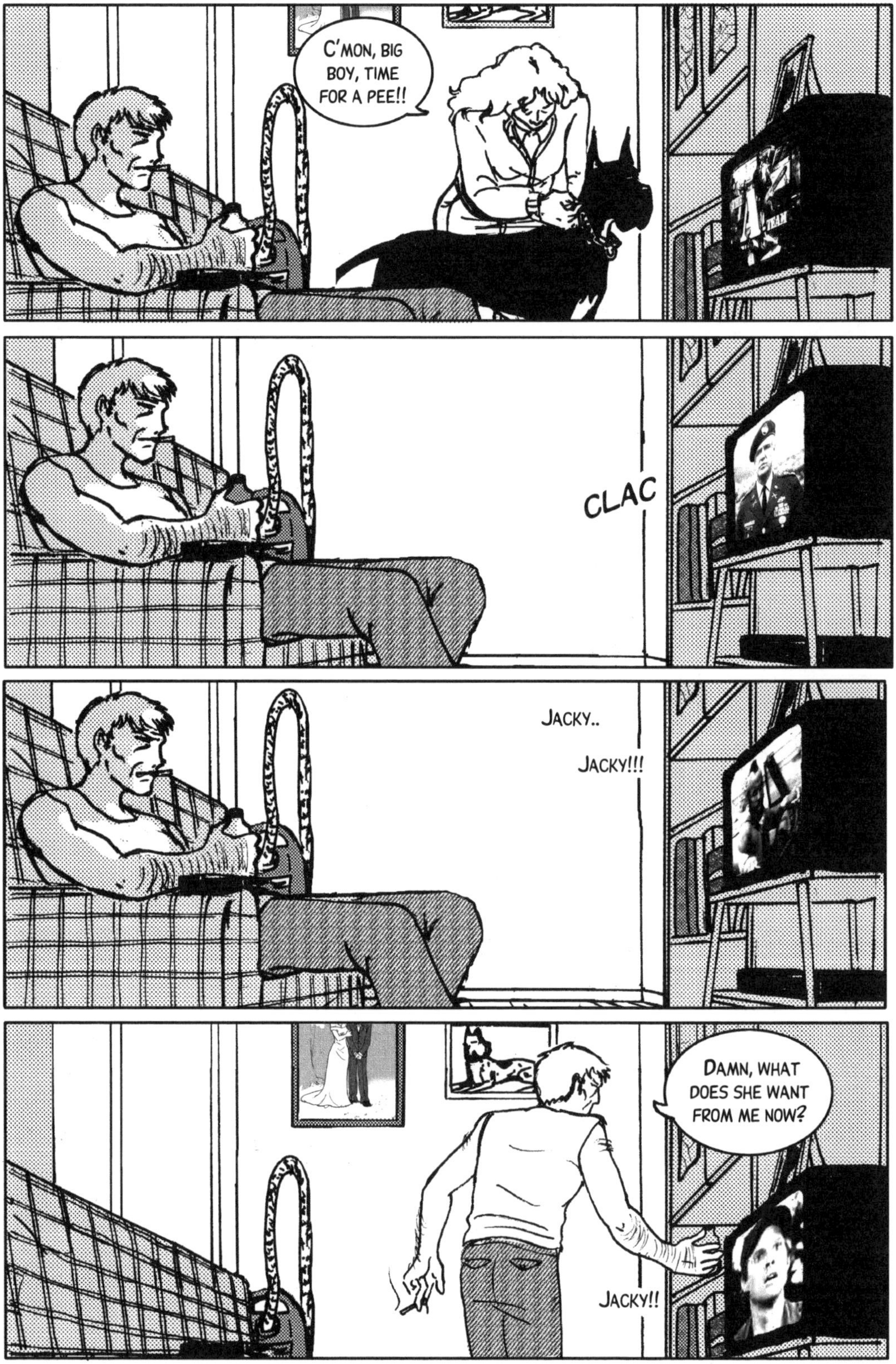
C'MON, BIG BOY, TIME FOR A PEE!!
CLAC
JACKY..
JACKY!!!
DAMN, WHAT DOES SHE WANT FROM ME NOW?
JACKY!!

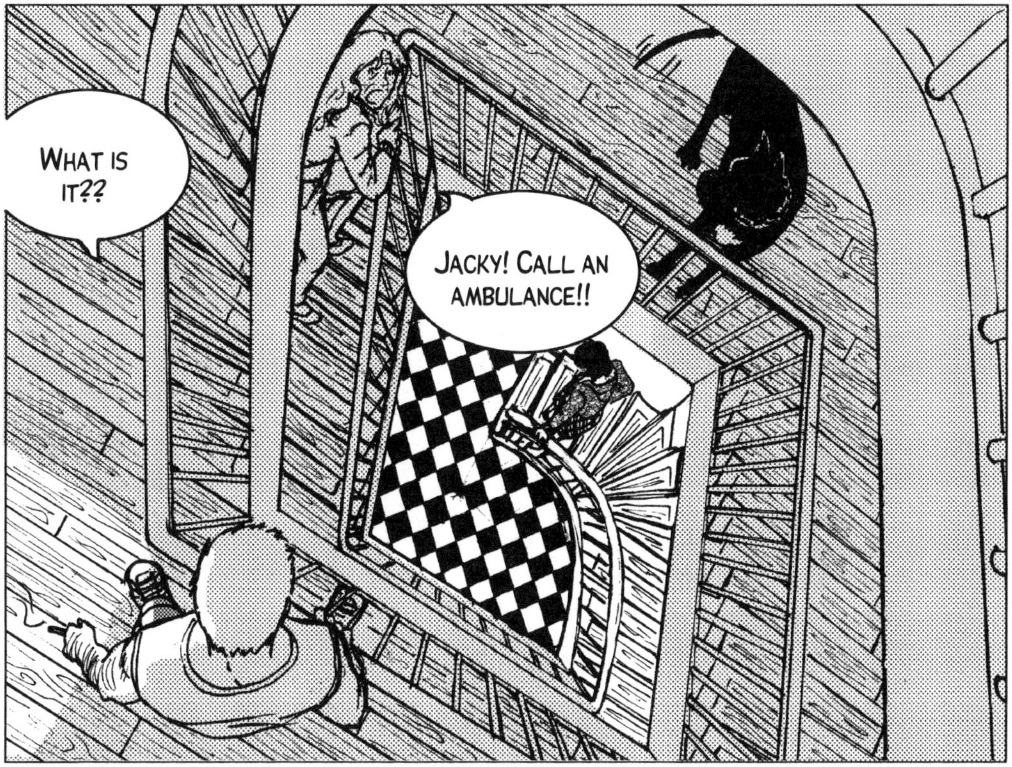
WHAT IS IT??
JACKY! CALL AN AMBULANCE!!

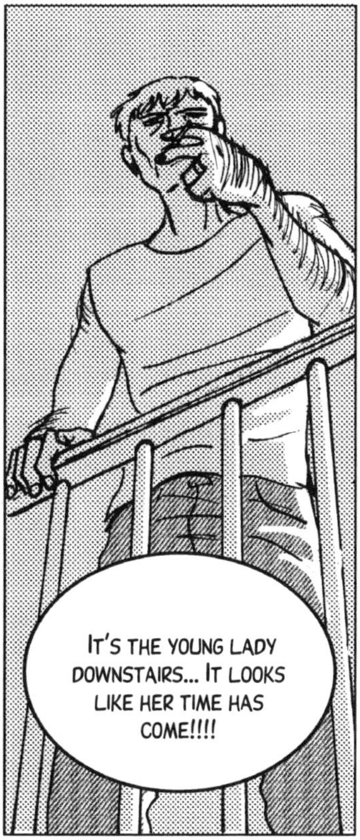
IT'S THE YOUNG LADY DOWNSTAIRS... IT LOOKS LIKE HER TIME HAS COME!!!!

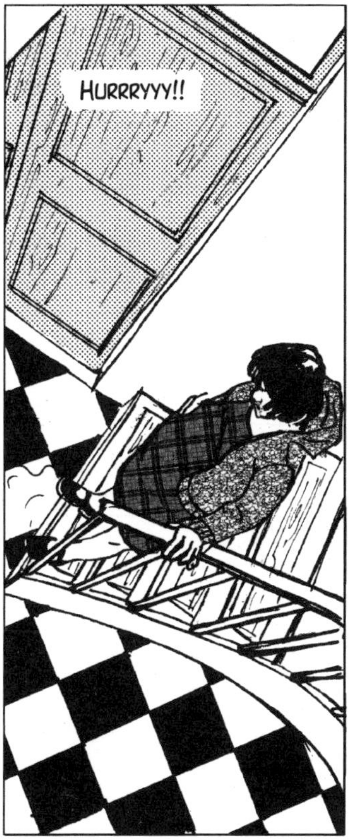
HURRRYYY!!

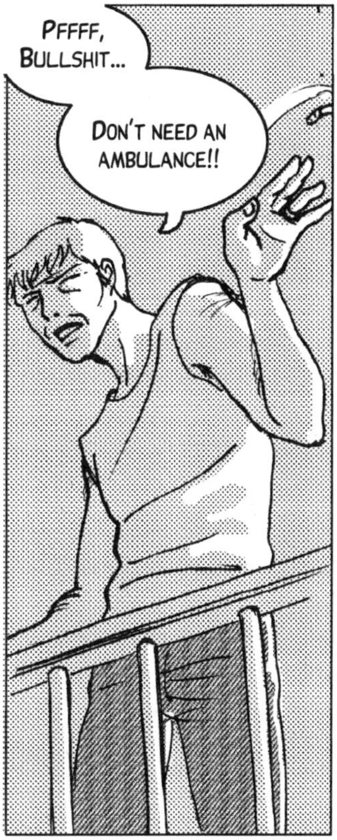
PFFFF, BULLSHIT...
DON'T NEED AN AMBULANCE!!

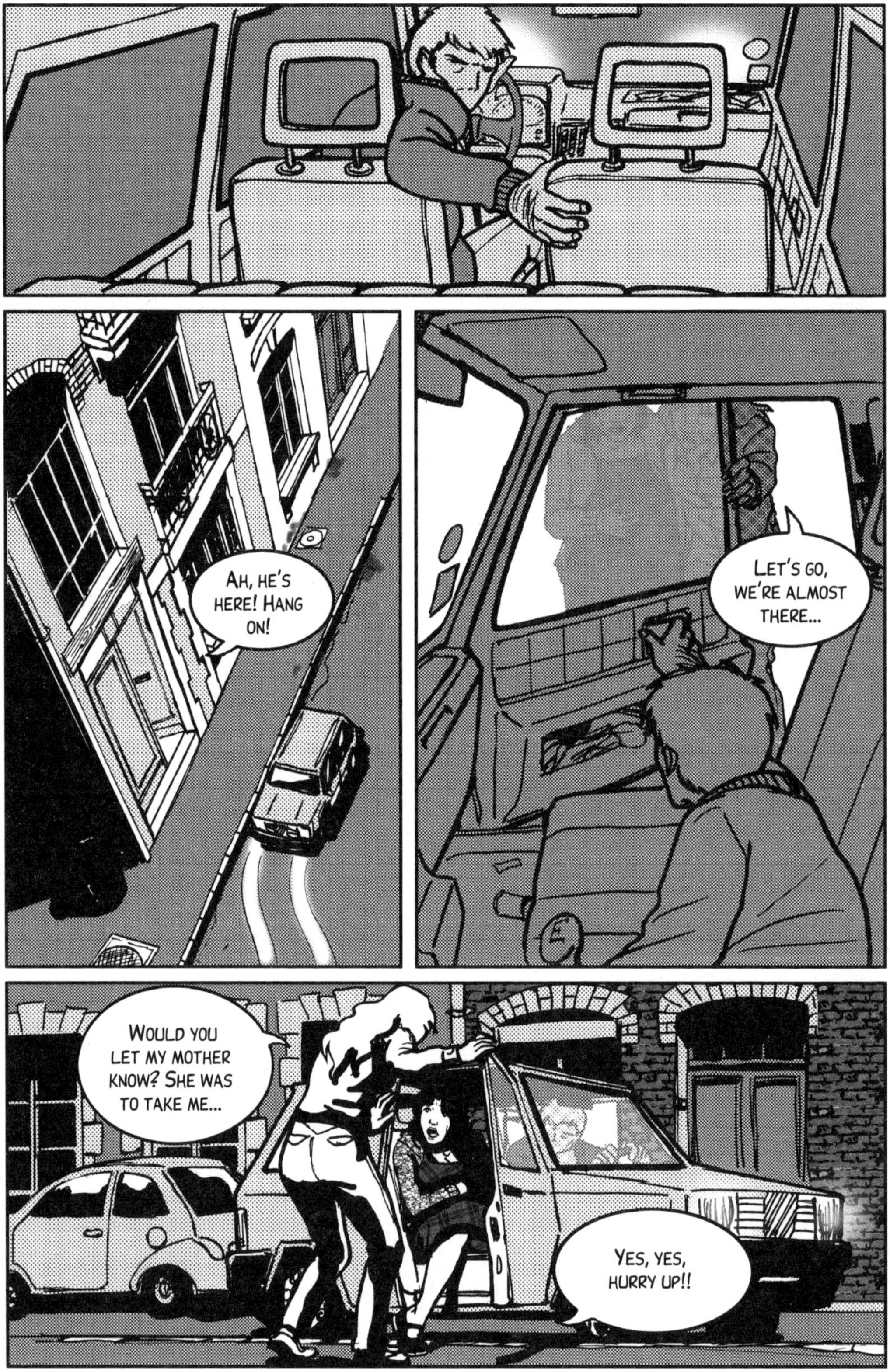
AH, HE'S HERE! HANG ON!
LET'S GO, WE'RE ALMOST THERE...
WOULD YOU LET MY MOTHER KNOW? SHE WAS TO TAKE ME...
YES, YES, HURRY UP!!

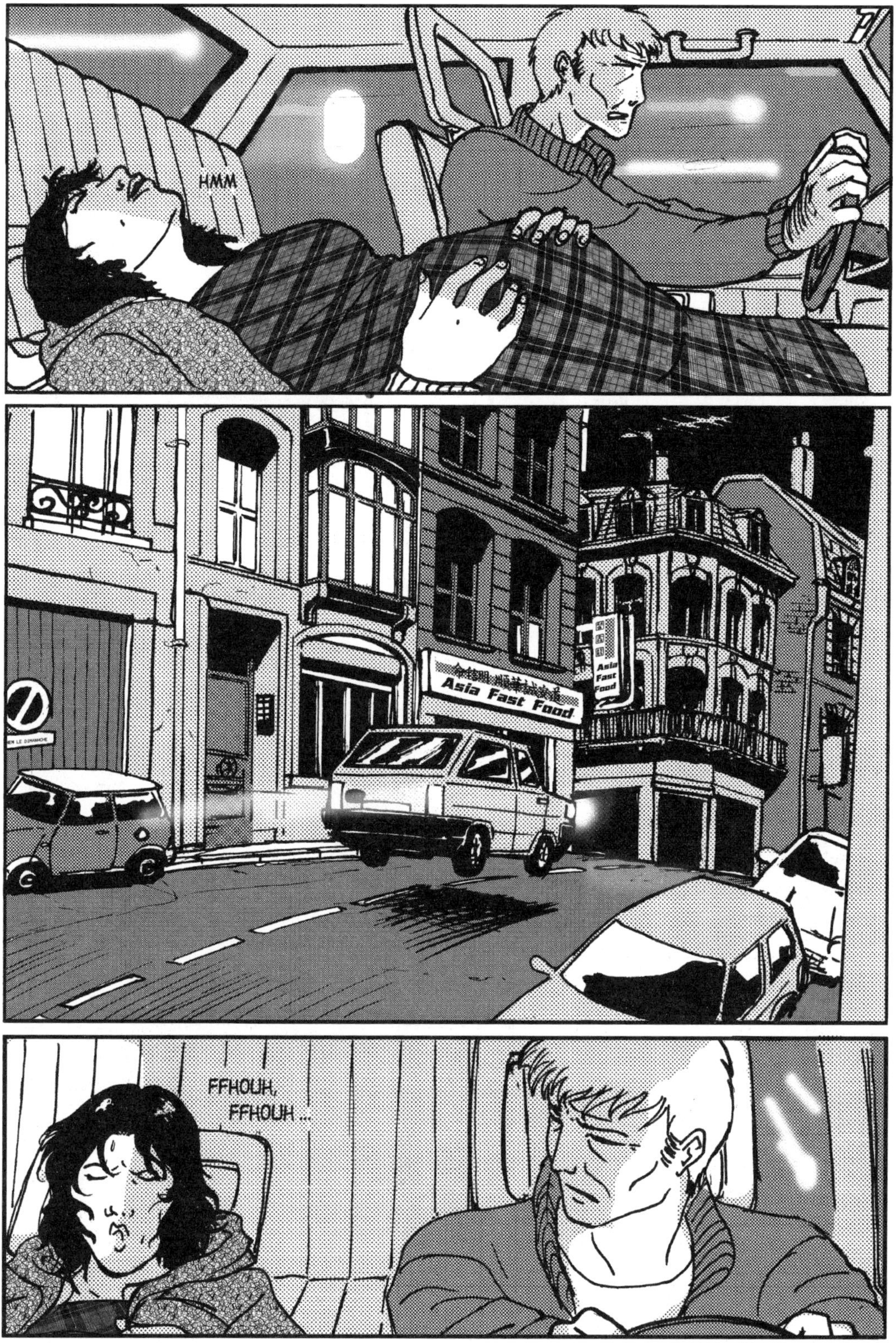
HMM
Asia Fast Food
Asia Fast Food
FFHOUH,
FFHOUH ...

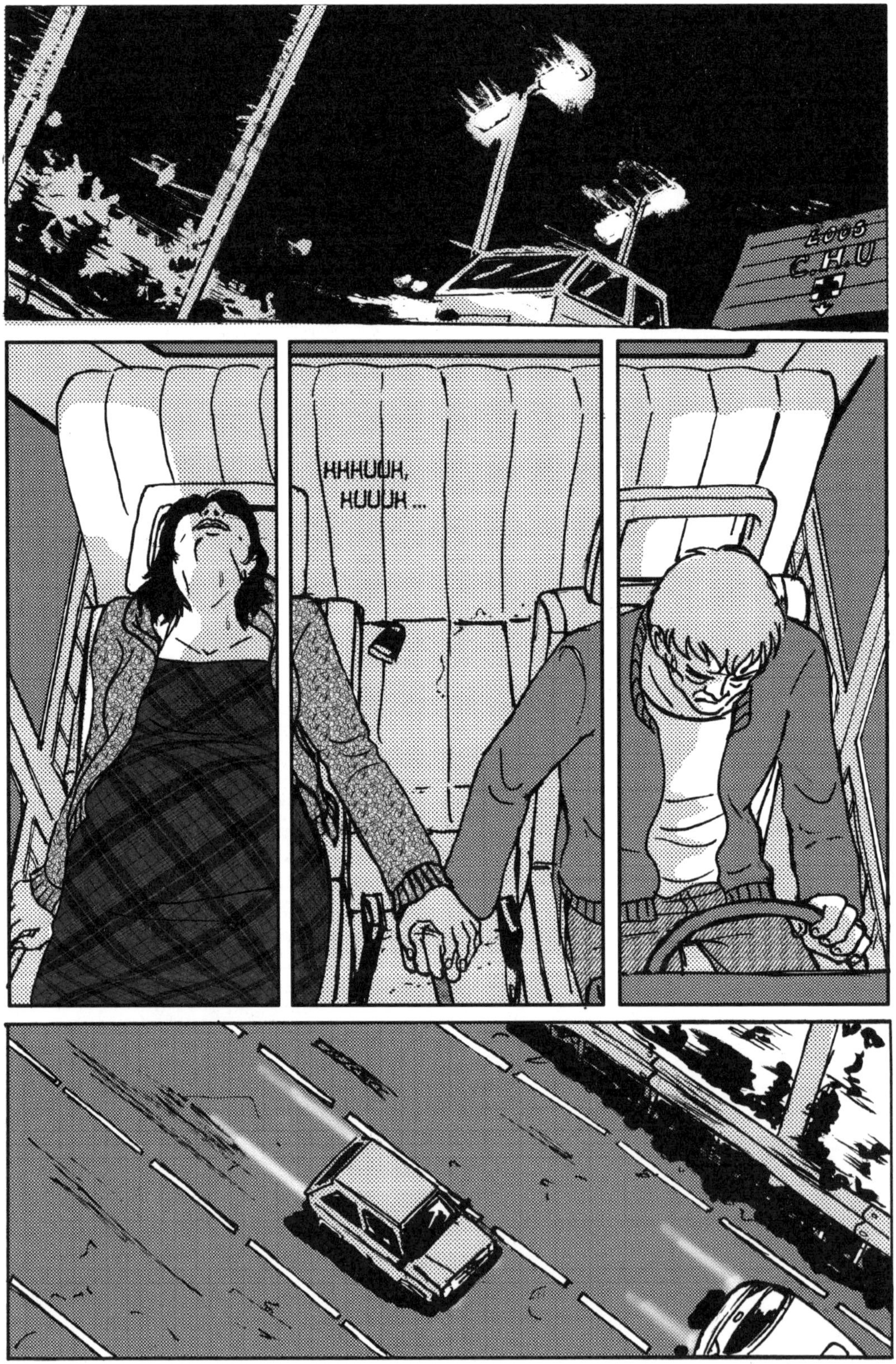
2005
C.H.U
HHHUUH,
HUUUH...

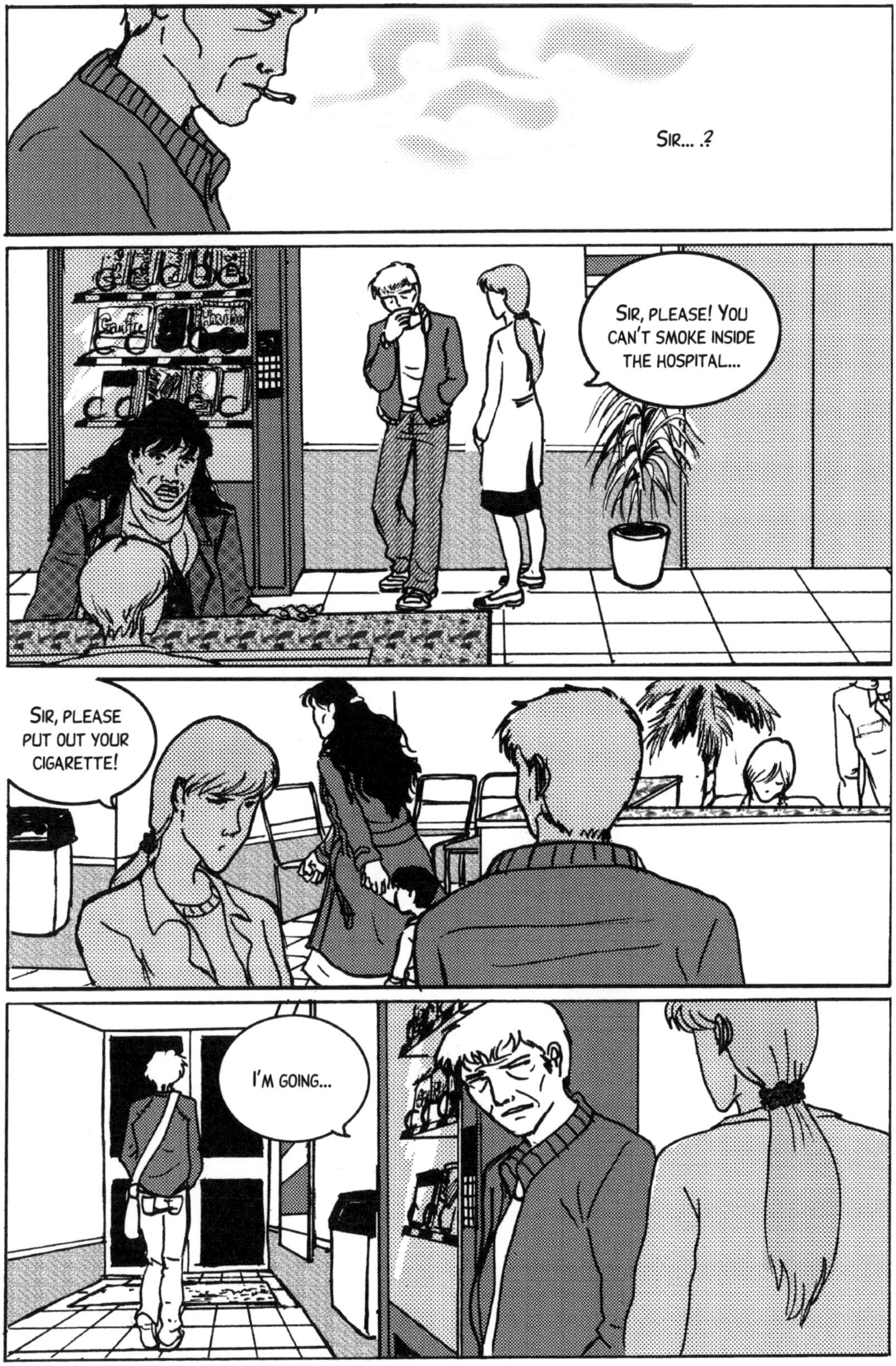
SIR... .?
SIR, PLEASE! YOU CAN'T SMOKE INSIDE THE HOSPITAL...
SIR, PLEASE PUT OUT YOUR CIGARETTE!
I'M GOING...

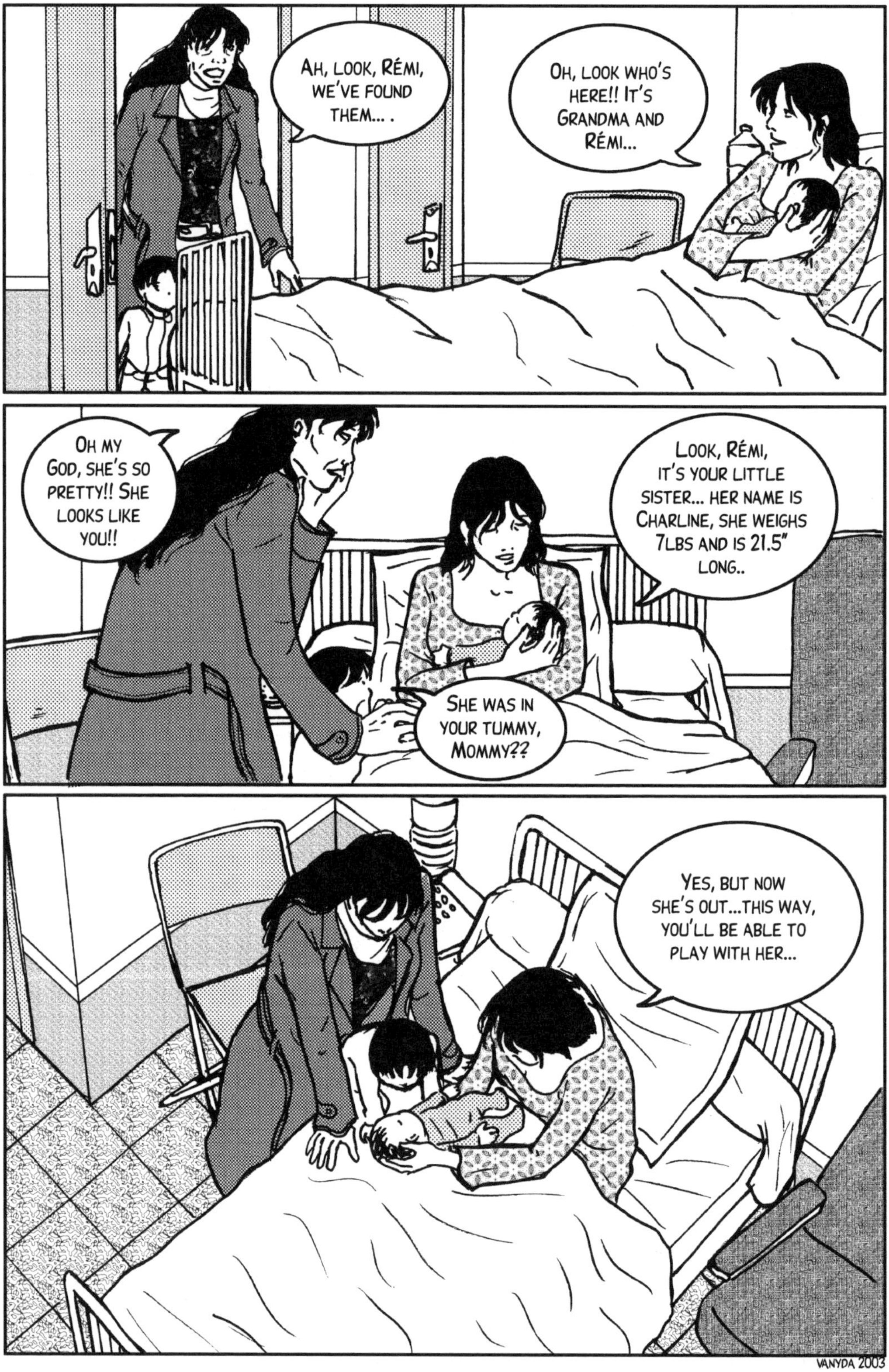
Ah, look, Rémi, we've found them... .
Oh, look who's here!! It's Grandma and Rémi...
Oh my God, she's so pretty!! She looks like you!!
Look, Rémi, it's your little sister... her name is Charline, she weighs 7lbs and is 21.5" long..
She was in your tummy, Mommy??
Yes, but now she's out...this way, you'll be able to play with her...

Vanyda 2003

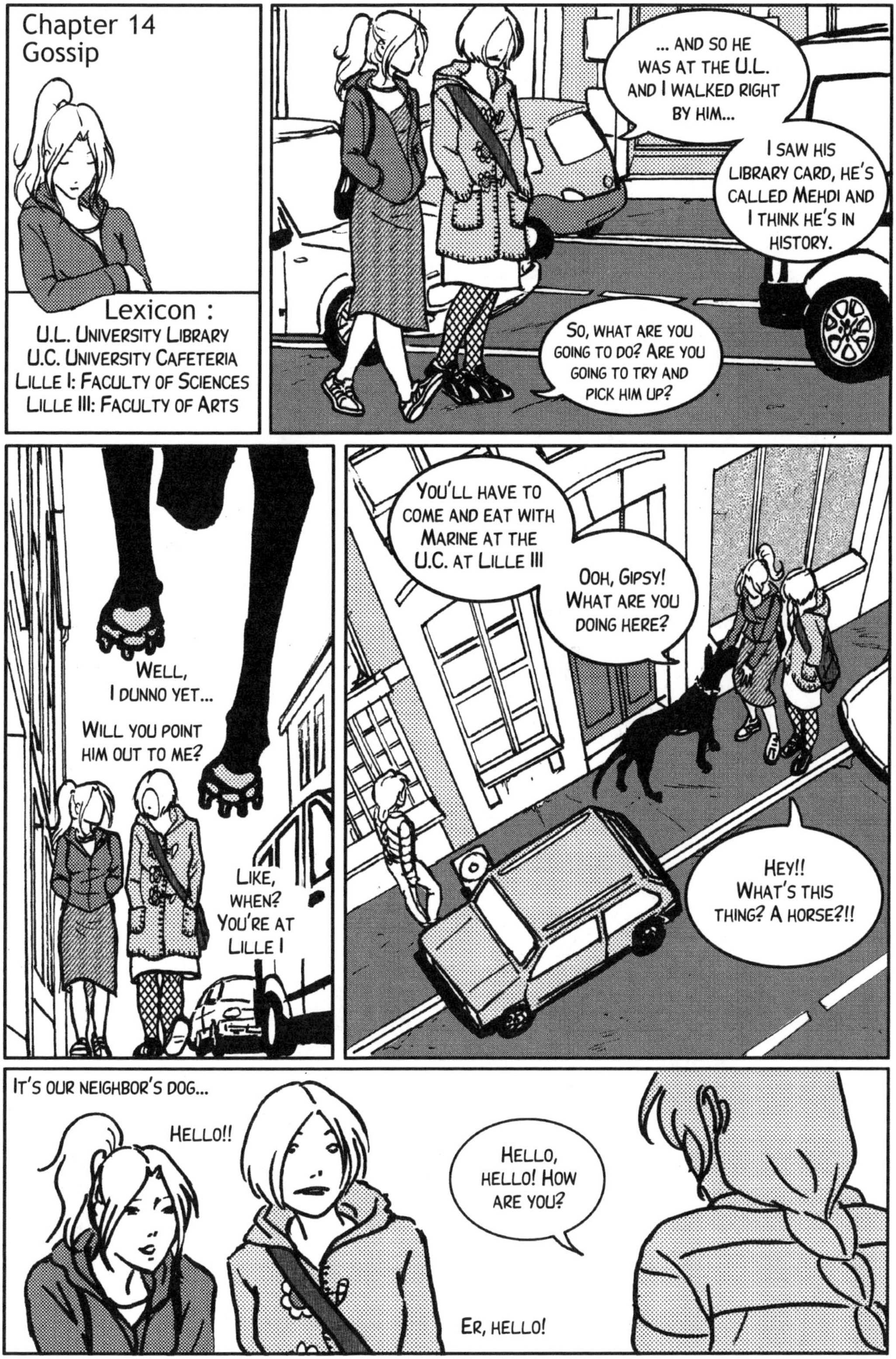
Chapter 14
Gossip
Lexicon :
U.L. University Library
U.C. University Cafeteria
Lille I: Faculty of Sciences
Lille III: Faculty of Arts
... AND SO HE WAS AT THE U.L. AND I WALKED RIGHT BY HIM...
I SAW HIS LIBRARY CARD, HE'S CALLED MEHDI AND I THINK HE'S IN HISTORY.
SO, WHAT ARE YOU GOING TO DO? ARE YOU GOING TO TRY AND PICK HIM UP?
WELL, I DUNNO YET...
WILL YOU POINT HIM OUT TO ME?
LIKE, WHEN? YOU'RE AT LILLE I
YOU'LL HAVE TO COME AND EAT WITH MARINE AT THE U.C. AT LILLE III
OOH, GIPSY! WHAT ARE YOU DOING HERE?
HEY!! WHAT'S THIS THING? A HORSE?!!
IT'S OUR NEIGHBOR'S DOG...
HELLO!!
HELLO, HELLO! HOW ARE YOU?
ER, HELLO!

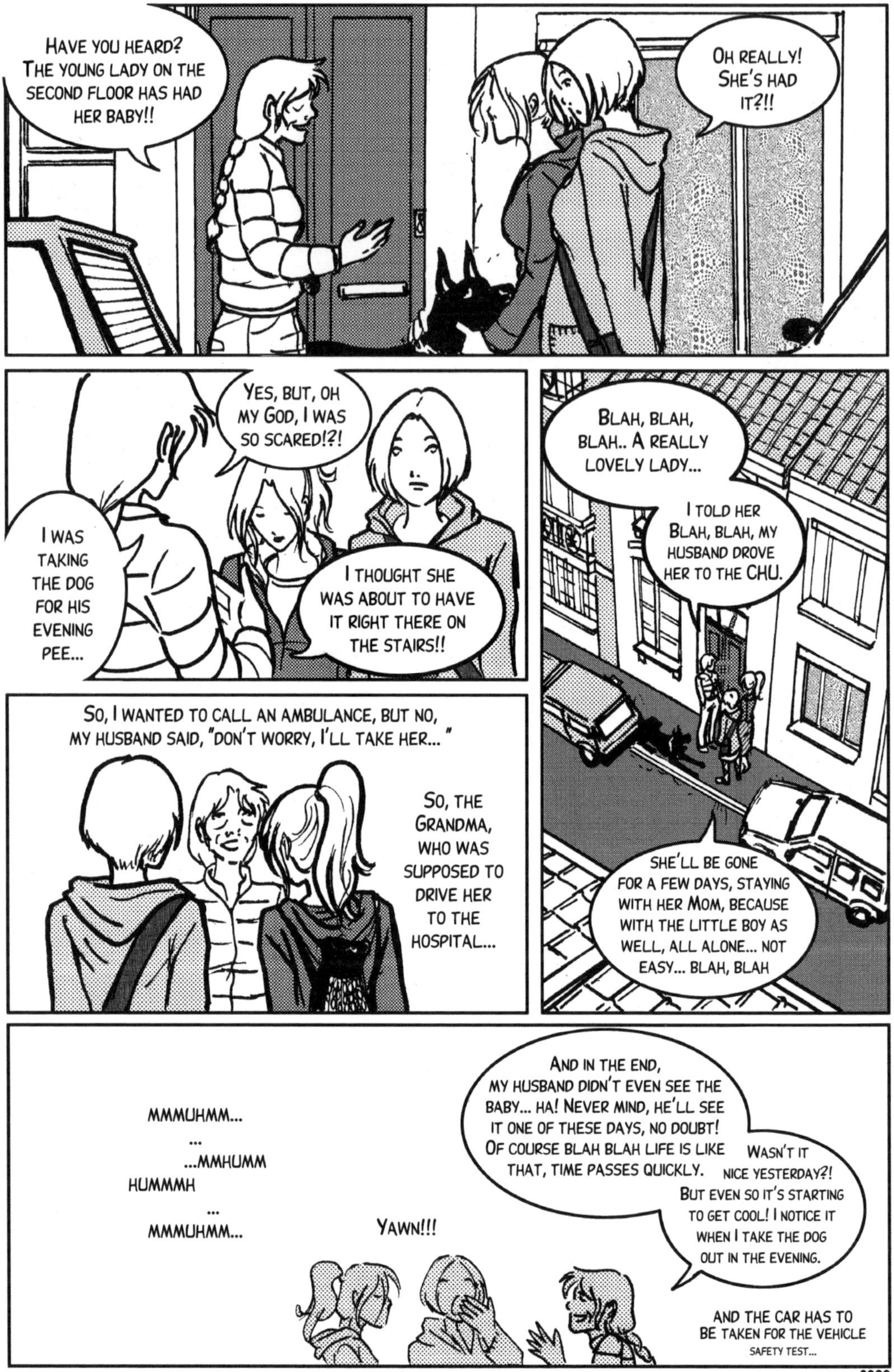
HAVE YOU HEARD? THE YOUNG LADY ON THE SECOND FLOOR HAS HAD HER BABY!!
OH REALLY! SHE'S HAD IT?!!
YES, BUT, OH MY GOD, I WAS SO SCARED!?!
I WAS TAKING THE DOG FOR HIS EVENING PEE...
I THOUGHT SHE WAS ABOUT TO HAVE IT RIGHT THERE ON THE STAIRS!!
SO, I WANTED TO CALL AN AMBULANCE, BUT NO, MY HUSBAND SAID, "DON'T WORRY, I'LL TAKE HER..."
SO, THE GRANDMA, WHO WAS SUPPOSED TO DRIVE HER TO THE HOSPITAL...
BLAH, BLAH, BLAH.. A REALLY LOVELY LADY...
I TOLD HER BLAH, BLAH, MY HUSBAND DROVE HER TO THE CHU.
SHE'LL BE GONE FOR A FEW DAYS, STAYING WITH HER MOM, BECAUSE WITH THE LITTLE BOY AS WELL, ALL ALONE... NOT EASY... BLAH, BLAH
MMMUHMM...
...
...MMHUMM
HUMMMH
...
MMMUHMM...
YAWN!!!
AND IN THE END, MY HUSBAND DIDN'T EVEN SEE THE BABY... HA! NEVER MIND, HE'LL SEE IT ONE OF THESE DAYS, NO DOUBT! OF COURSE BLAH BLAH LIFE IS LIKE THAT, TIME PASSES QUICKLY.
WASN'T IT NICE YESTERDAY?! BUT EVEN SO IT'S STARTING TO GET COOL! I NOTICE IT WHEN I TAKE THE DOG OUT IN THE EVENING.
AND THE CAR HAS TO BE TAKEN FOR THE VEHICLE SAFETY TEST...

VANYDA 2003

Chapter 15 Breakfast

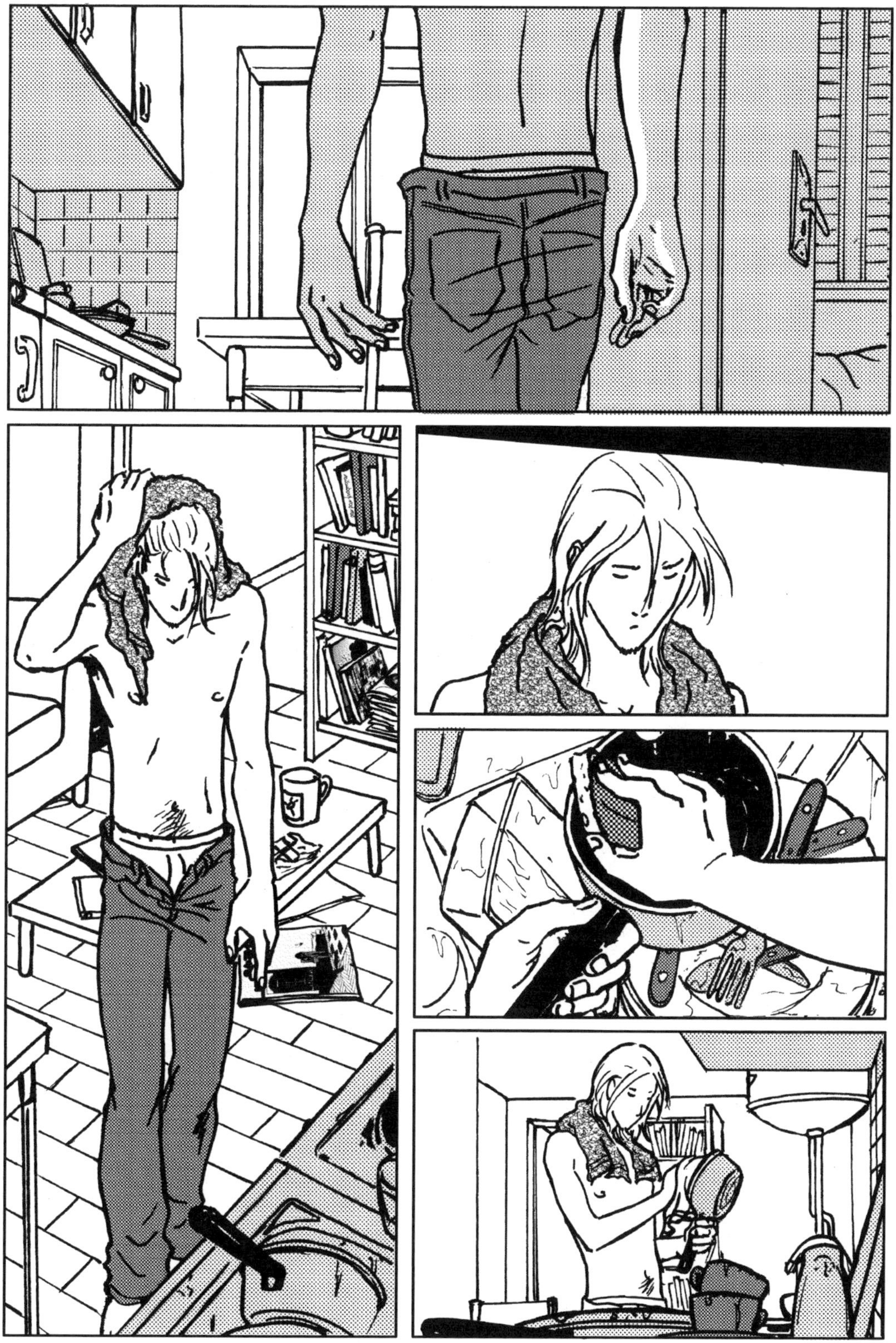

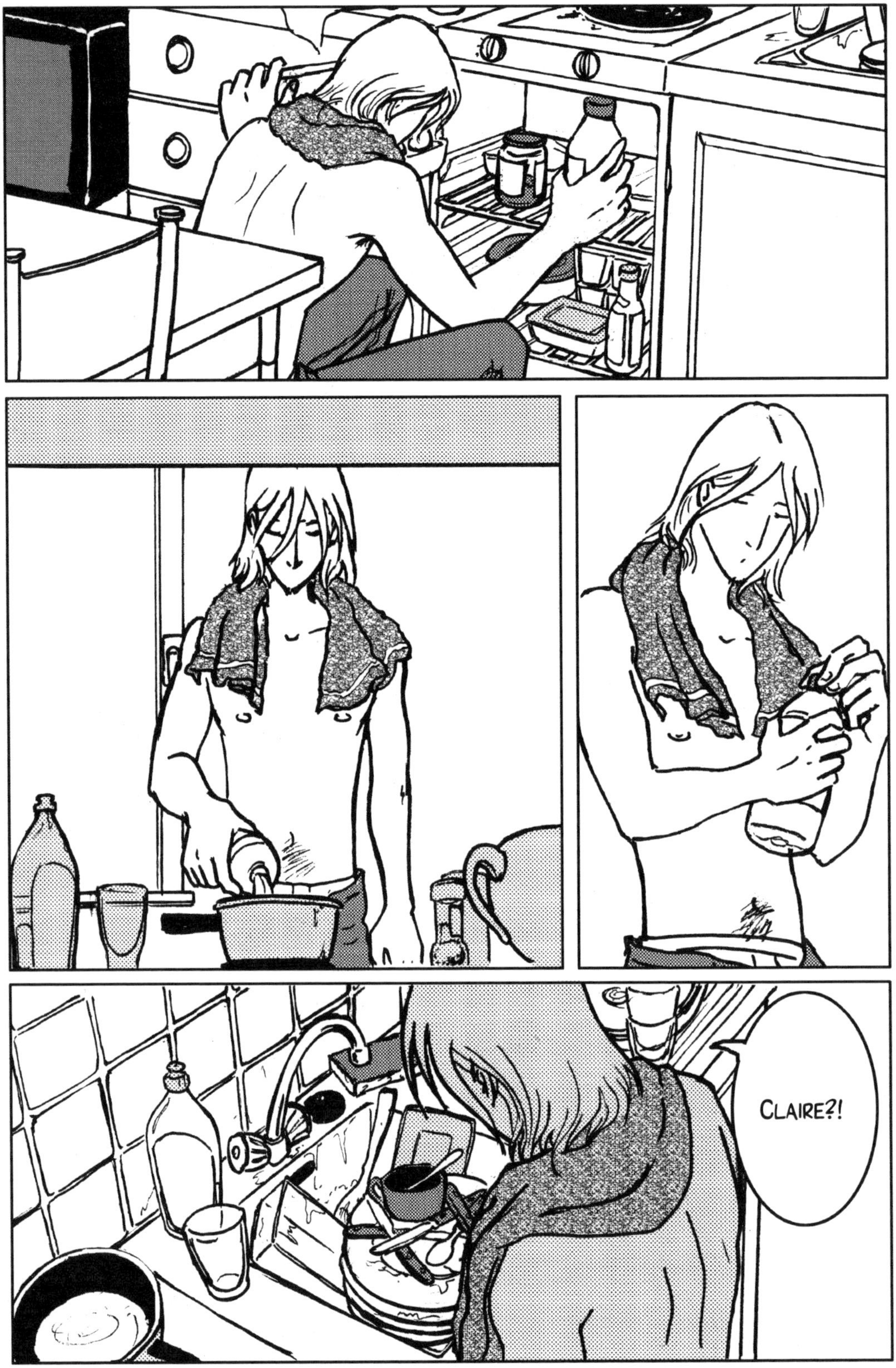
CLAIRE?!

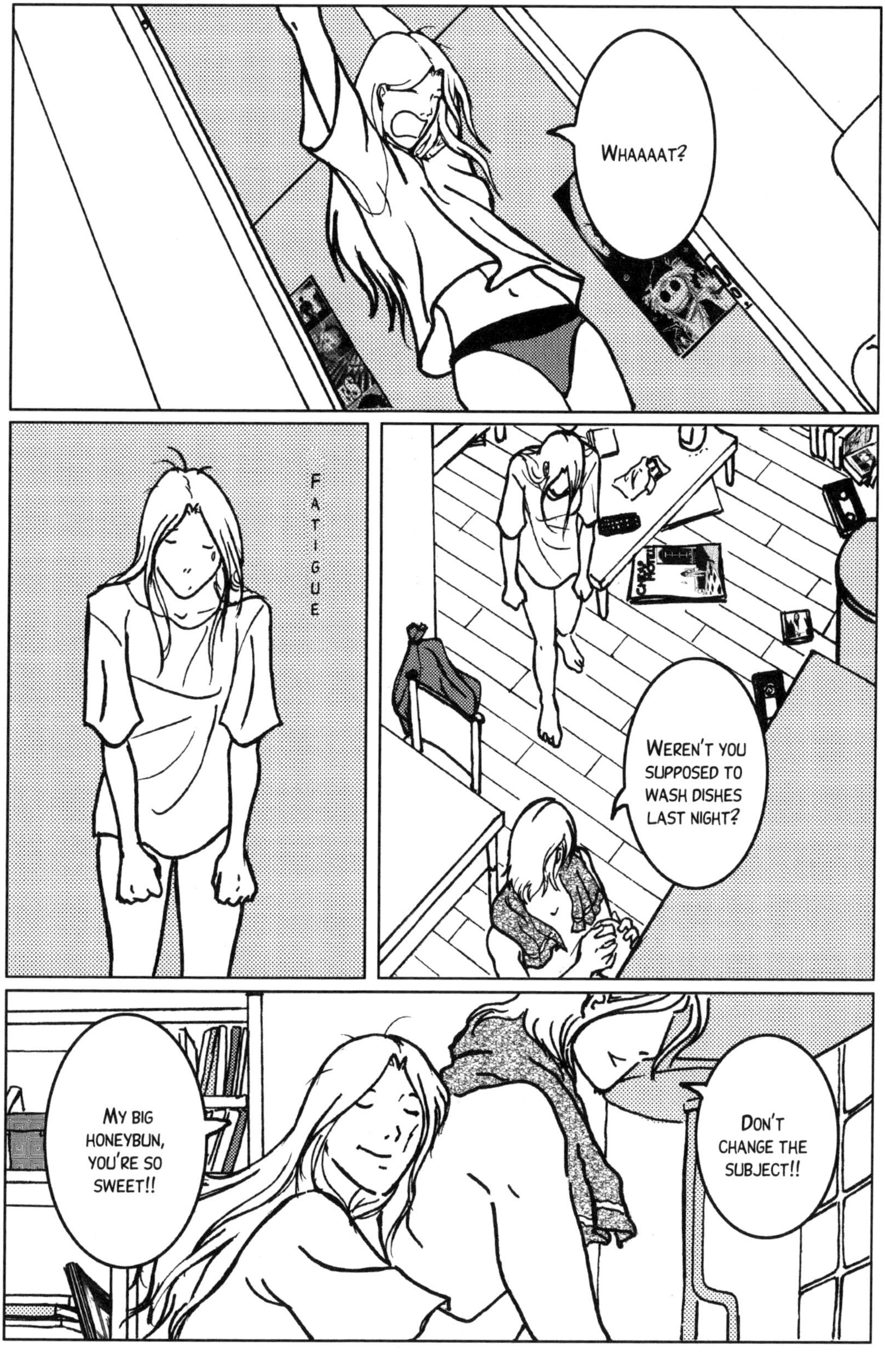
WHAAAAT?
FATIGUE
WEREN'T YOU SUPPOSED TO WASH DISHES LAST NIGHT?
MY BIG HONEYBUN, YOU'RE SO SWEET!!
DON'T CHANGE THE SUBJECT!!

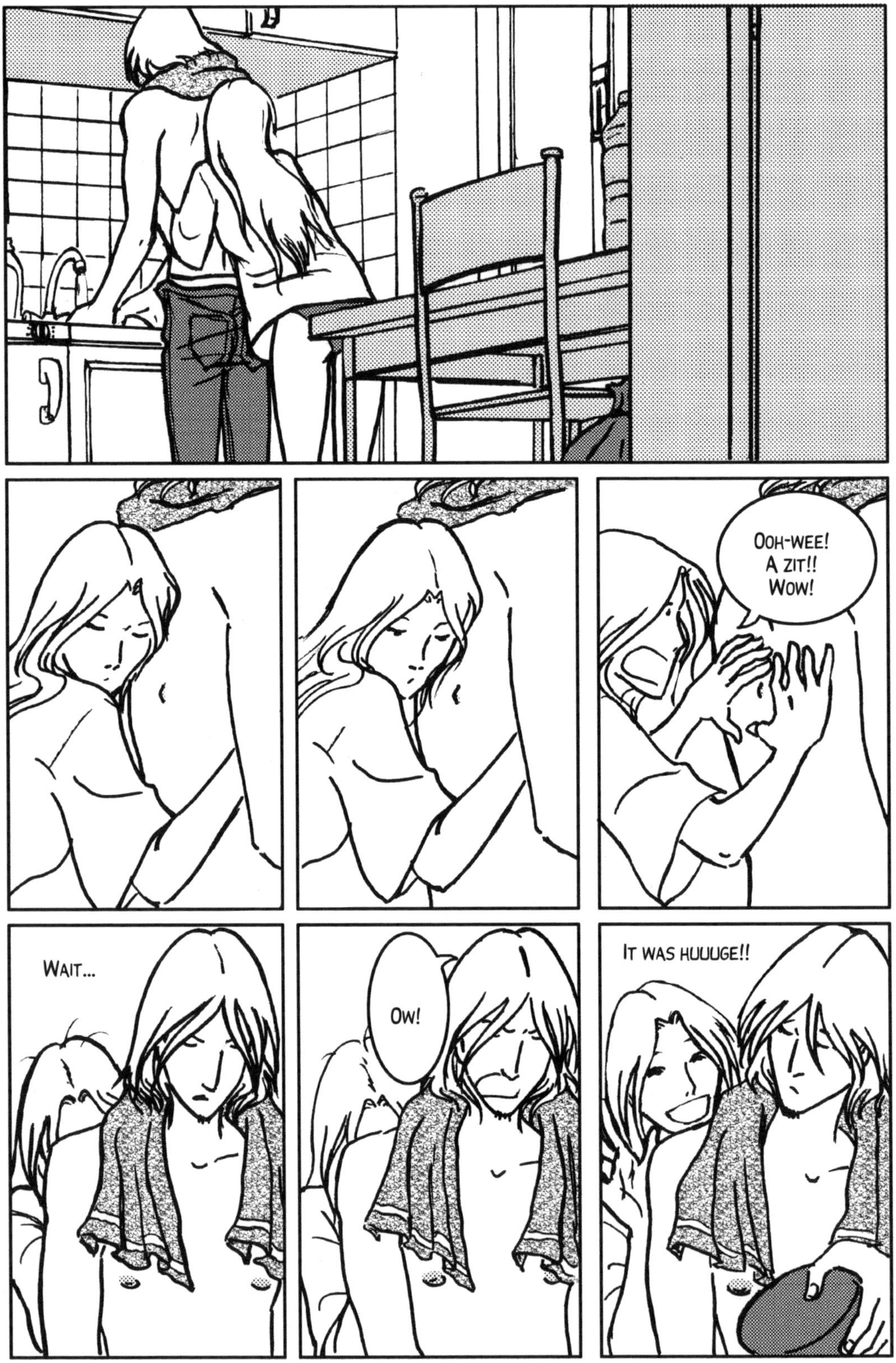
OOH-WEE! A ZIT!! WOW!
WAIT...
OW!
IT WAS HUUUGE!!

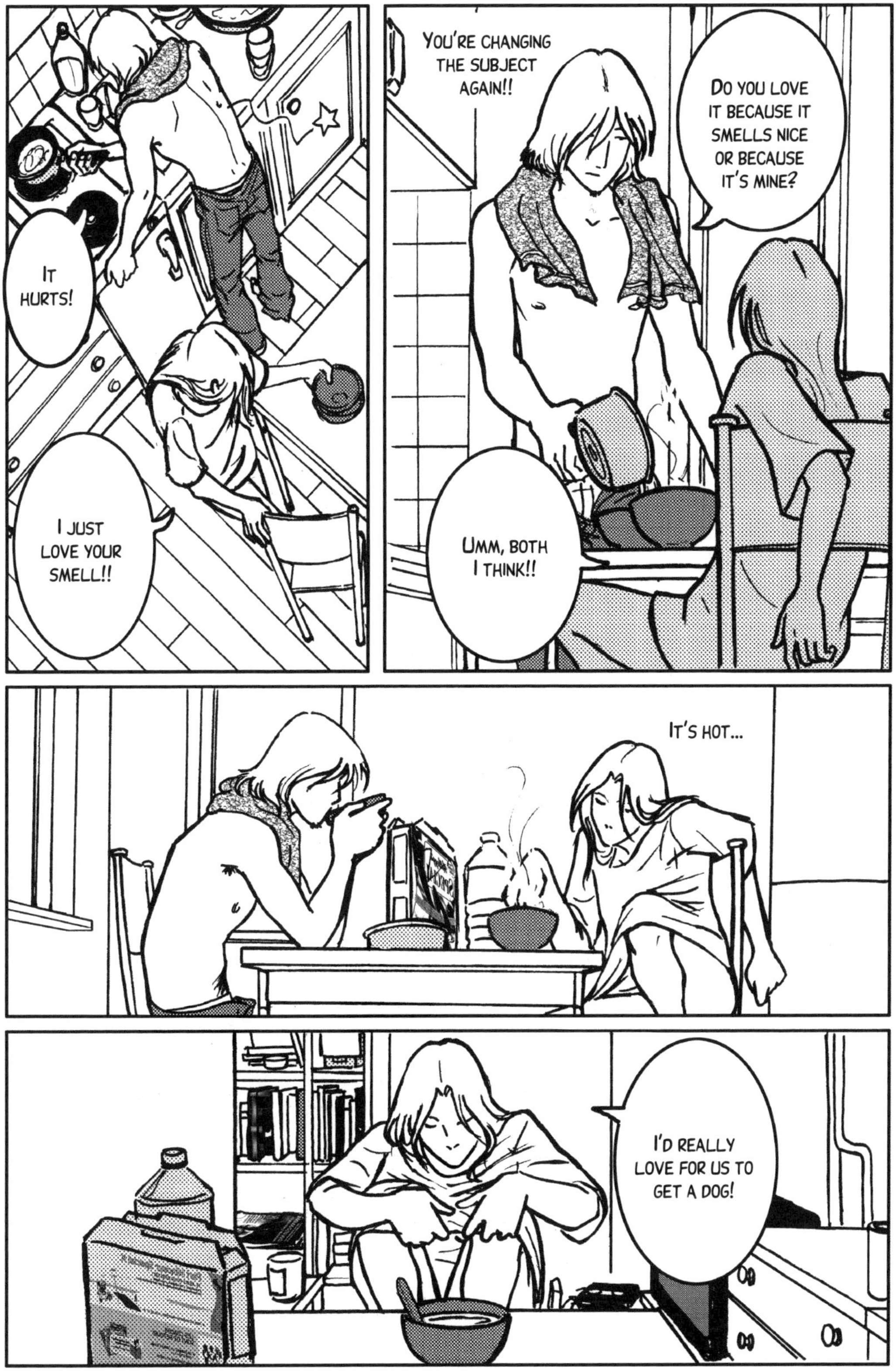
It hurts!
I just love your smell!!
You're changing the subject again!!
Do you love it because it smells nice or because it's mine?
Umm, both I think!!
It's hot...
I'd really love for us to get a dog!

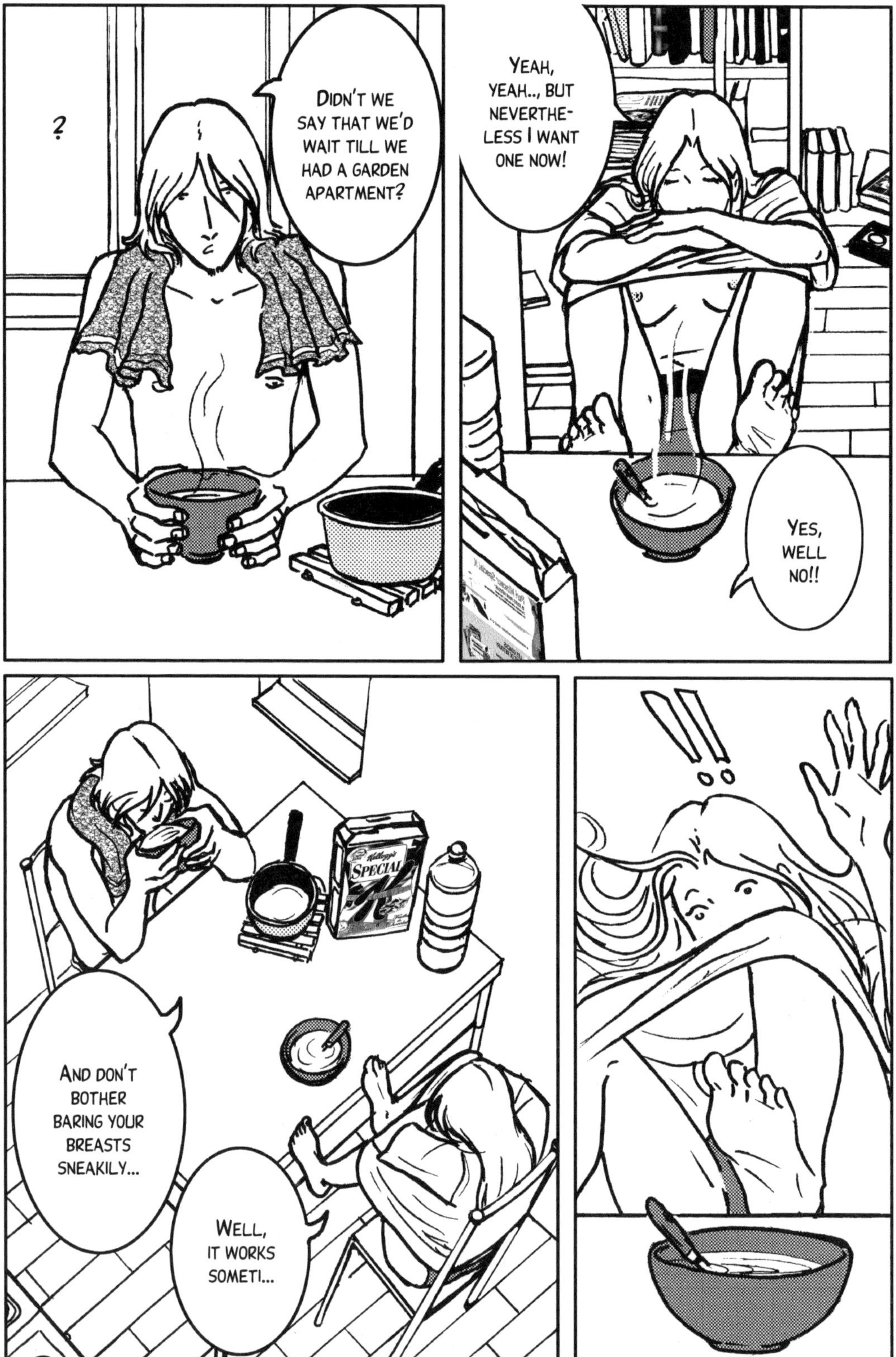
?
DIDN'T WE SAY THAT WE'D WAIT TILL WE HAD A GARDEN APARTMENT?
YEAH, YEAH.., BUT NEVERTHE-LESS I WANT ONE NOW!
YES, WELL NO!!
Kellogg's
SPECIAL K
AND DON'T BOTHER BARING YOUR BREASTS SNEAKILY...
WELL, IT WORKS SOMETI...
!!

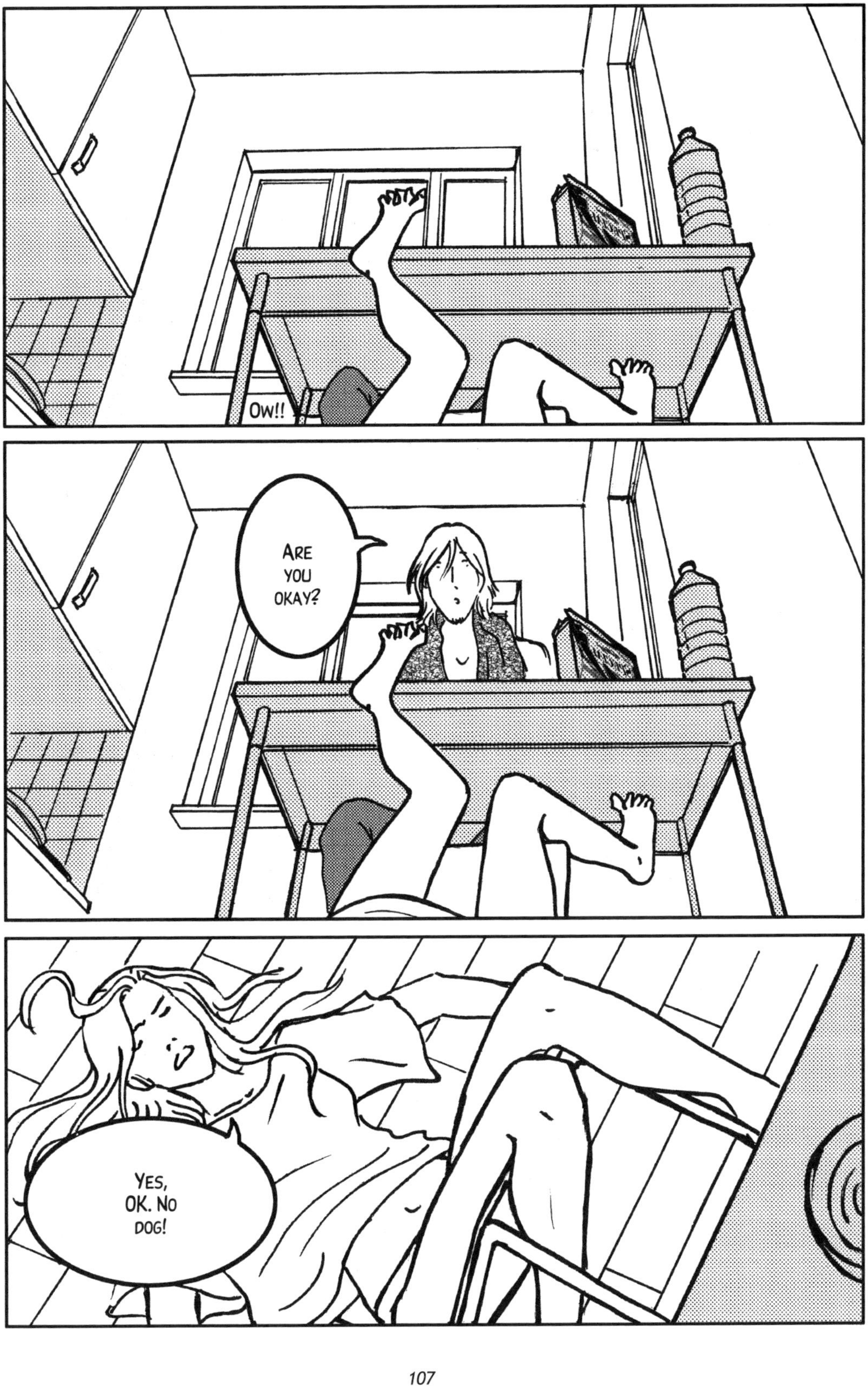
OW!!
ARE YOU OKAY?
YES, OK. NO DOG!

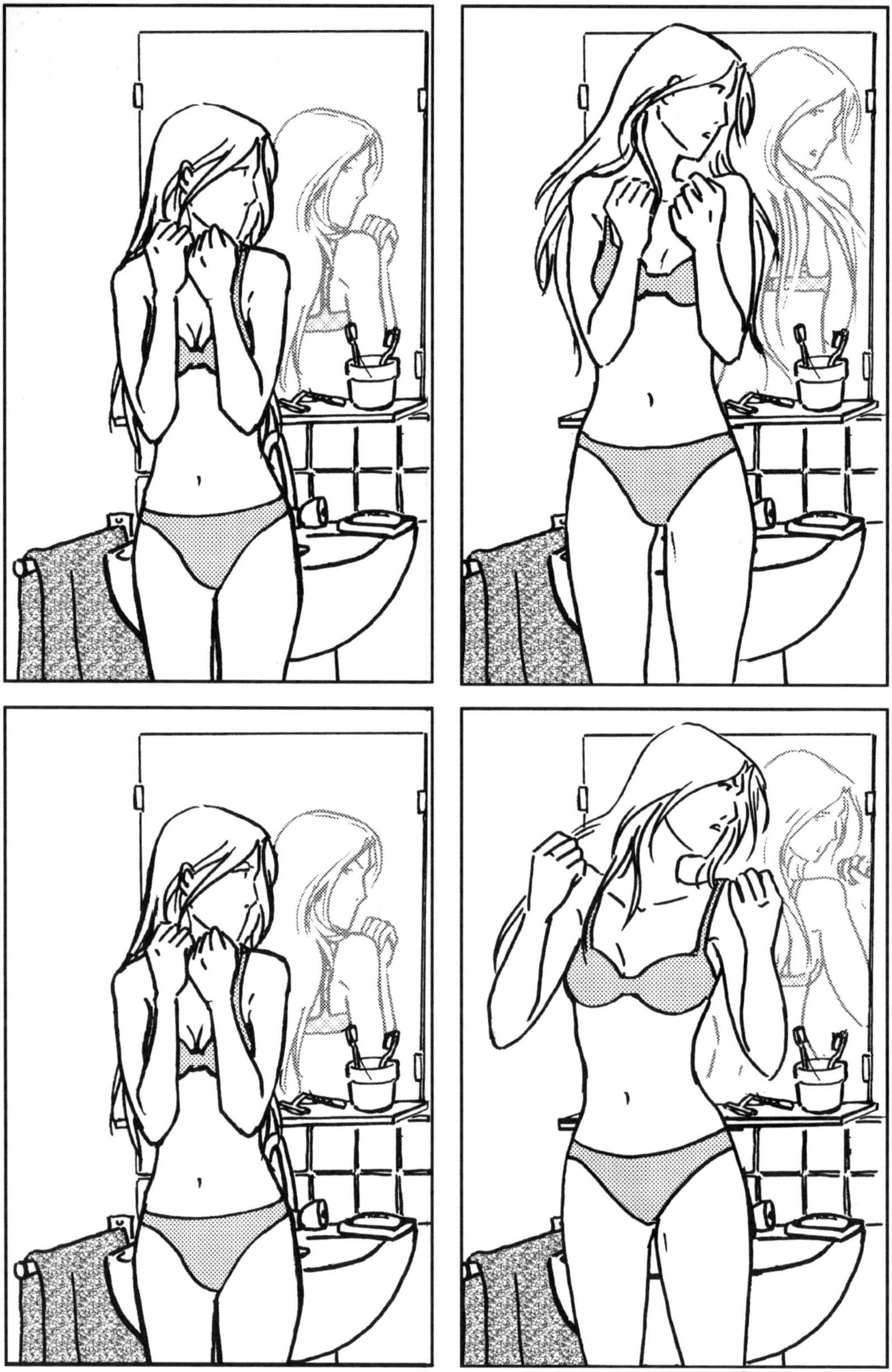

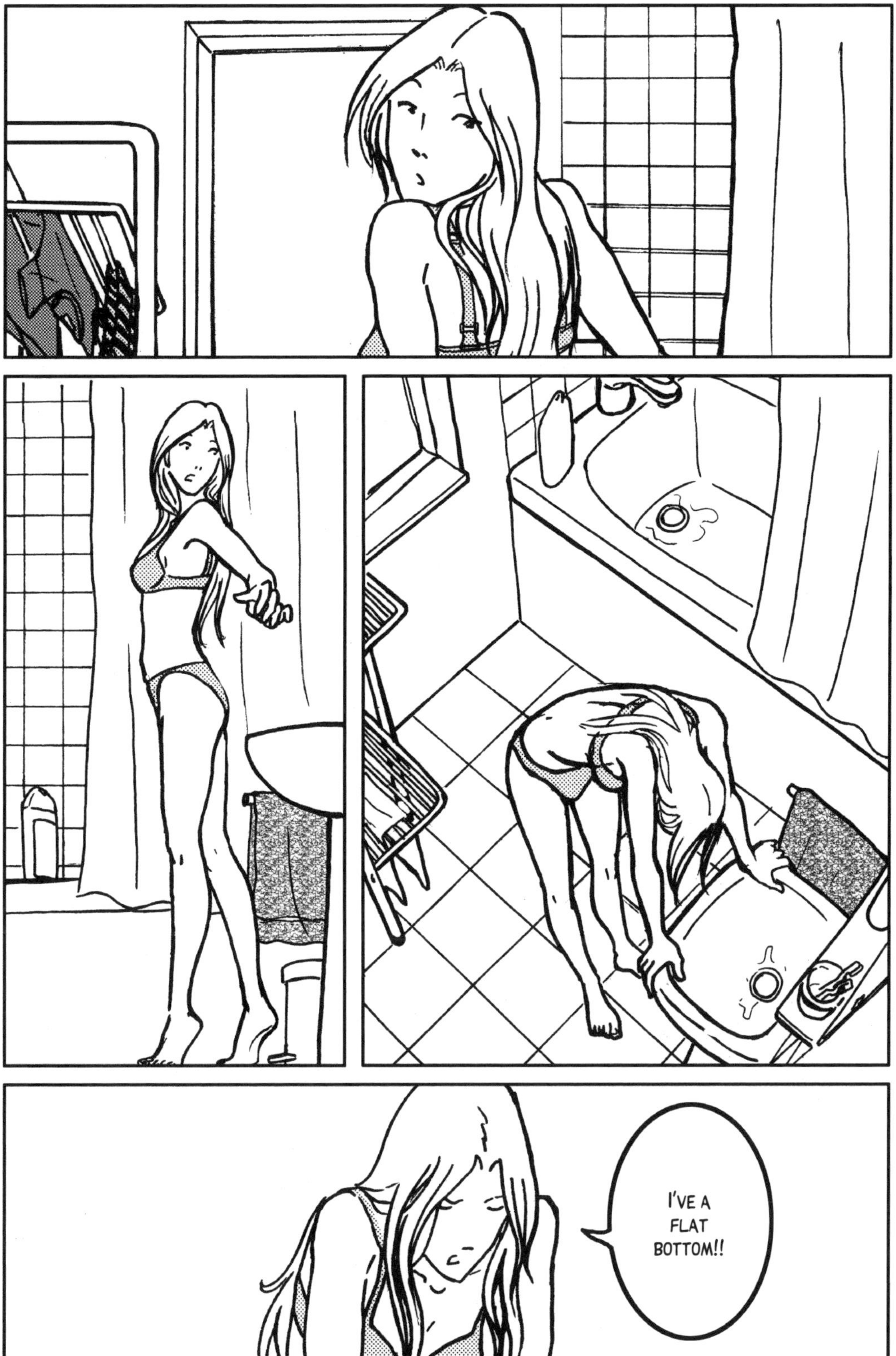
I'VE A FLAT BOTTOM!!

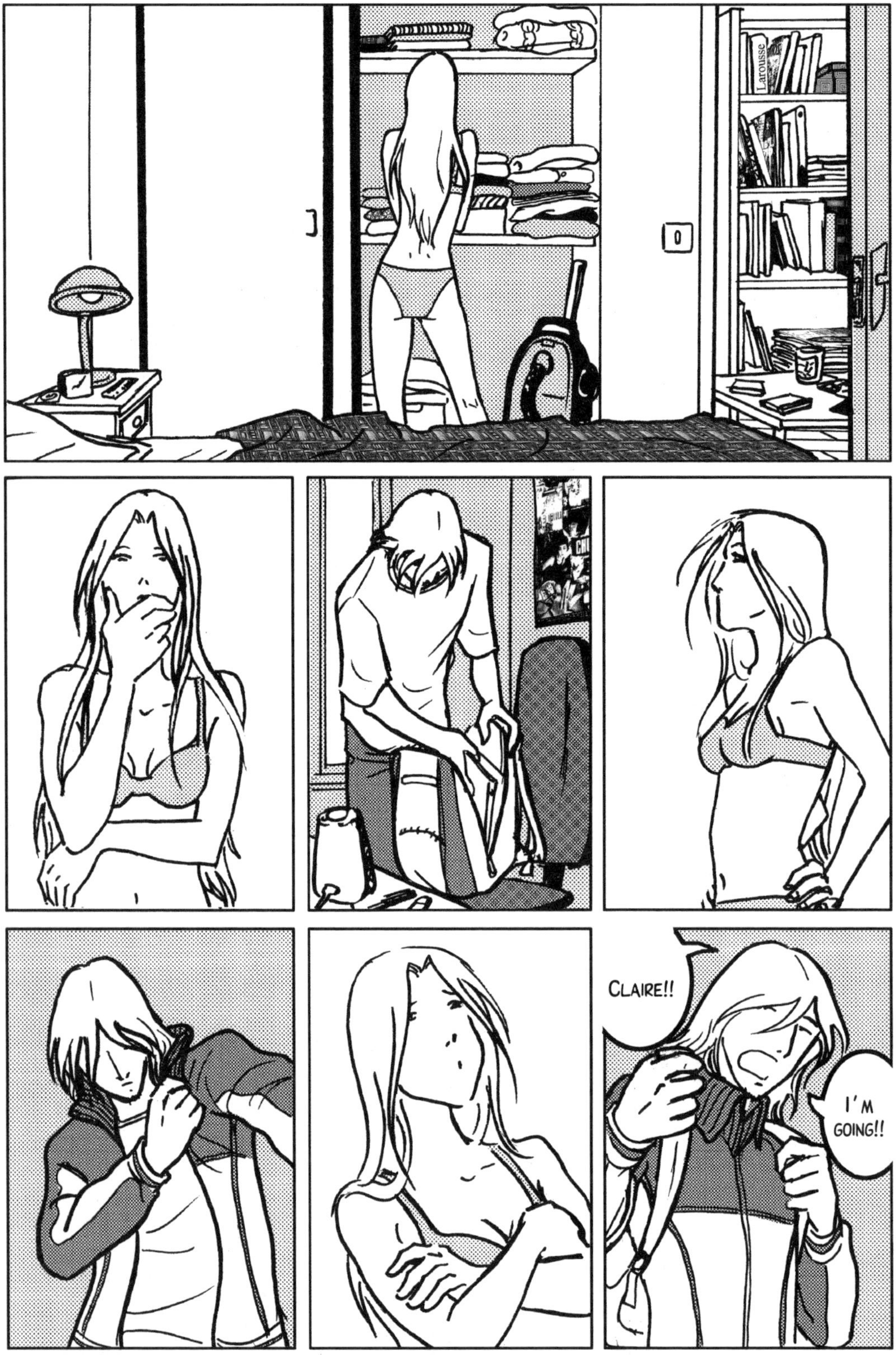
Larousse
CLAIRE!!
I'M GOING!!

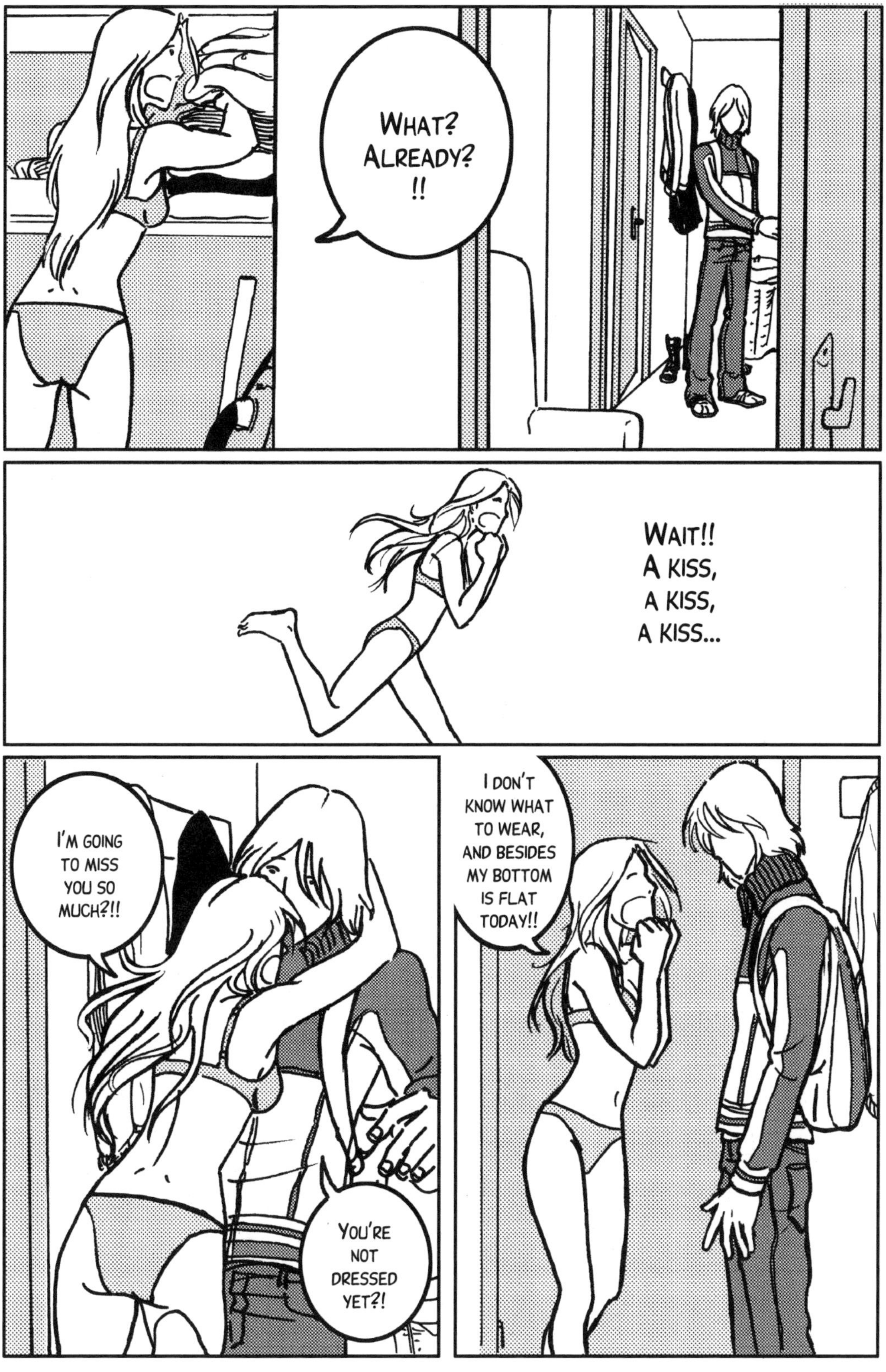
WHAT? ALREADY? !!
WAIT!! A KISS, A KISS, A KISS...
I'M GOING TO MISS YOU SO MUCH?!!
YOU'RE NOT DRESSED YET?!
I DON'T KNOW WHAT TO WEAR, AND BESIDES MY BOTTOM IS FLAT TODAY!!

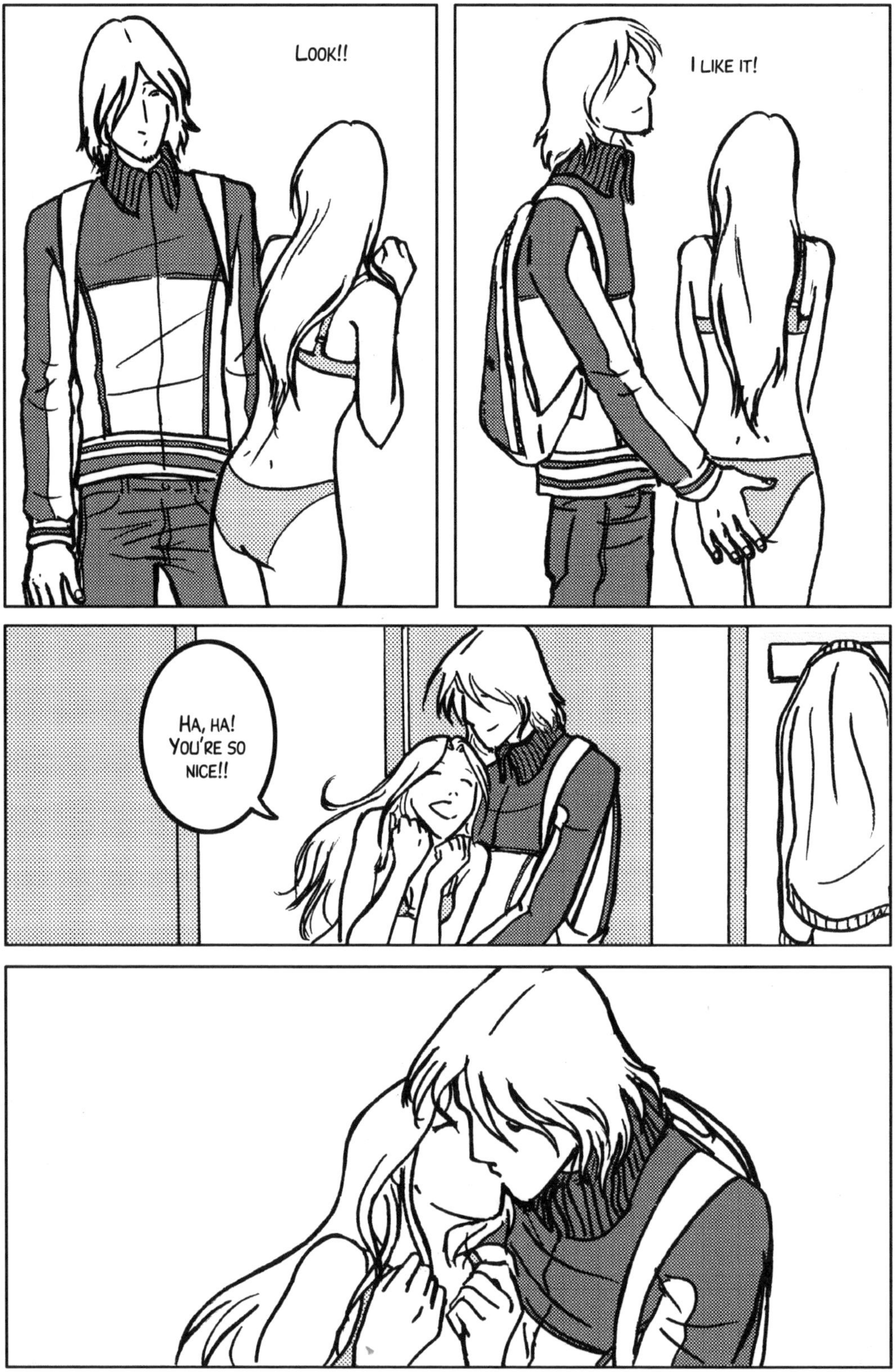
LOOK!!
I LIKE IT!
HA, HA! YOU'RE SO NICE!!

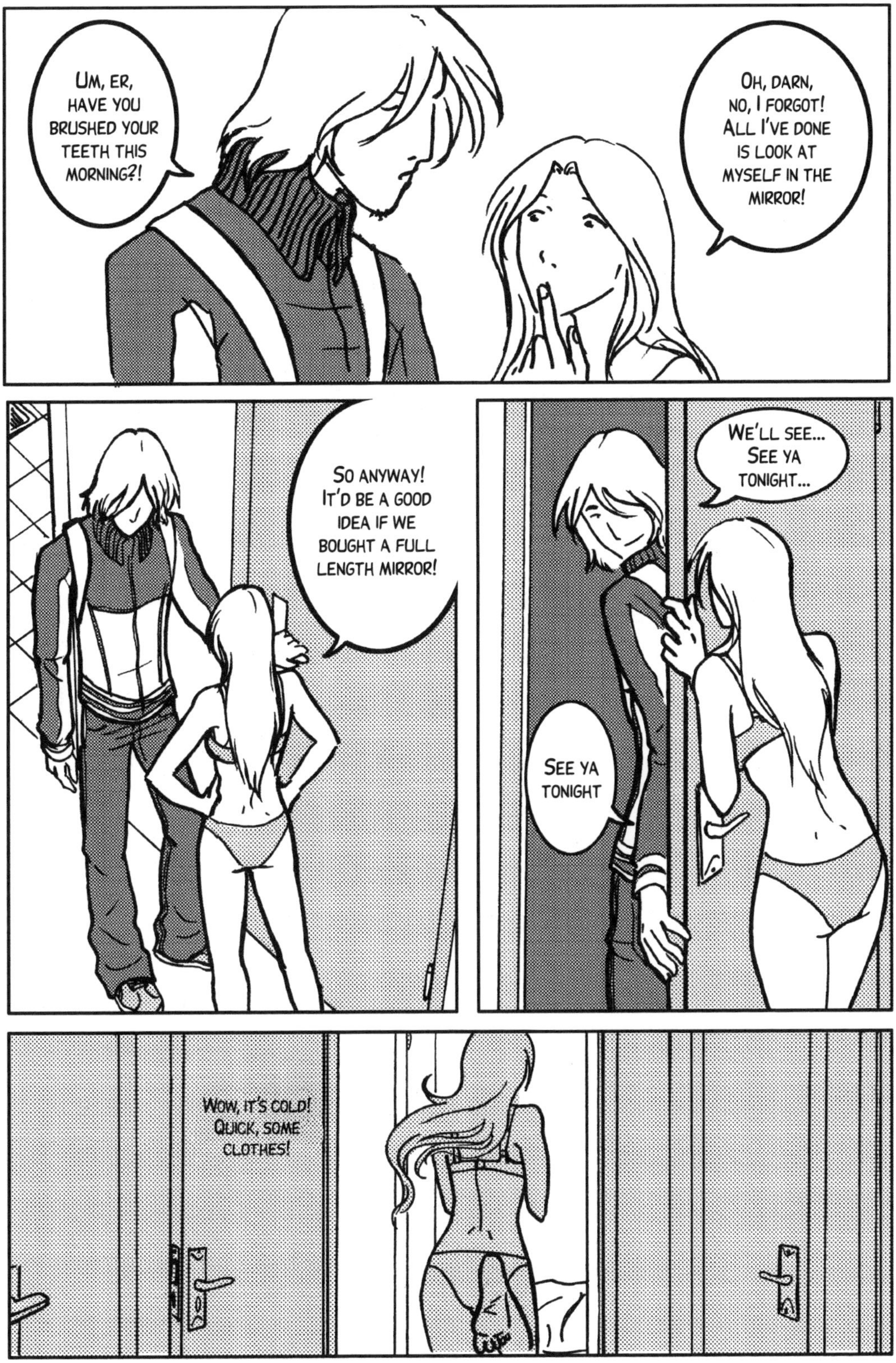
Um, er, have you brushed your teeth this morning?!
Oh, darn, no, I forgot! All I've done is look at myself in the mirror!
So anyway! It'd be a good idea if we bought a full length mirror!
We'll see... See ya tonight...
See ya tonight
Wow, it's cold! Quick, some clothes!

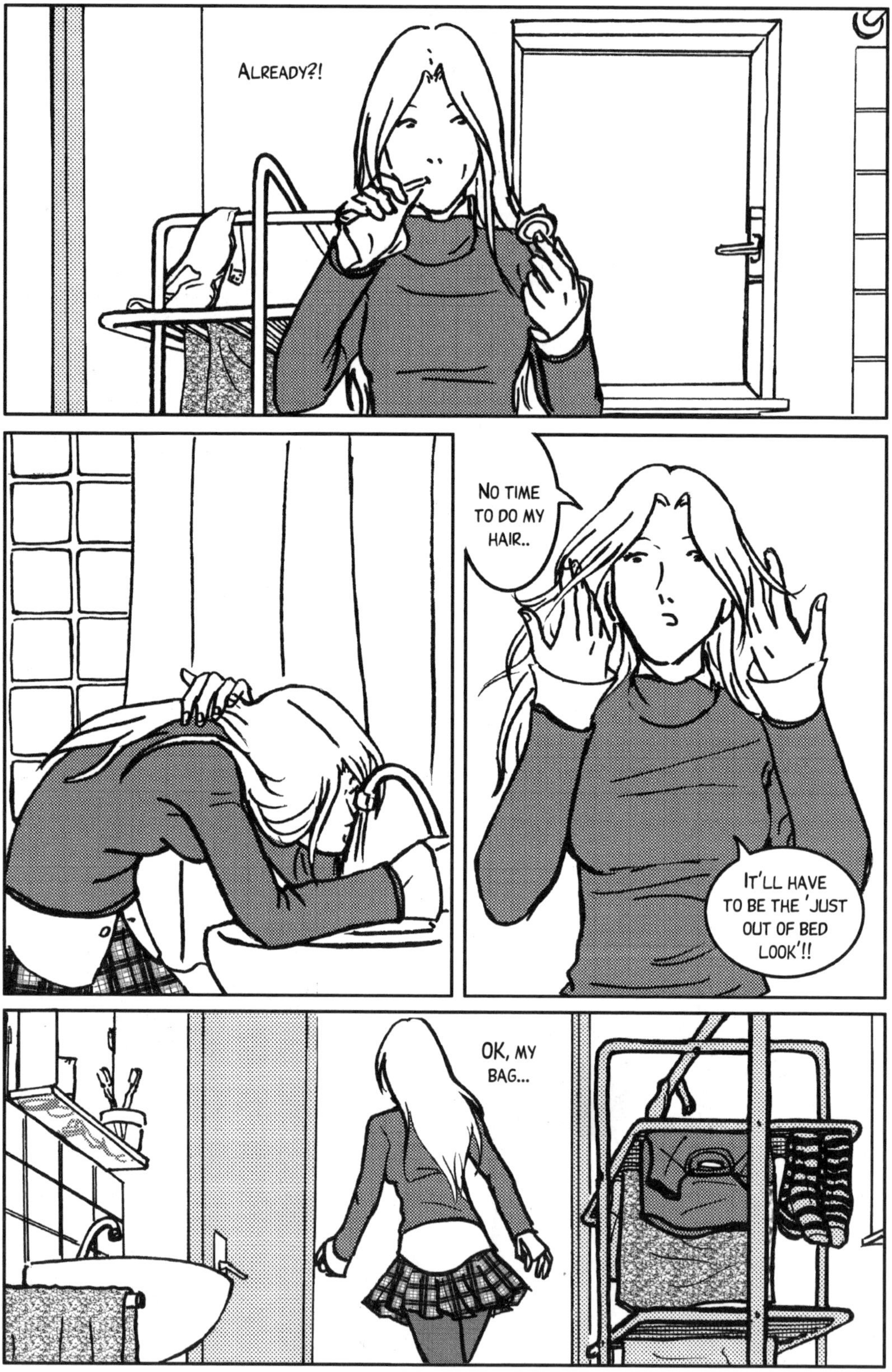
ALREADY?!
NO TIME TO DO MY HAIR..
IT'LL HAVE TO BE THE 'JUST OUT OF BED LOOK'!!
OK, MY BAG...

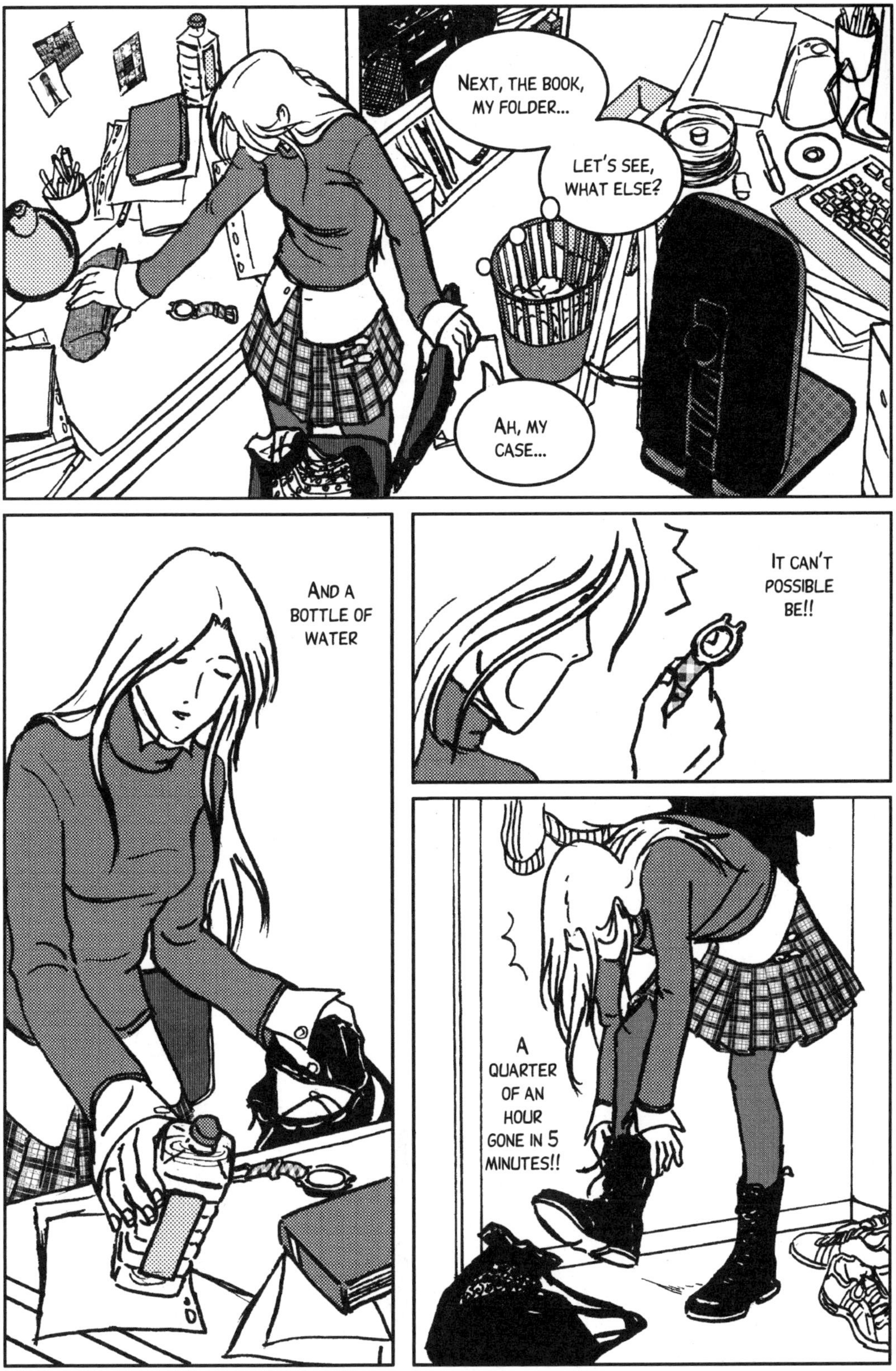

NEXT, THE BOOK, MY FOLDER...
LET'S SEE, WHAT ELSE?
AH, MY CASE...
AND A BOTTLE OF WATER
IT CAN'T POSSIBLE BE!!
A QUARTER OF AN HOUR GONE IN 5 MINUTES!!

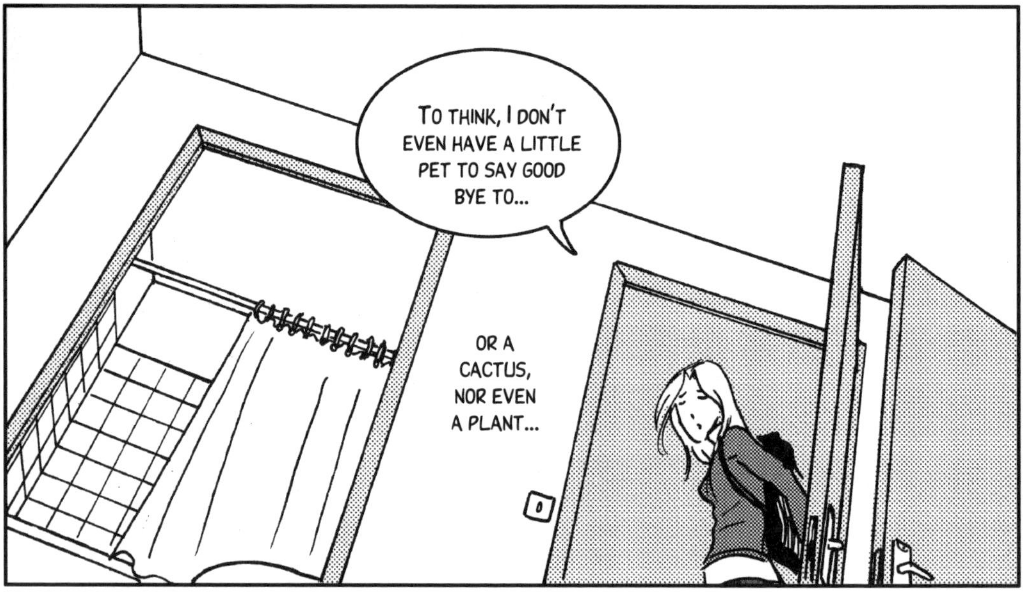
TO THINK, I DON'T EVEN HAVE A LITTLE PET TO SAY GOOD BYE TO...
OR A CACTUS, NOR EVEN A PLANT...
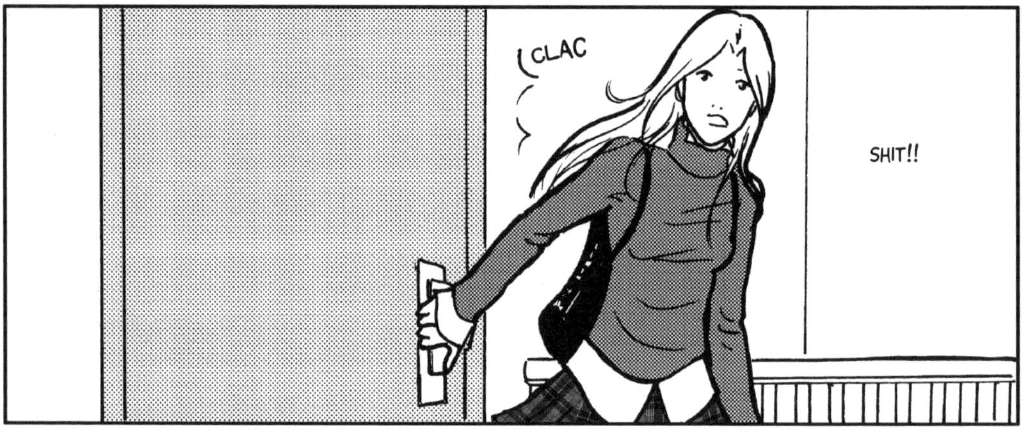
CLAC
SHIT!!
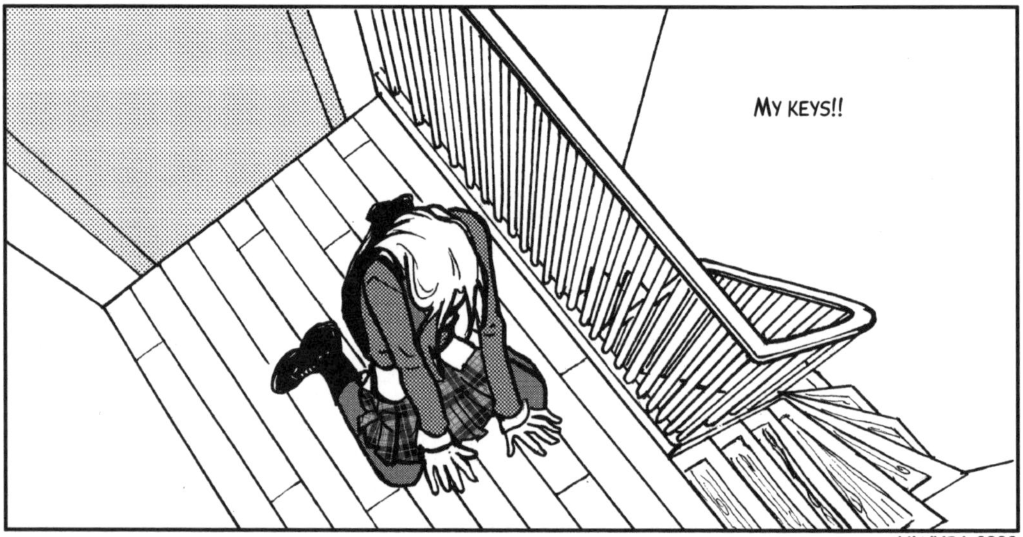
MY KEYS!!

VANYDA 2003

Chapter 16
Special Moments

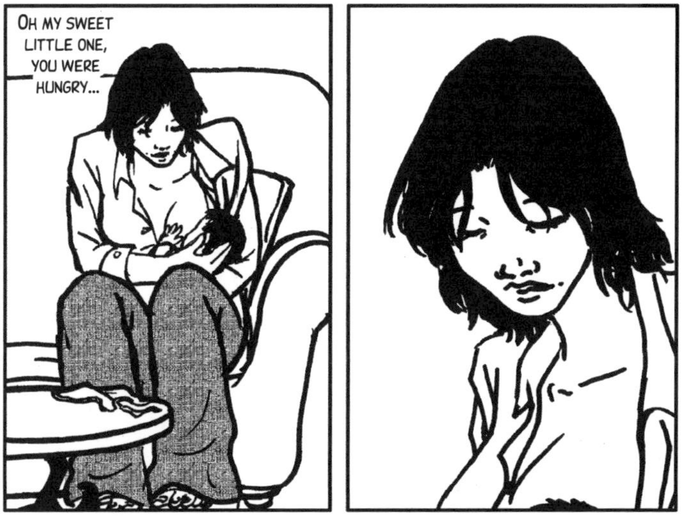
OH MY SWEET LITTLE ONE, YOU WERE HUNGRY...

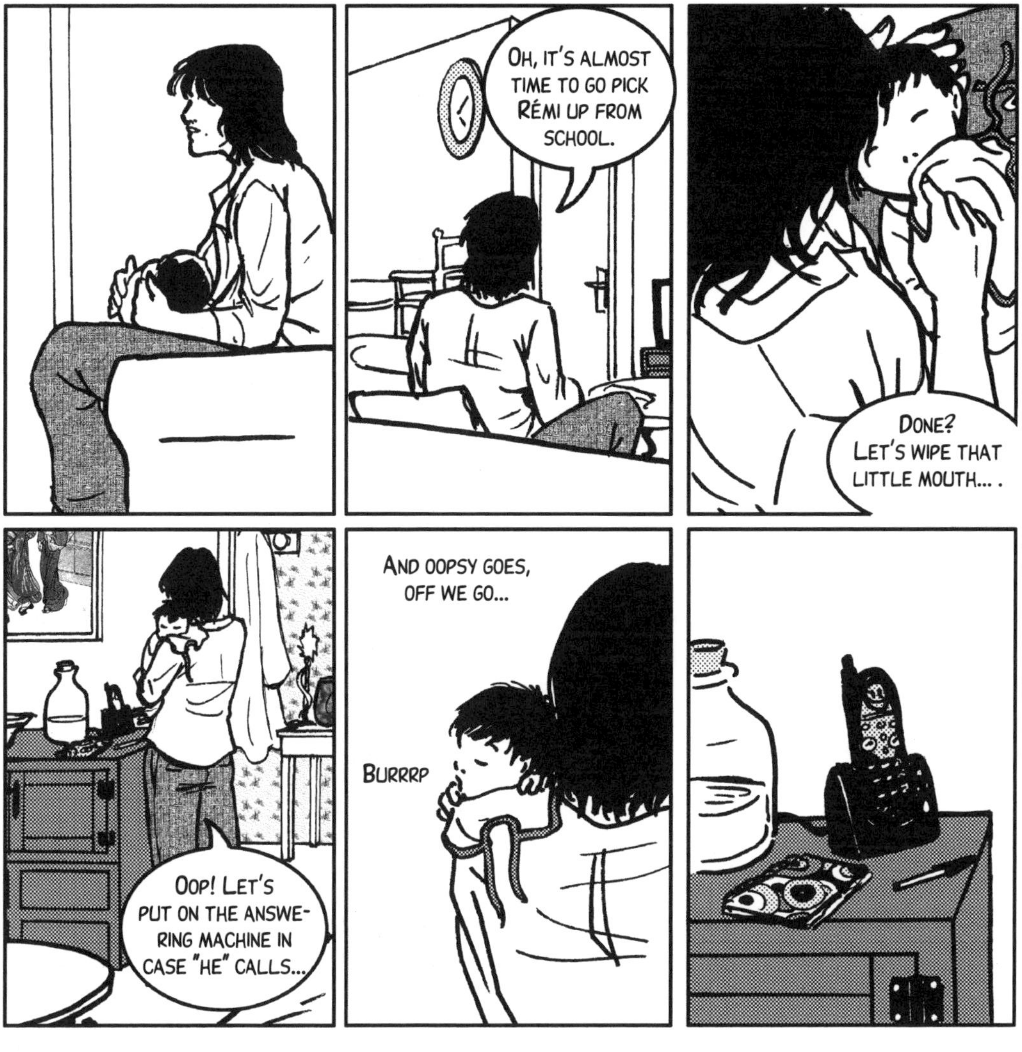
OH, IT'S ALMOST TIME TO GO PICK RÉMI UP FROM SCHOOL.
DONE? LET'S WIPE THAT LITTLE MOUTH... .
OOP! LET'S PUT ON THE ANSWE-RING MACHINE IN CASE "HE" CALLS...
AND OOPSY GOES, OFF WE GO...
BURRRP

Chapter 17
Tea with the Nuts...

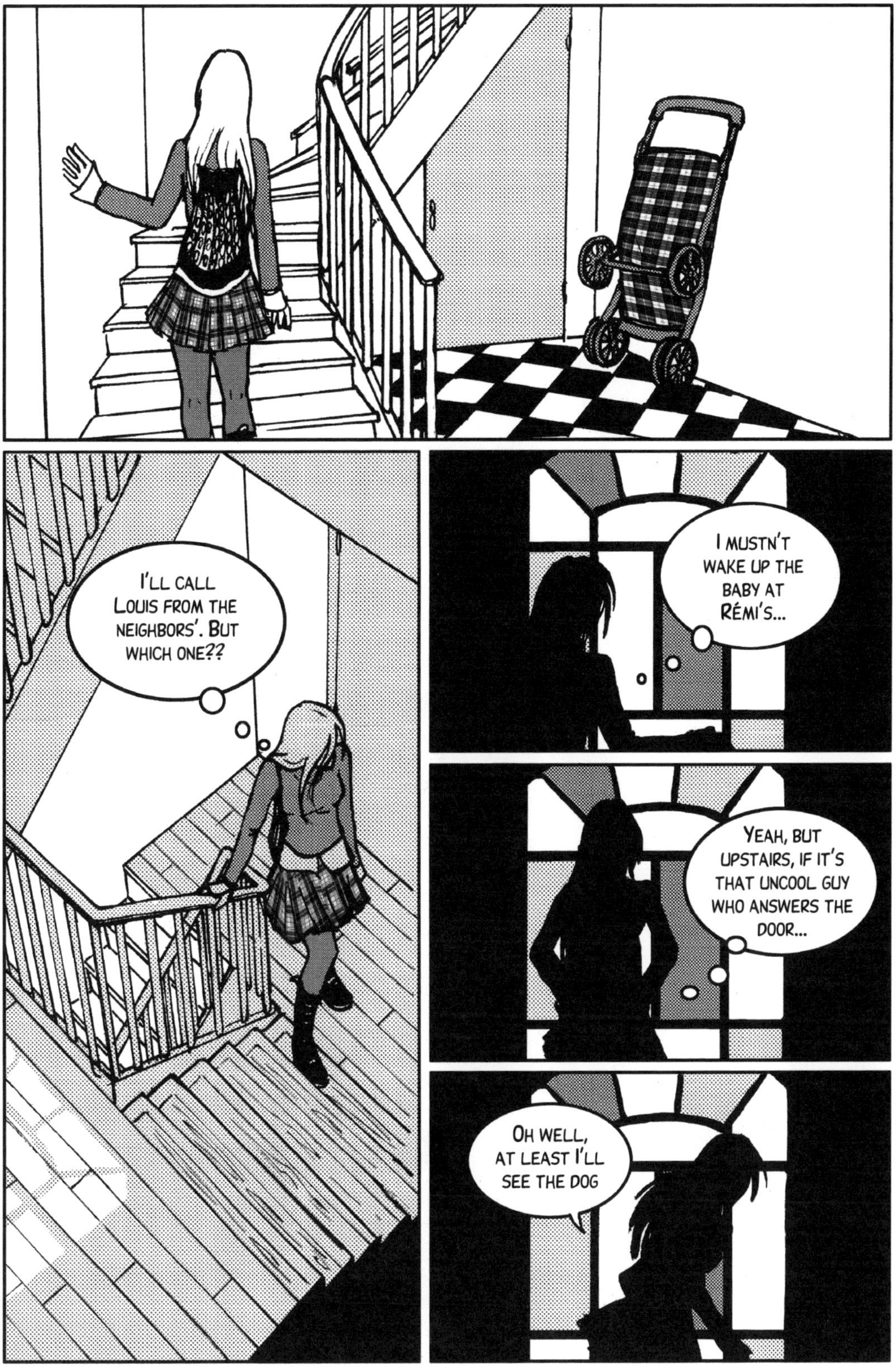
I'll call Louis from the neighbors'. But which one??
I mustn't wake up the baby at Rémi's...
Yeah, but upstairs, if it's that uncool guy who answers the door...
Oh well, at least I'll see the dog

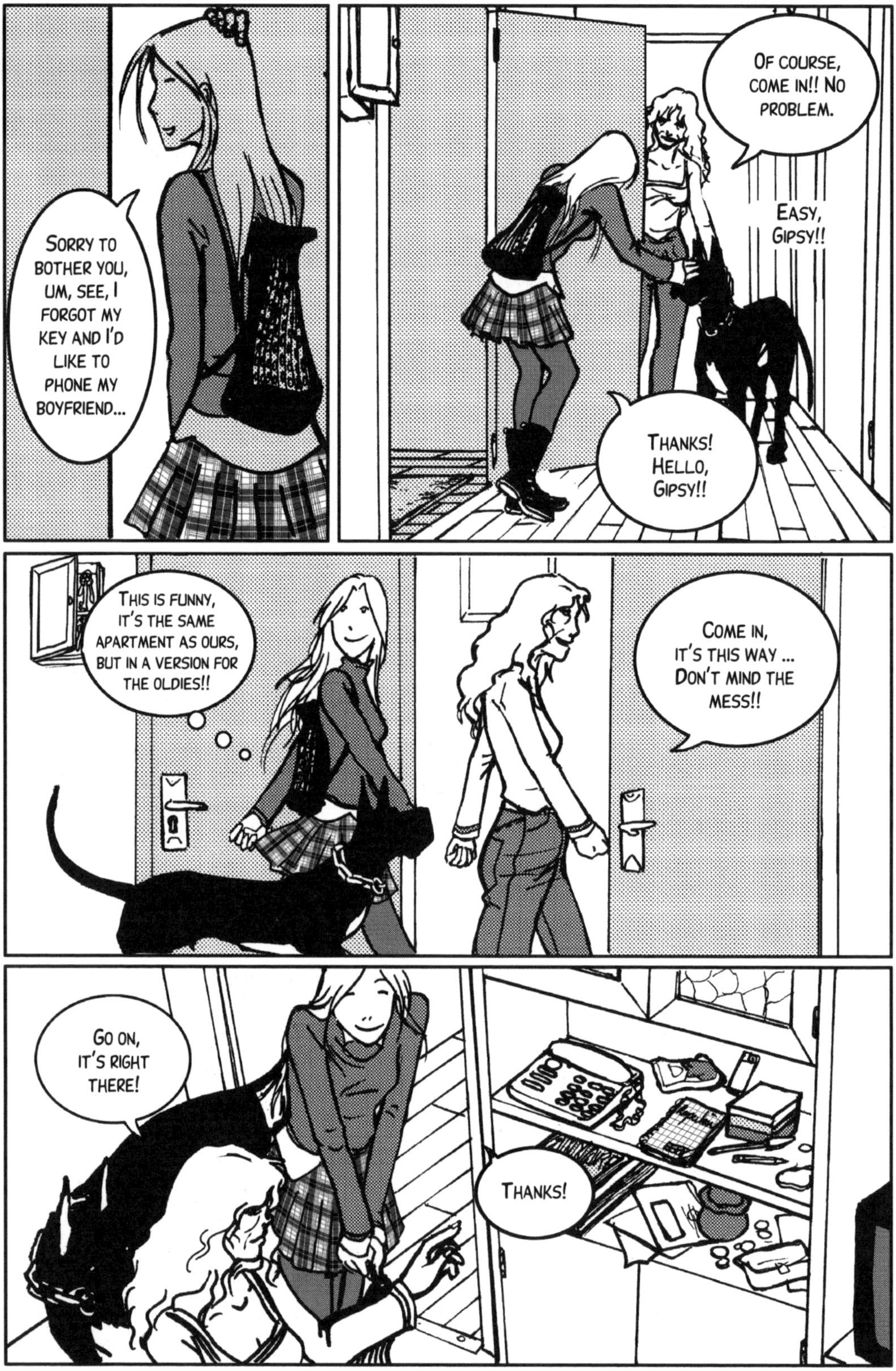
Sorry to bother you, um, see, I forgot my key and I'd like to phone my boyfriend...
Of course, come in!! No problem.
Easy, Gipsy!!
Thanks! Hello, Gipsy!!
This is funny, it's the same apartment as ours, but in a version for the oldies!!
Come in, it's this way ... Don't mind the mess!!
Go on, it's right there!
Thanks!

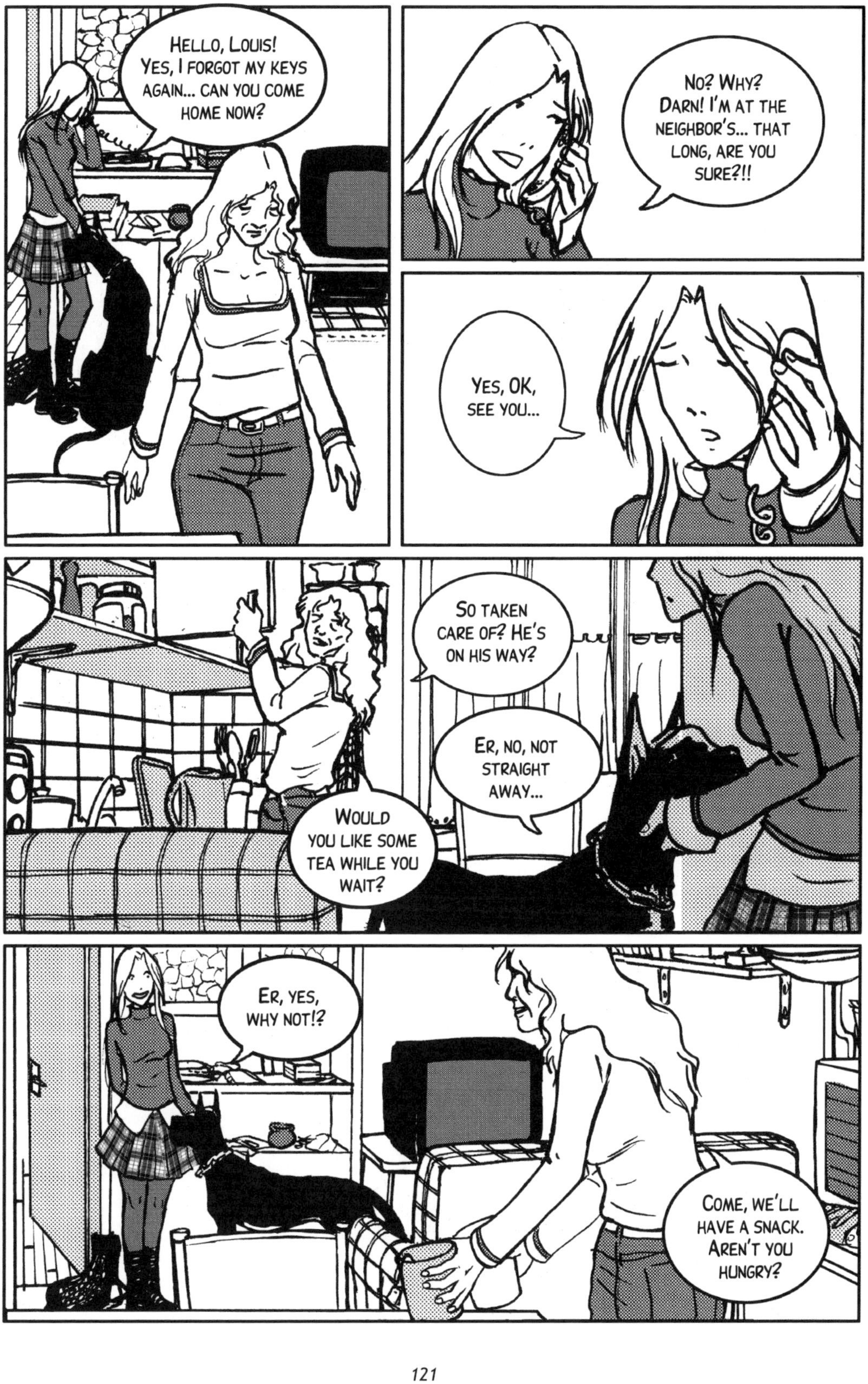
HELLO, LOUIS! YES, I FORGOT MY KEYS AGAIN... CAN YOU COME HOME NOW?
NO? WHY? DARN! I'M AT THE NEIGHBOR'S... THAT LONG, ARE YOU SURE?!!
YES, OK, SEE YOU...
SO TAKEN CARE OF? HE'S ON HIS WAY?
ER, NO, NOT STRAIGHT AWAY...
WOULD YOU LIKE SOME TEA WHILE YOU WAIT?
ER, YES, WHY NOT!?
COME, WE'LL HAVE A SNACK. AREN'T YOU HUNGRY?

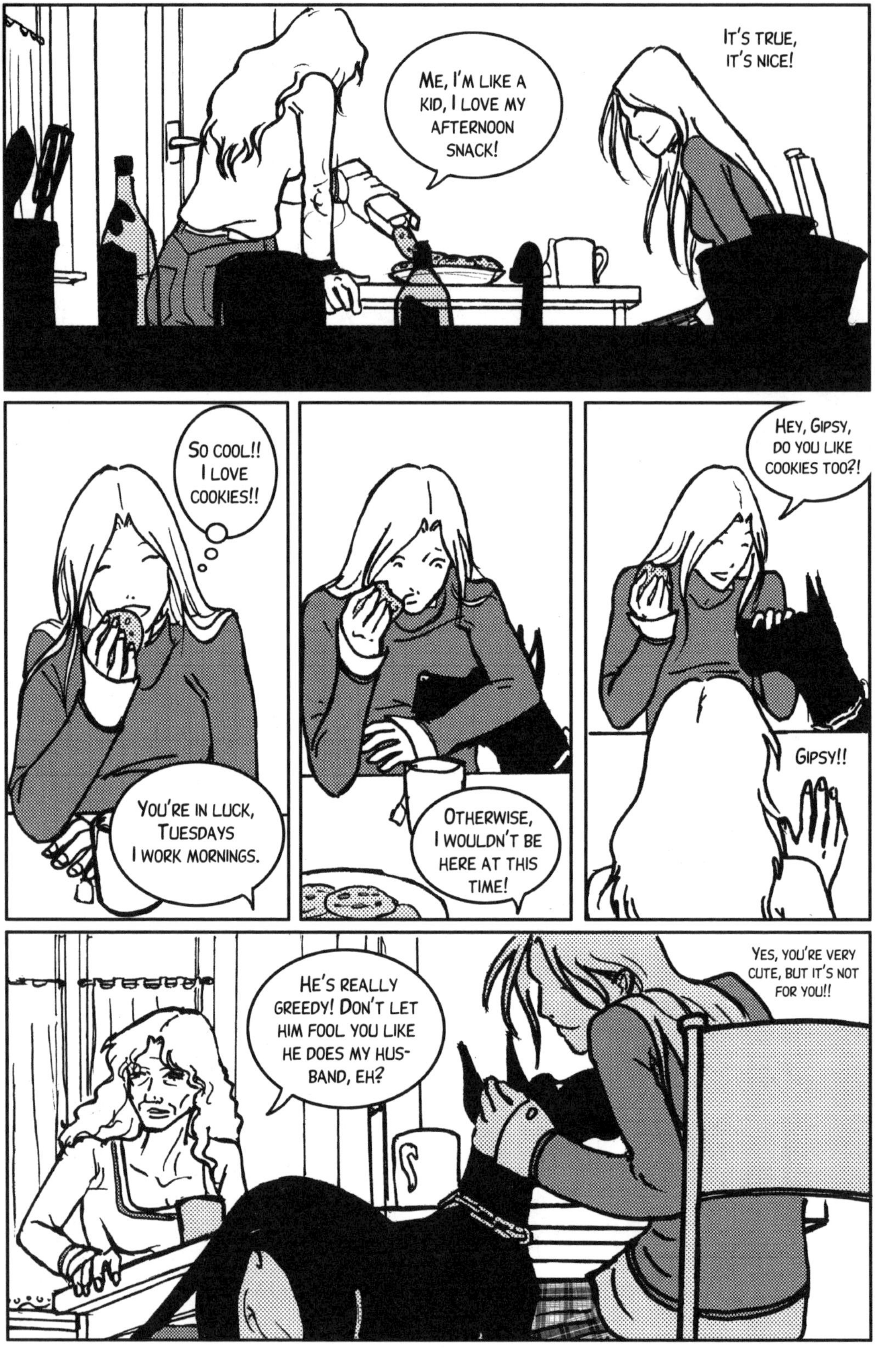
Me, I'm like a kid, I love my afternoon snack!
It's true, it's nice!
So cool!! I love cookies!!
You're in luck, Tuesdays I work mornings.
Otherwise, I wouldn't be here at this time!
Hey, Gipsy, do you like cookies too?!
Gipsy!!
He's really greedy! Don't let him fool you like he does my hus-band, eh?
Yes, you're very cute, but it's not for you!!

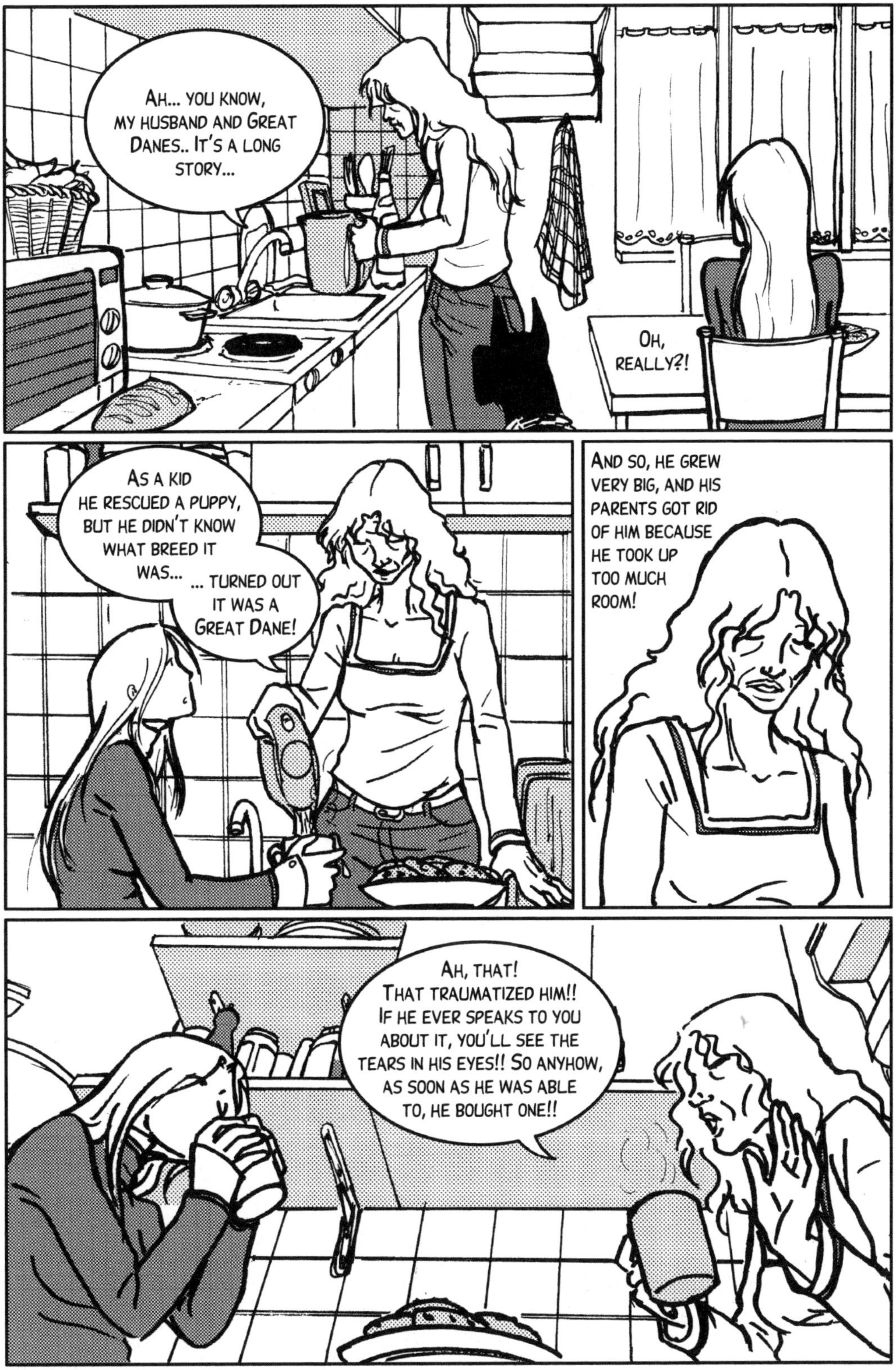
AH... YOU KNOW, MY HUSBAND AND GREAT DANES.. IT'S A LONG STORY...
OH, REALLY?!
AS A KID HE RESCUED A PUPPY, BUT HE DIDN'T KNOW WHAT BREED IT WAS...
... TURNED OUT IT WAS A GREAT DANE!
AND SO, HE GREW VERY BIG, AND HIS PARENTS GOT RID OF HIM BECAUSE HE TOOK UP TOO MUCH ROOM!
AH, THAT! THAT TRAUMATIZED HIM!! IF HE EVER SPEAKS TO YOU ABOUT IT, YOU'LL SEE THE TEARS IN HIS EYES!! SO ANYHOW, AS SOON AS HE WAS ABLE TO, HE BOUGHT ONE!!

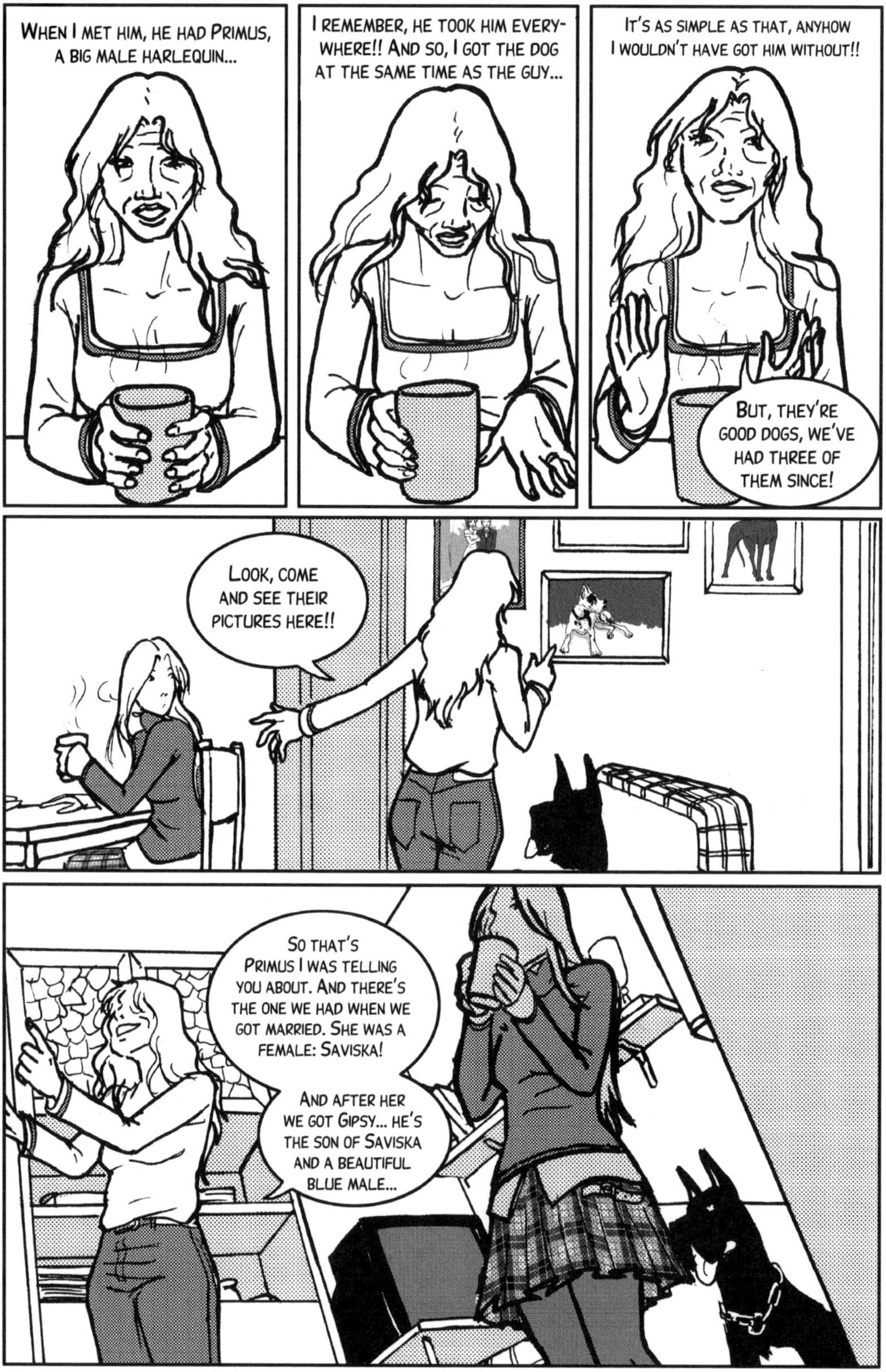
When I met him, he had Primus, a big male harlequin...
I remember, he took him everywhere!! And so, I got the dog at the same time as the guy...
It's as simple as that, anyhow I wouldn't have got him without!!
But, they're good dogs, we've had three of them since!
Look, come and see their pictures here!!
So that's Primus I was telling you about. And there's the one we had when we got married. She was a female: Saviska!
And after her we got Gipsy... he's the son of Saviska and a beautiful blue male...

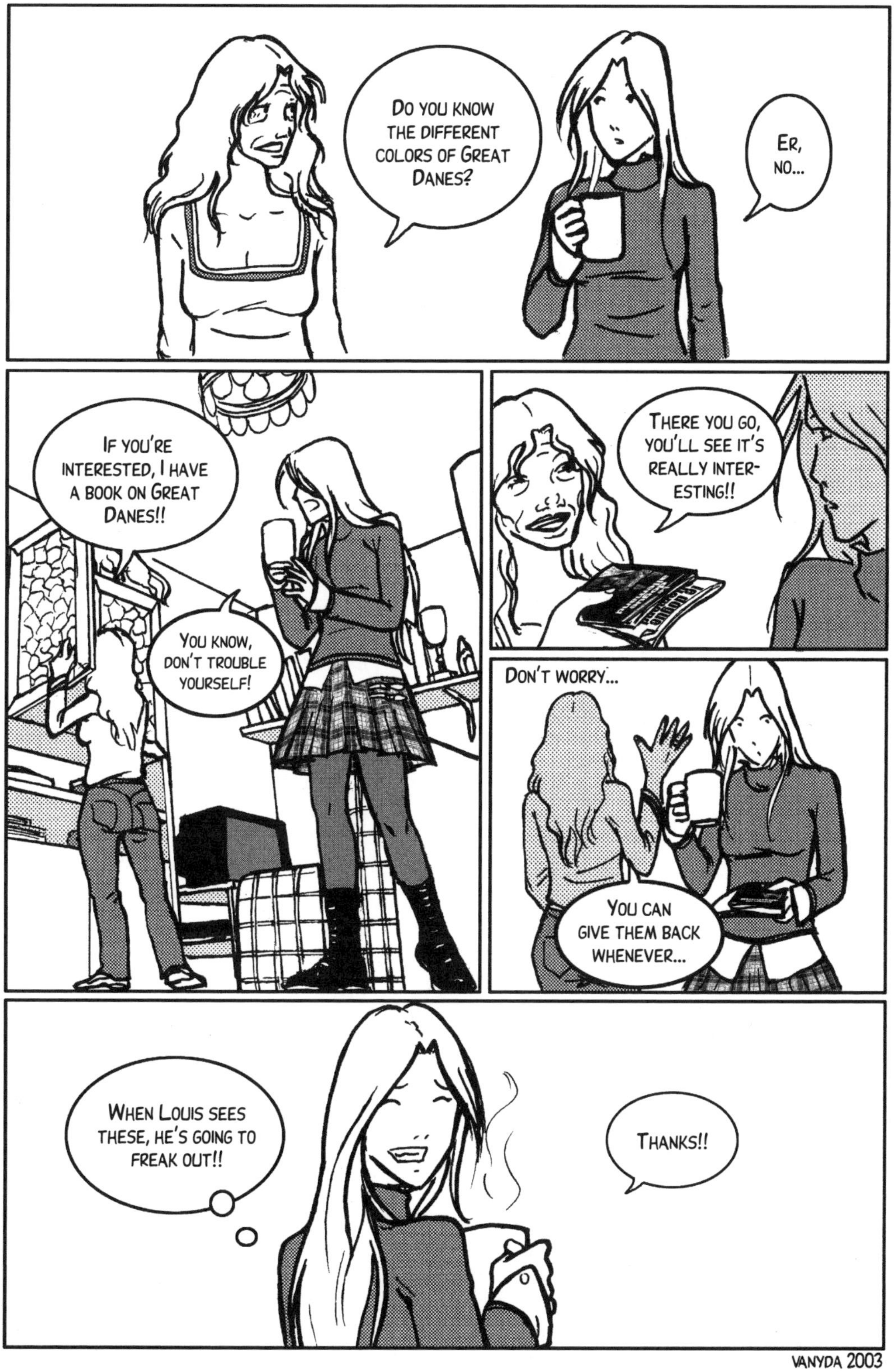
Do you know the different colors of Great Danes?
Er, no...
If you're interested, I have a book on Great Danes!!
You know, don't trouble yourself!
There you go, you'll see it's really inter-esting!!
Don't worry...
You can give them back whenever...
When Louis sees these, he's going to freak out!!
Thanks!!
VANYDA 2003

Chapter 18
Thanks

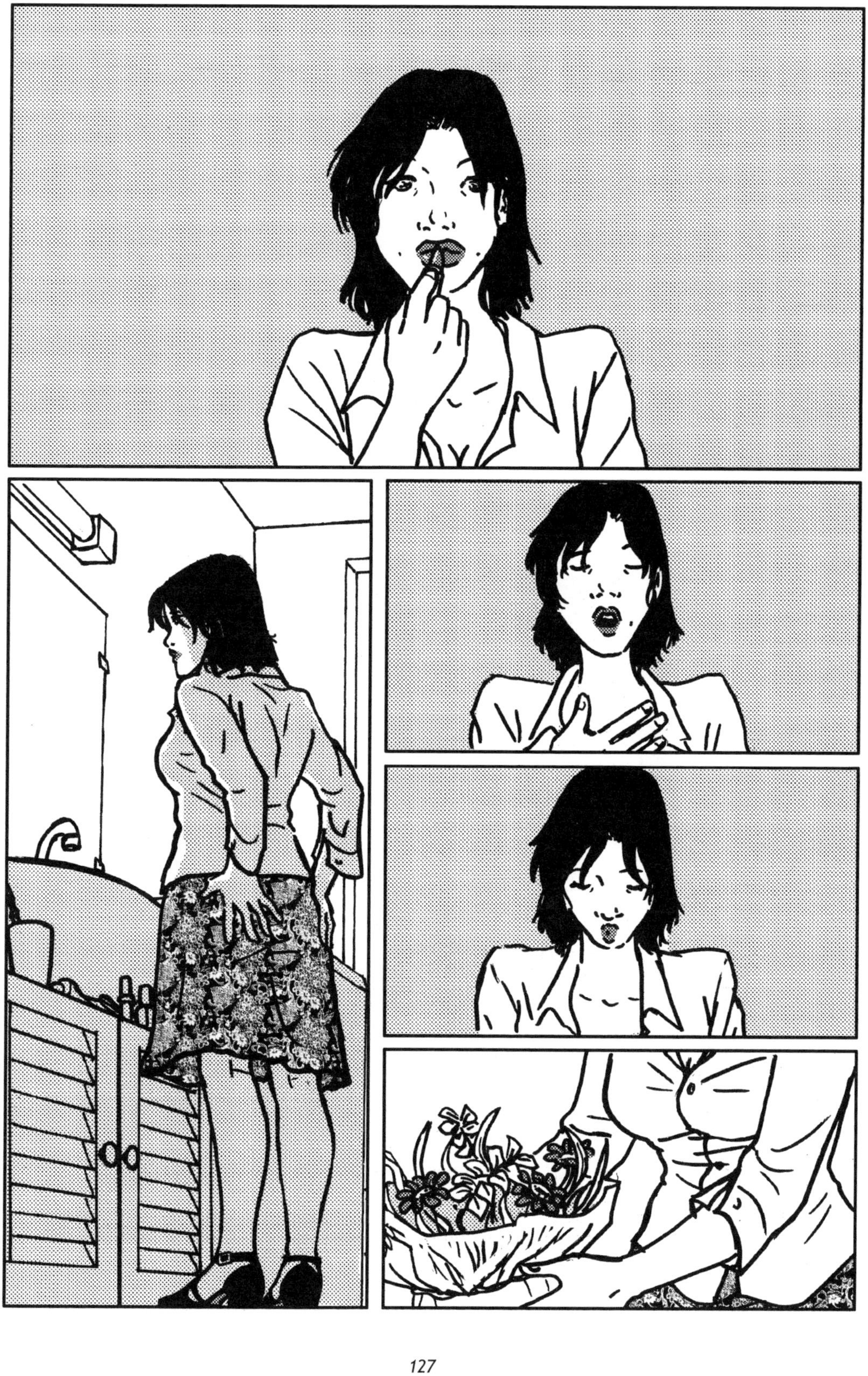

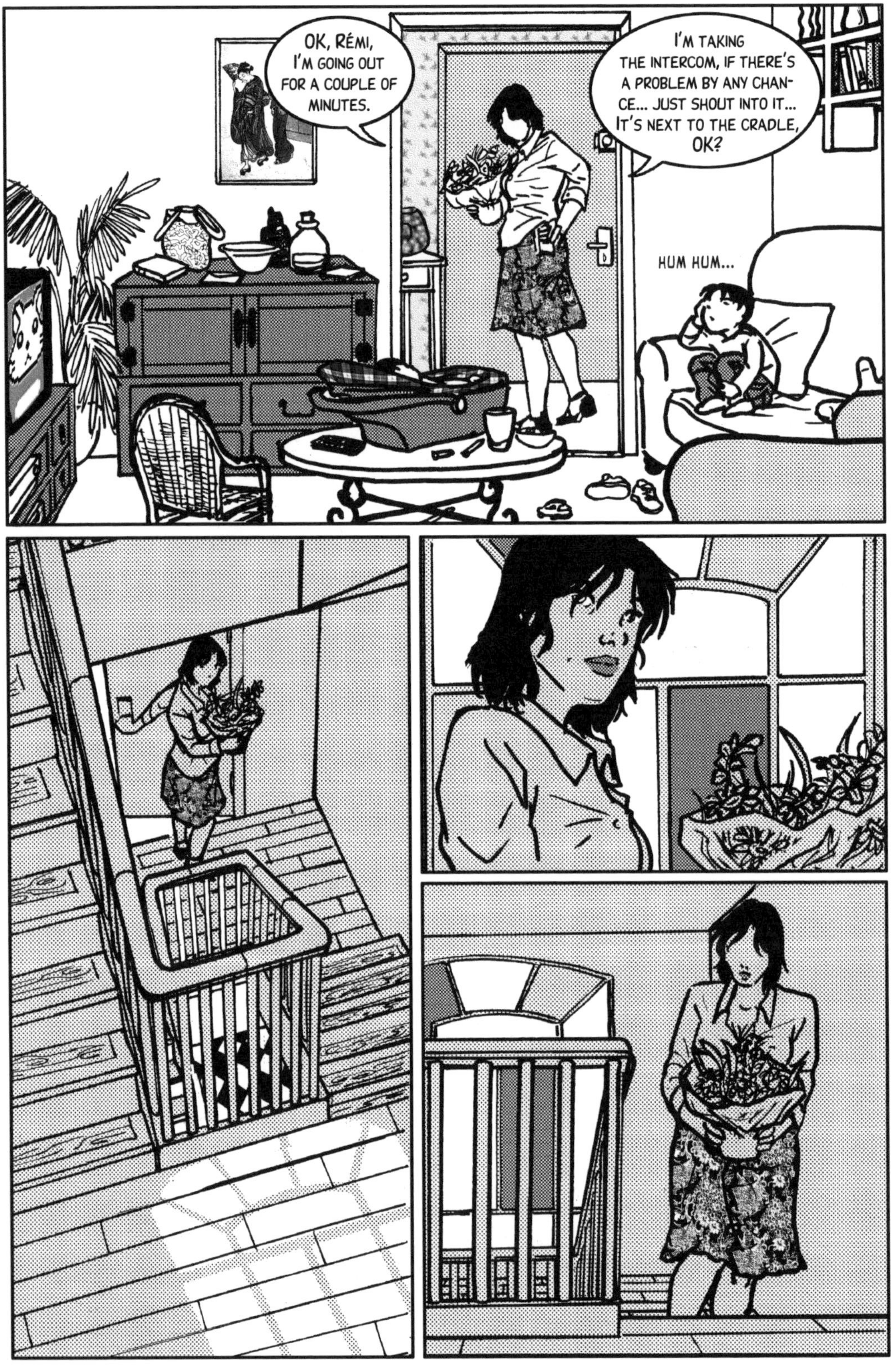
OK, RÉMI, I'M GOING OUT FOR A COUPLE OF MINUTES.
I'M TAKING THE INTERCOM, IF THERE'S A PROBLEM BY ANY CHANCE... JUST SHOUT INTO IT... IT'S NEXT TO THE CRADLE, OK?
HUM HUM...

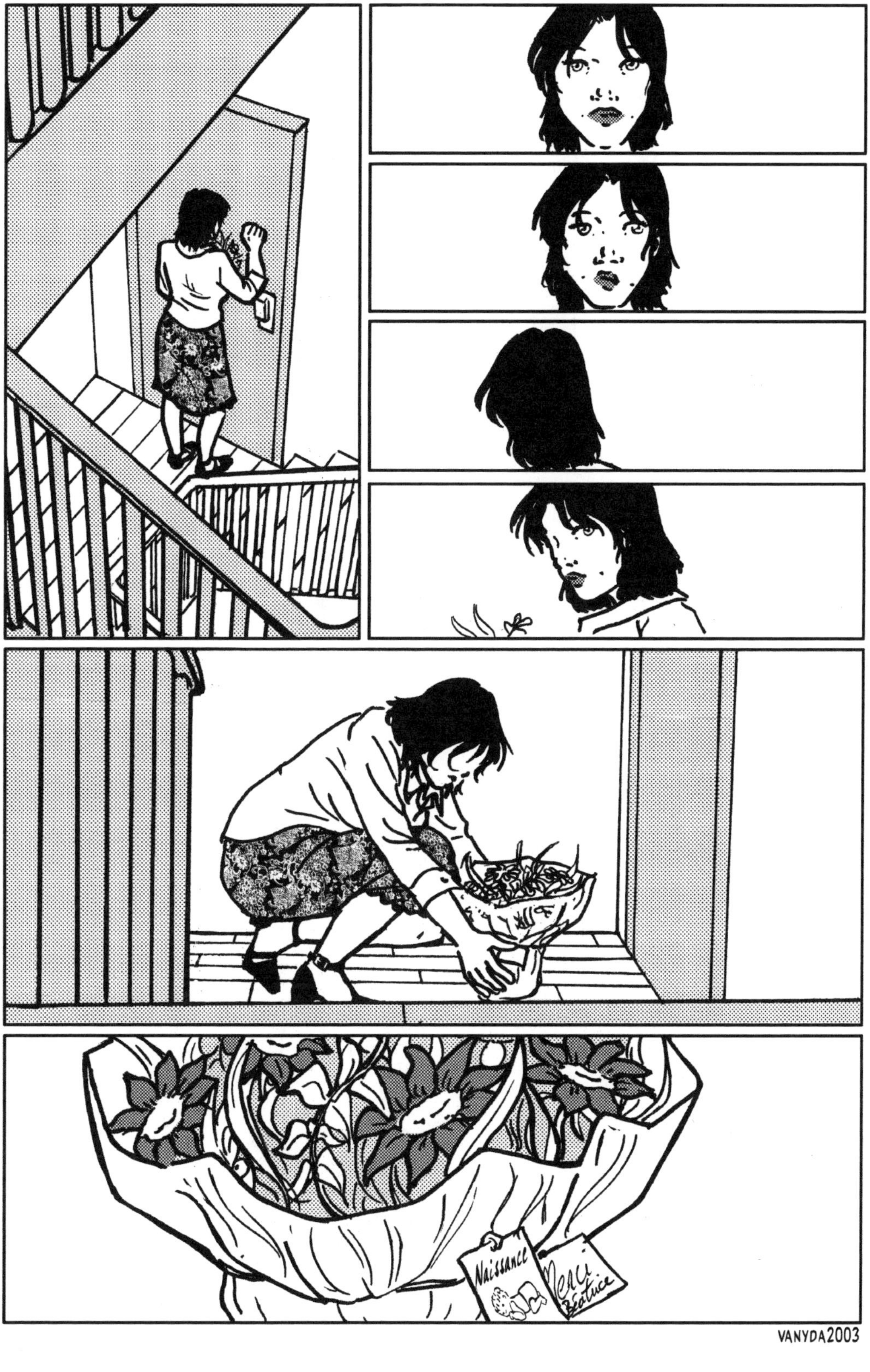
Naissance
Merci Béatrice

VANYDA2003

Chapter 19

TELEPHONE CONVERSATION

5:48 PM
HELLO, SARAH? YEAH, I'M OK, AND YOU?... SCHOOL OK?... HMM, HMM... SAME HERE... YEAH, DID YOU SEE THAT STUPID PROGRAM ON TV YESTERDAY, WITH THE SINGLES LOOKING FOR THEIR SOUL MATE THROUGH AN AGENCY... .? THAT DUDE WAS SUCH A TWIT, REALLY.. AND THE CHICK, WAS SO PITIFUL!!

6:03 PM
HAVE YOU SEEN MEHDI?... SO WHAT'S THE STORY? HMM, HMM, YOU'RE HAVING LUNCH TOGETHER TOMORROW? GETTING SERIOUS, EH?... HMM, HMM... THAT'S SO COOL! HMM.. JEEZ, I'VE GOT TO SEE THIS GUY!!

6:14 PM
YEAH, APPARENTLY YOU'VE GOT TO SLEEP WITH YOUR FEET RAISED UP, AND SOAK THEM IN COLD WATER FOR 5 MINUTES IN THE MORNING AND EVENING... A REAL PAIN! OH, YOU CAN ALSO MASSAGE THEM WITH ESSENTIAL OILS..

HMM.. MY MOM TOLD ME ABOUT IT...

I DON'T KNOW WHERE YOU BUY IT.

6:27 PM
JEROME CAME OVER SUNDAY. YEAH, HE ALWAYS JUST DROPS IN WITHOUT WARNING, LIKE WE'RE ONLY WAITING FOR HIM AND HE'S SOOO WELCOME... WELL, NO, NOT REALLY, BUT... AND LOUIS NEVER TELLS HIM THAT AT TIMES HE'S A PAIN ...

REALLY, BIG TIME SOMETIMES...

6:42 PM

YOUR GRANDMA?

SHE SAID THAT?... REALLY, SHE'S AWFUL!! WHAT'S IT GOT TO DO WITH HER?... BESIDES IT'S GOT NOTHING TO DO WITH.. HMM...

6:56 PM

SATURDAY, THERE'LL BE SOME OF LOUIS' PALS AS WELL, YEAH... I THINK.. YES, AND MARTIN AND CECILE ARE COMING TOO...

7:07 PM
HMM...
HMM...
YES...
HMM...
HMM...

IT'S OBVIOUS, HMM, HMM... .OH YEAH?... HMM

7:22 PM

OK, SEE YOU TOMORROW? YEAH?... 'BYE...

VANYDA 2003

Chapter 20 "Go Fetch !!"

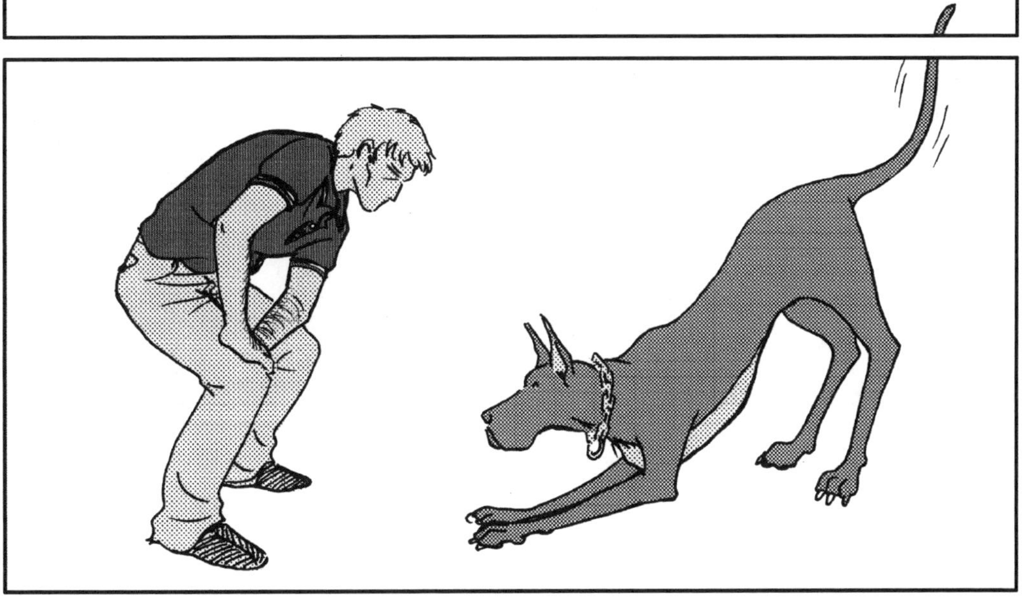

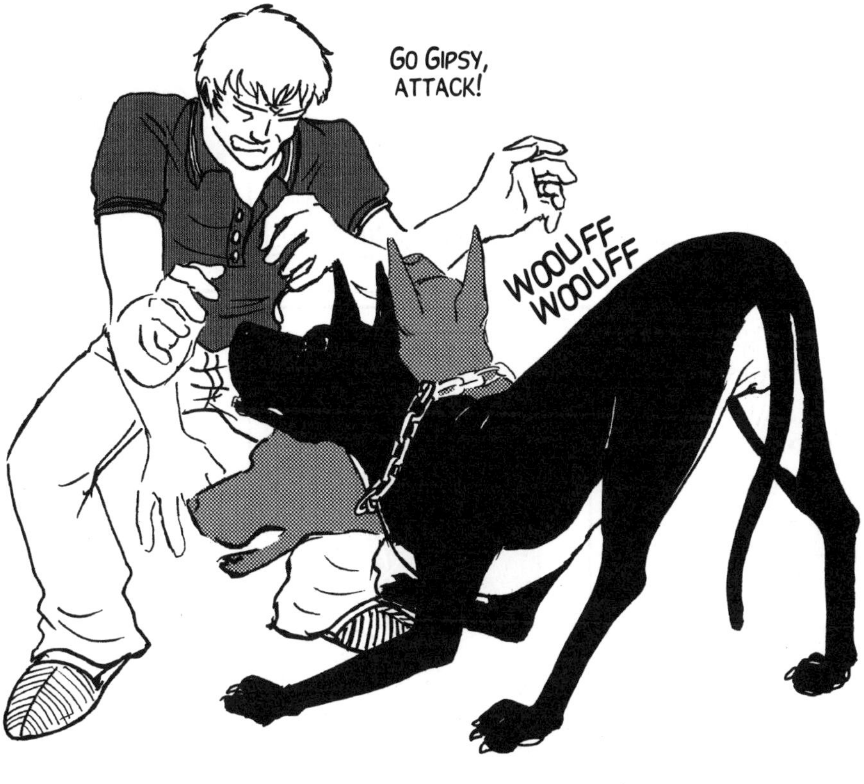
GO GIPSY, ATTACK!
WOOUFF WOOUFF

GRRR !
YAAAH!
Beethoven
ARHHH, BAD BOY!

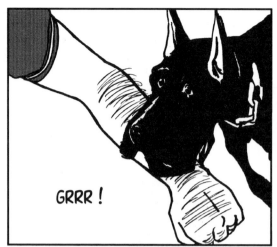

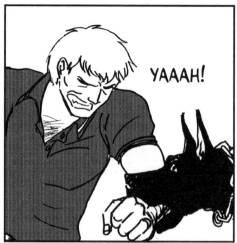

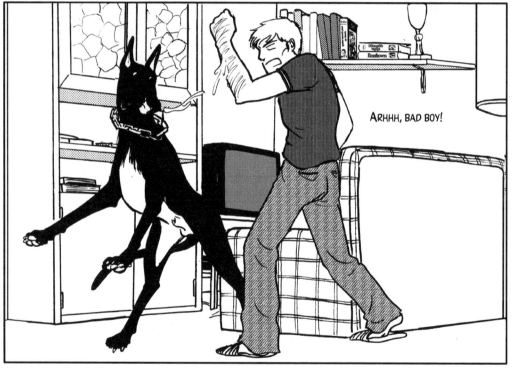

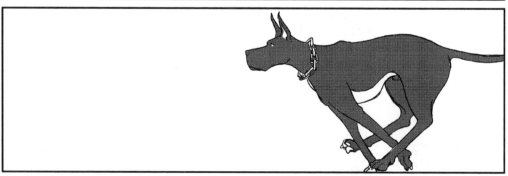

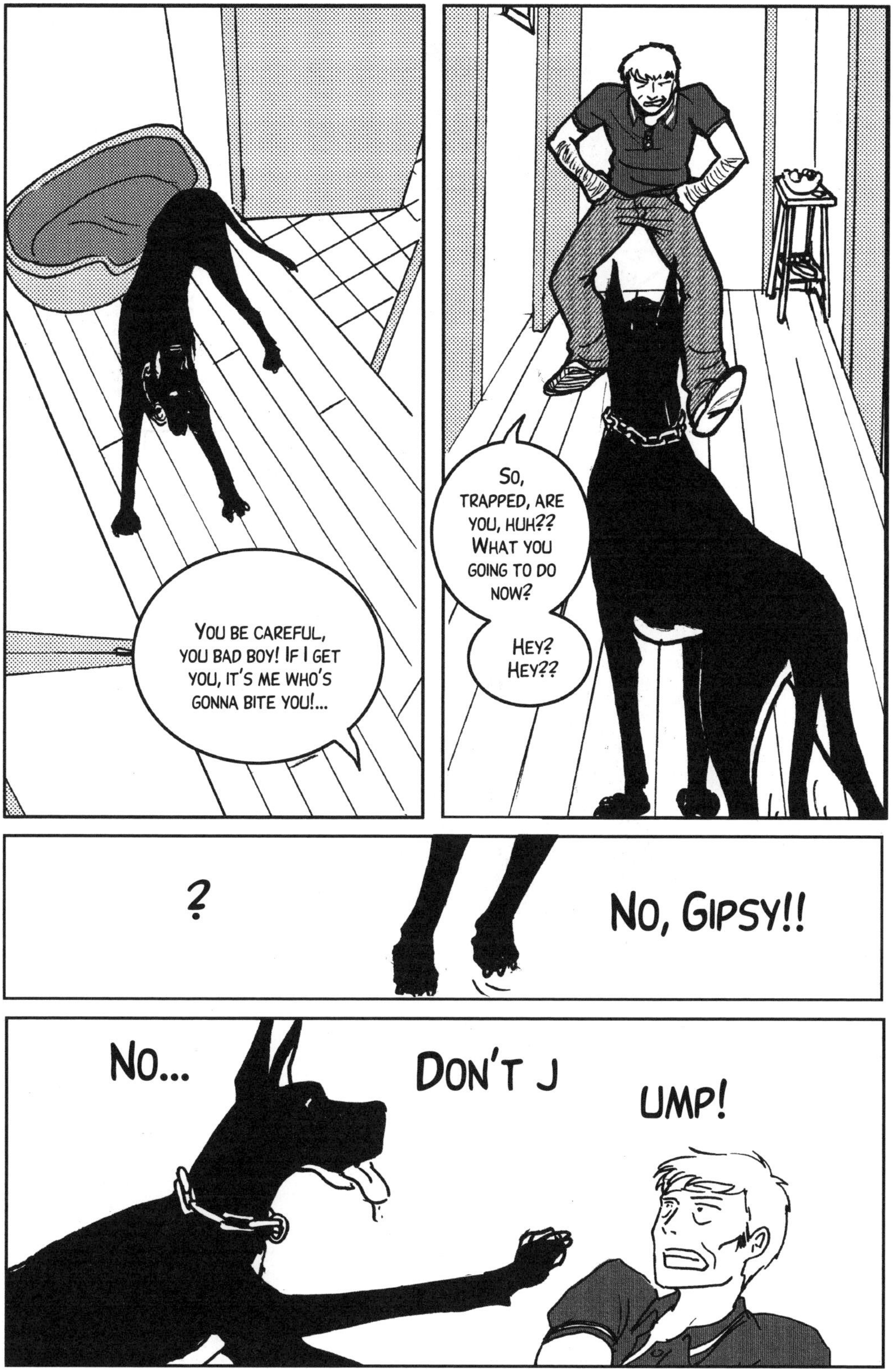
You be careful, you bad boy! If I get you, it's me who's gonna bite you!...
So, trapped, are you, huh?? What you going to do now?
Hey? Hey??
?
No, Gipsy!!
No...
Don't j
ump!

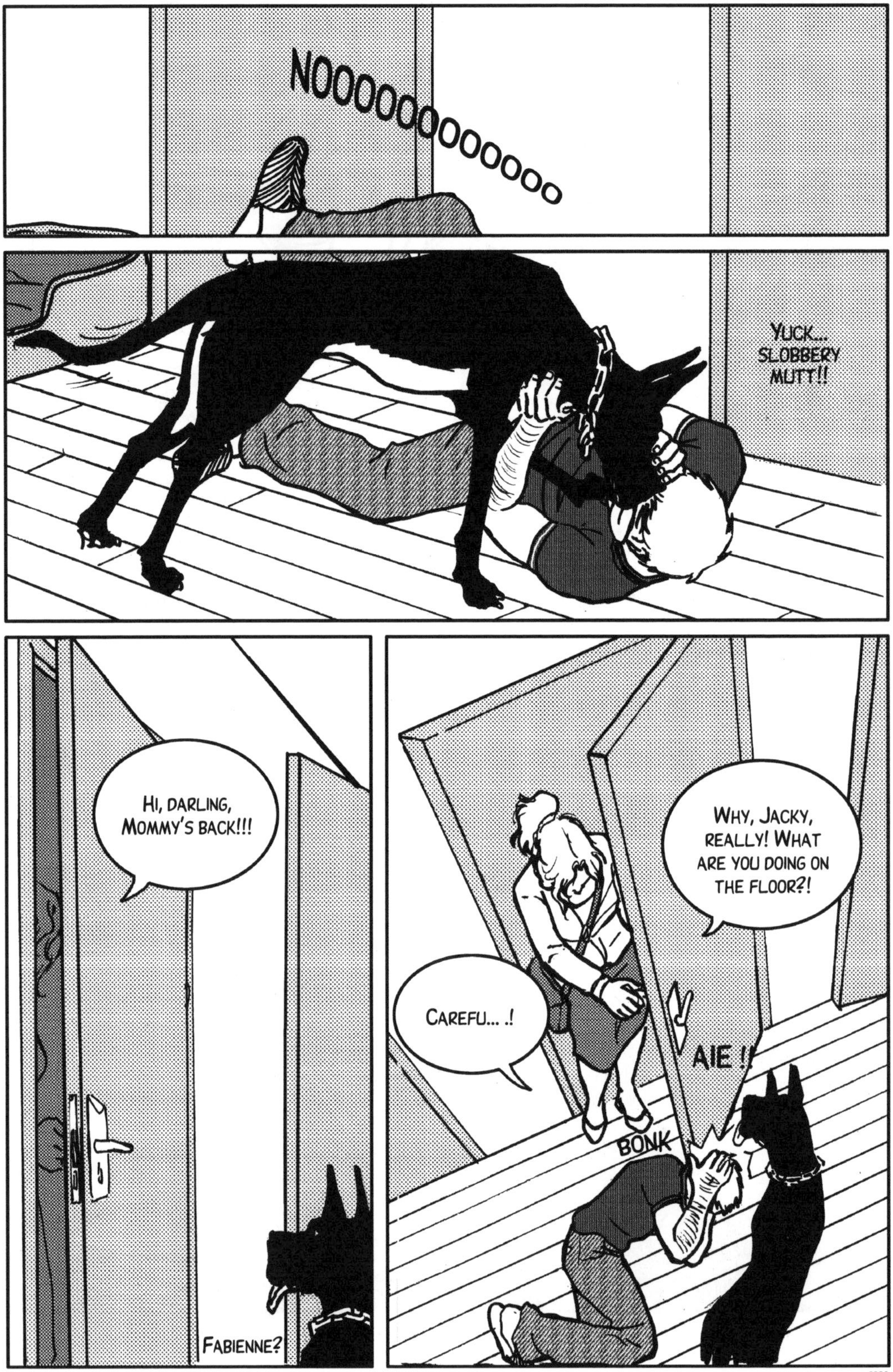
NOOOOOOOOOOOOO
YUCK... SLOBBERY MUTT!!
HI, DARLING, MOMMY'S BACK!!!
FABIENNE?
WHY, JACKY, REALLY! WHAT ARE YOU DOING ON THE FLOOR?!
CAREFU... .!
AIE !!
BONK
VANYDA 2003

Chapter 21 Welcome Baby

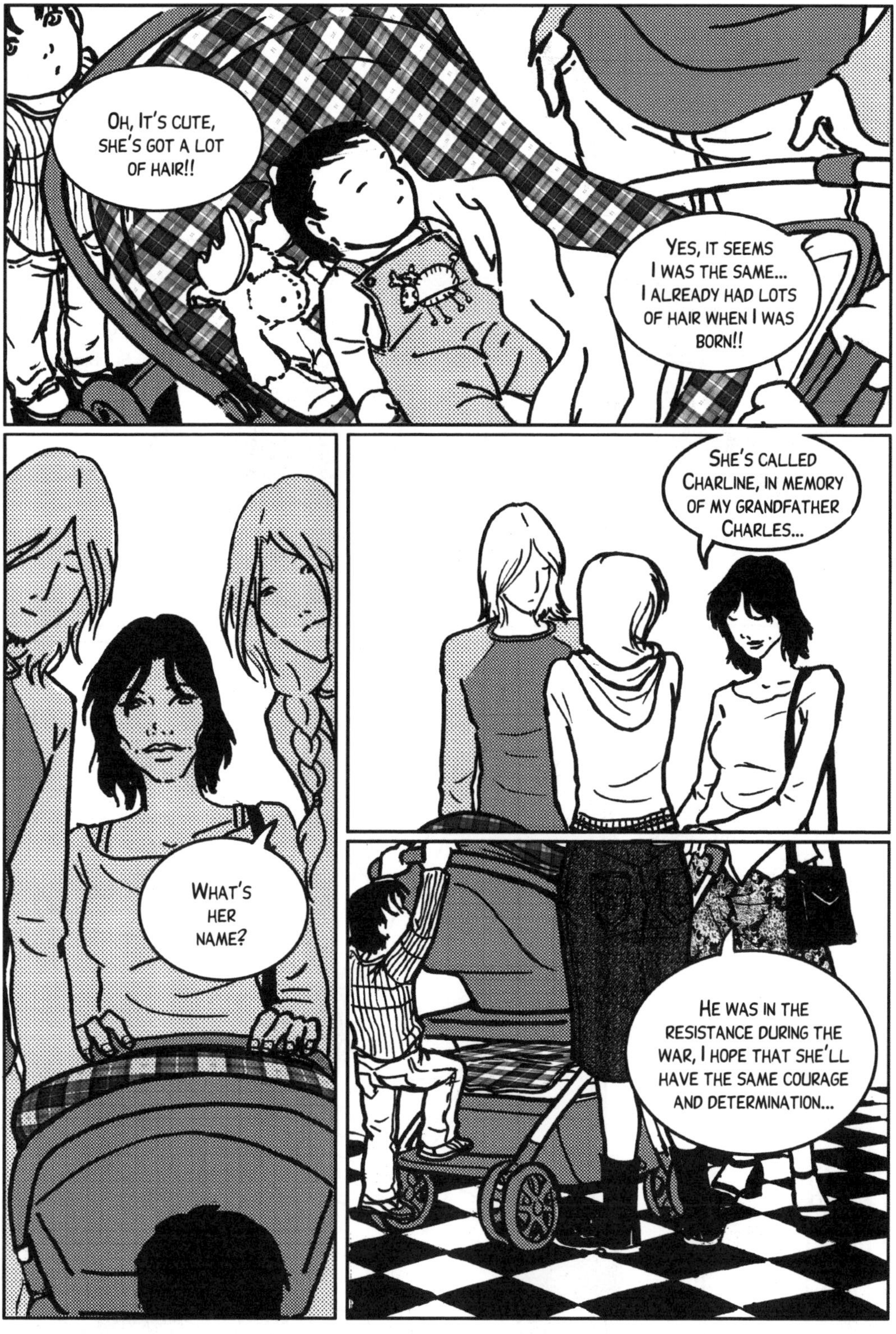

OH, IT'S CUTE, SHE'S GOT A LOT OF HAIR!!
YES, IT SEEMS I WAS THE SAME... I ALREADY HAD LOTS OF HAIR WHEN I WAS BORN!!
WHAT'S HER NAME?
SHE'S CALLED CHARLINE, IN MEMORY OF MY GRANDFATHER CHARLES...
HE WAS IN THE RESISTANCE DURING THE WAR, I HOPE THAT SHE'LL HAVE THE SAME COURAGE AND DETERMINATION...

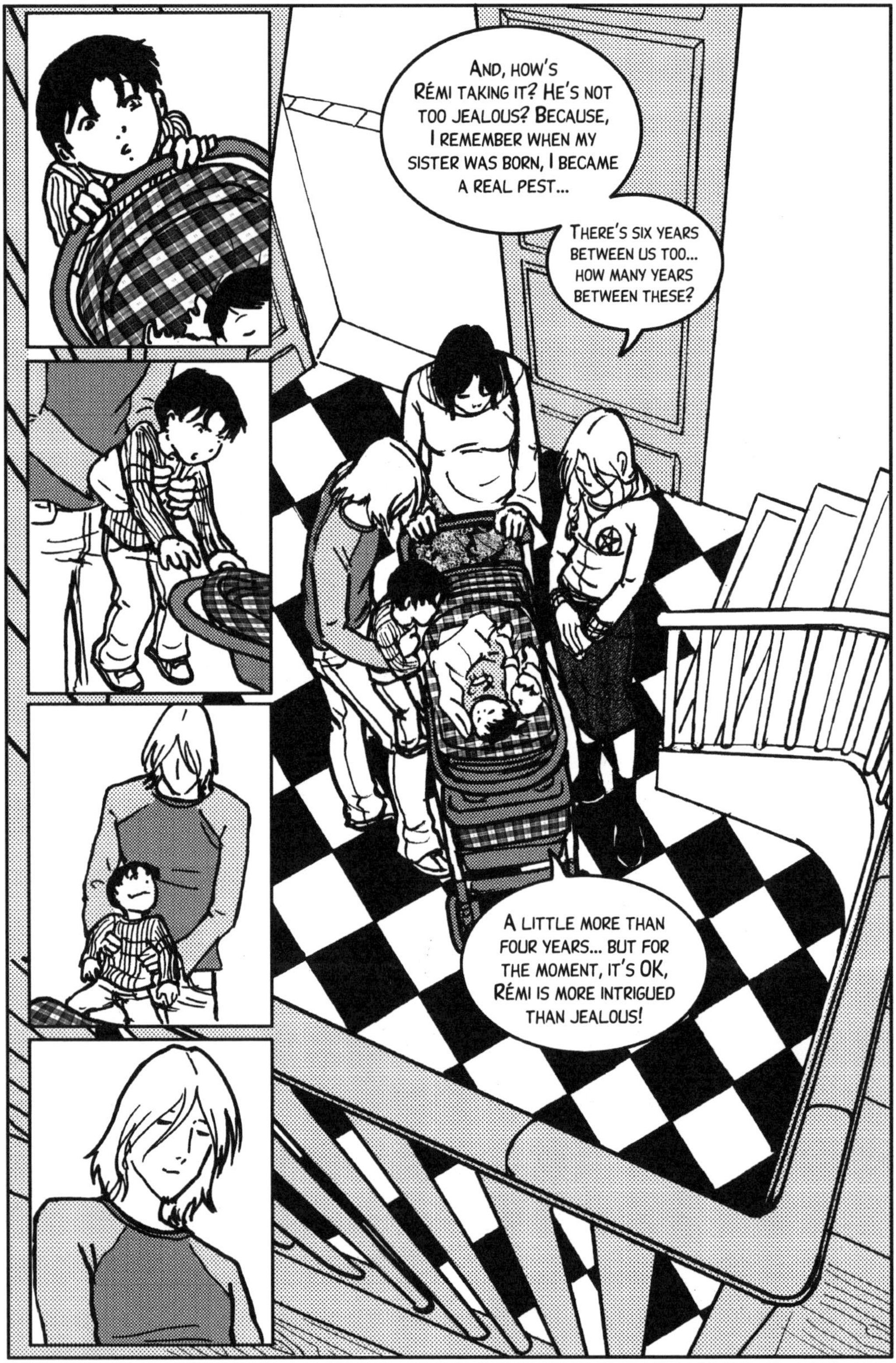
AND, HOW'S RÉMI TAKING IT? HE'S NOT TOO JEALOUS? BECAUSE, I REMEMBER WHEN MY SISTER WAS BORN, I BECAME A REAL PEST...
THERE'S SIX YEARS BETWEEN US TOO... HOW MANY YEARS BETWEEN THESE?
A LITTLE MORE THAN FOUR YEARS... BUT FOR THE MOMENT, IT'S OK, RÉMI IS MORE INTRIGUED THAN JEALOUS!

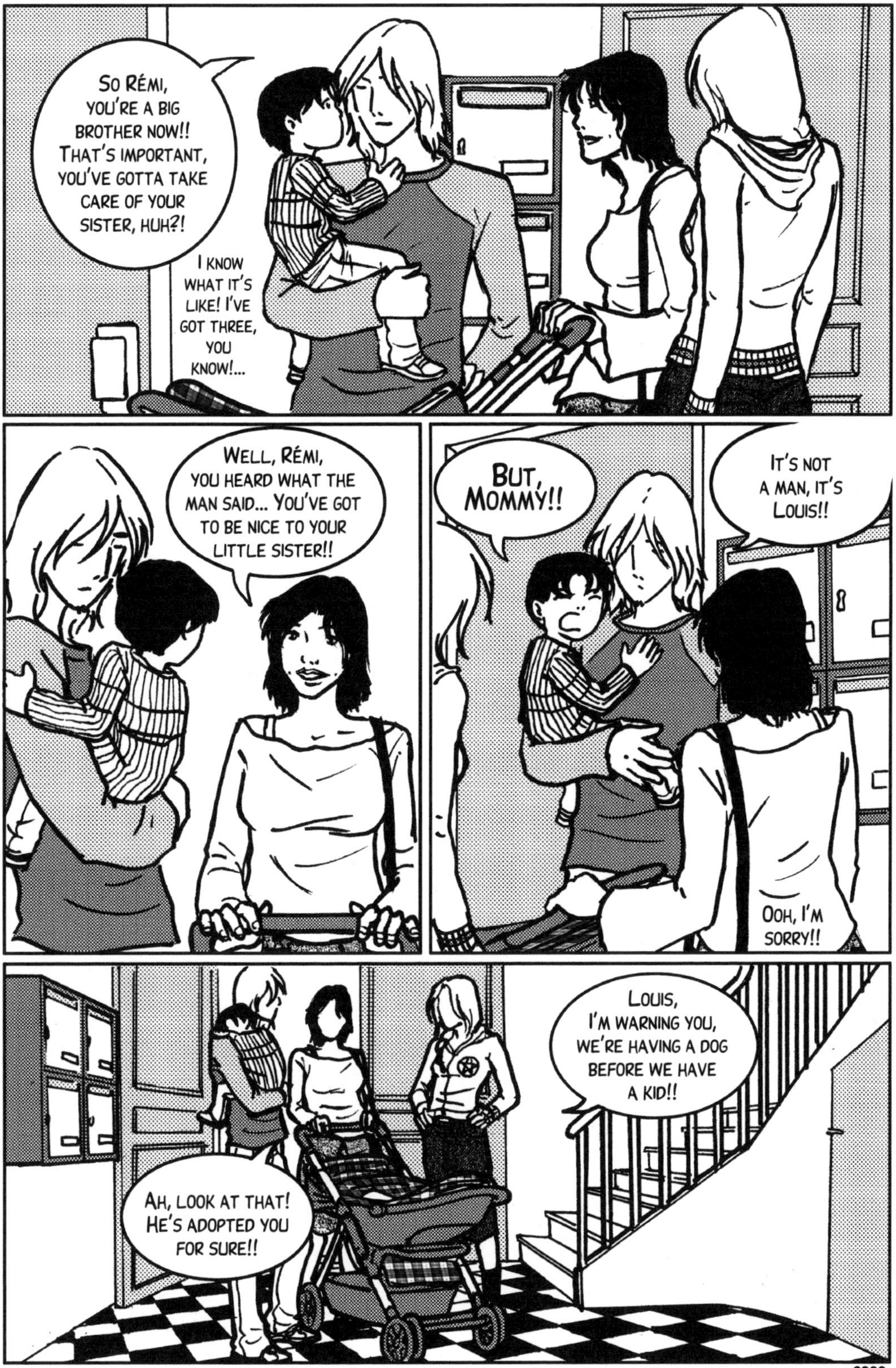
SO RÉMI, YOU'RE A BIG BROTHER NOW!! THAT'S IMPORTANT, YOU'VE GOTTA TAKE CARE OF YOUR SISTER, HUH?!
I KNOW WHAT IT'S LIKE! I'VE GOT THREE, YOU KNOW!...
WELL, RÉMI, YOU HEARD WHAT THE MAN SAID... YOU'VE GOT TO BE NICE TO YOUR LITTLE SISTER!!
BUT, MOMMY!!
IT'S NOT A MAN, IT'S LOUIS!!
OOH, I'M SORRY!!
AH, LOOK AT THAT! HE'S ADOPTED YOU FOR SURE!!
LOUIS, I'M WARNING YOU, WE'RE HAVING A DOG BEFORE WE HAVE A KID!!

VANYDA 2003

Chapter 22
The Lord of the Pancakes Versus Kiki from Space...

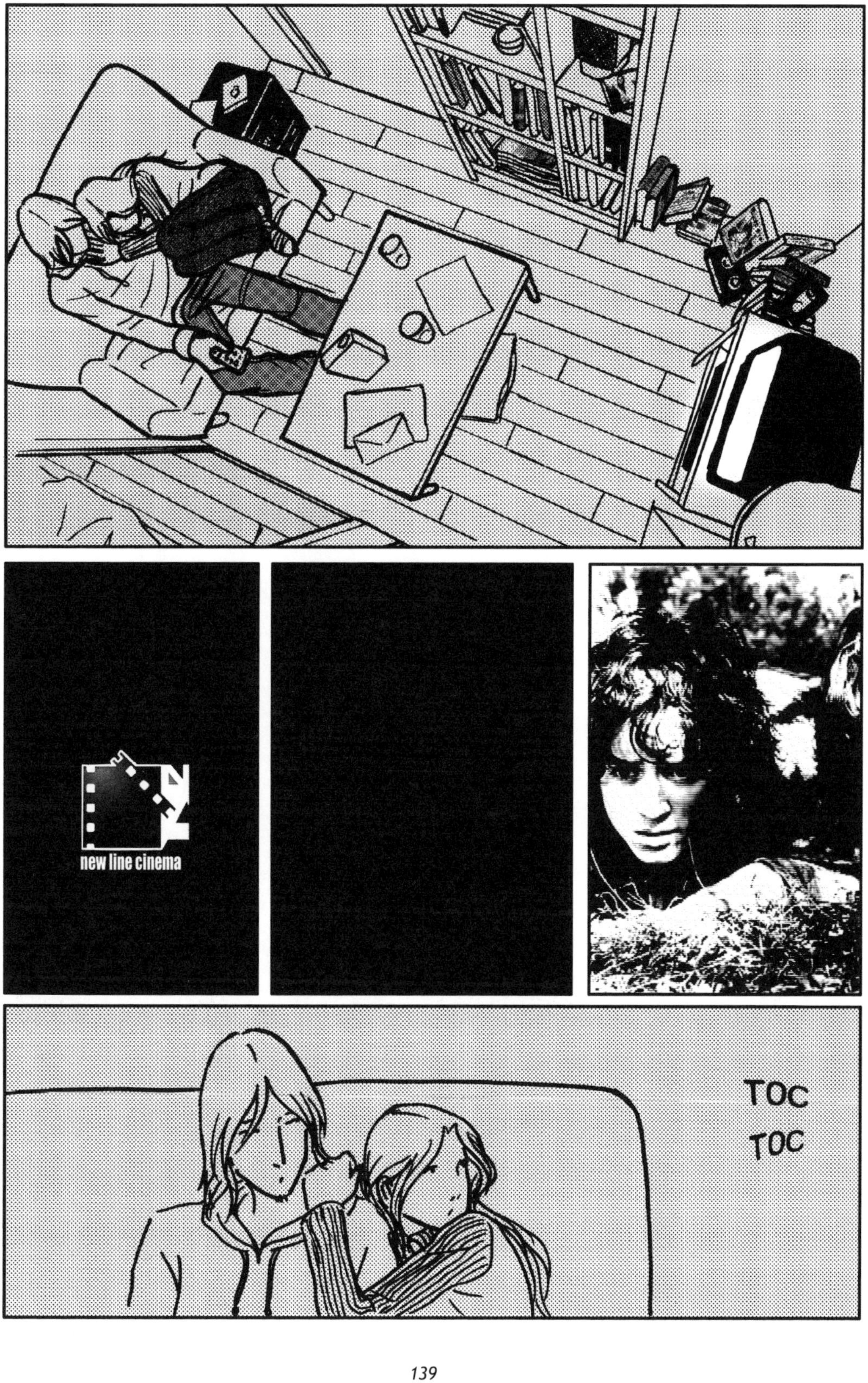
new line cinema
TOC
TOC

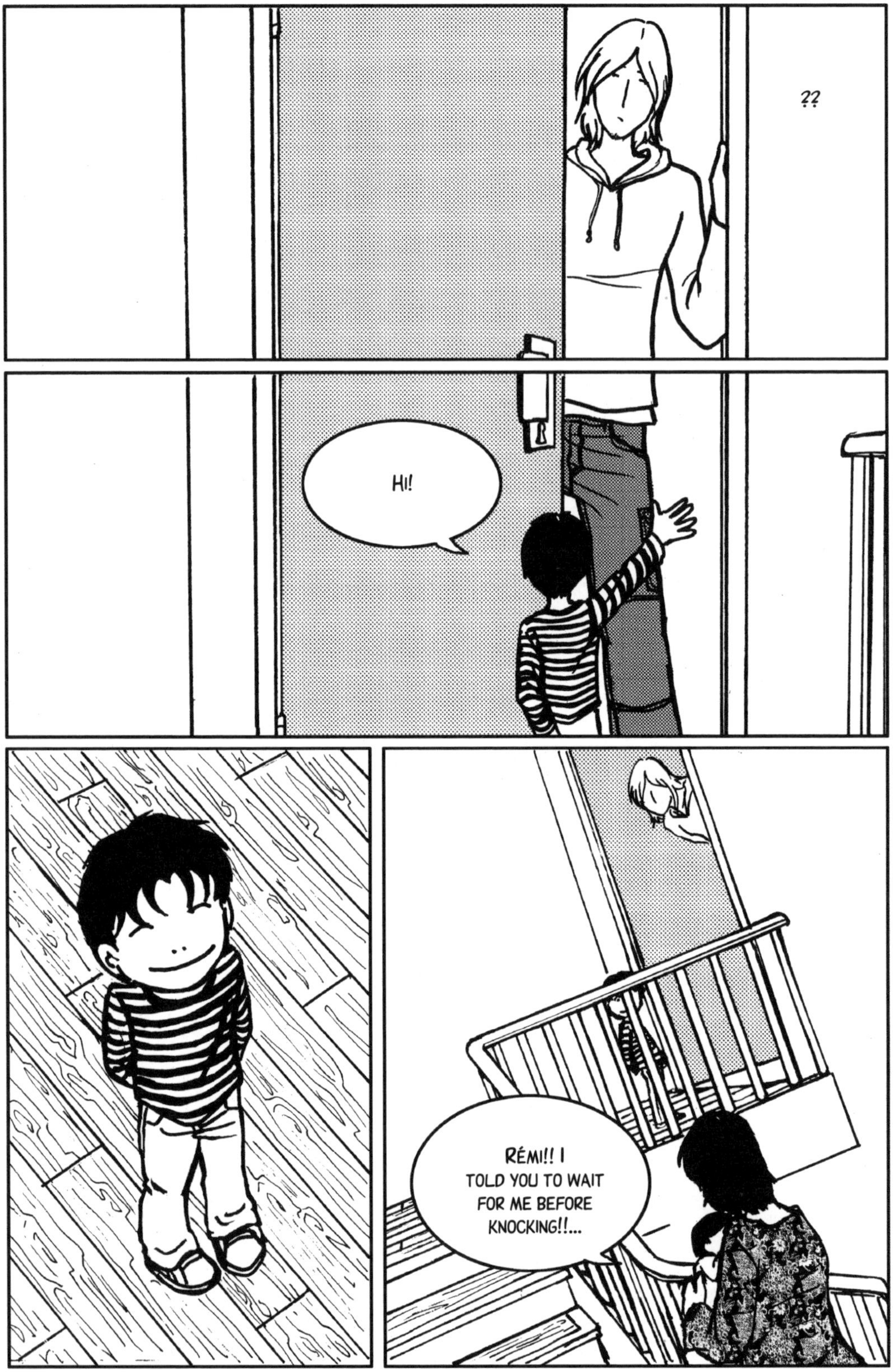
??
HI!
RÉMI!! I TOLD YOU TO WAIT FOR ME BEFORE KNOCKING!!...

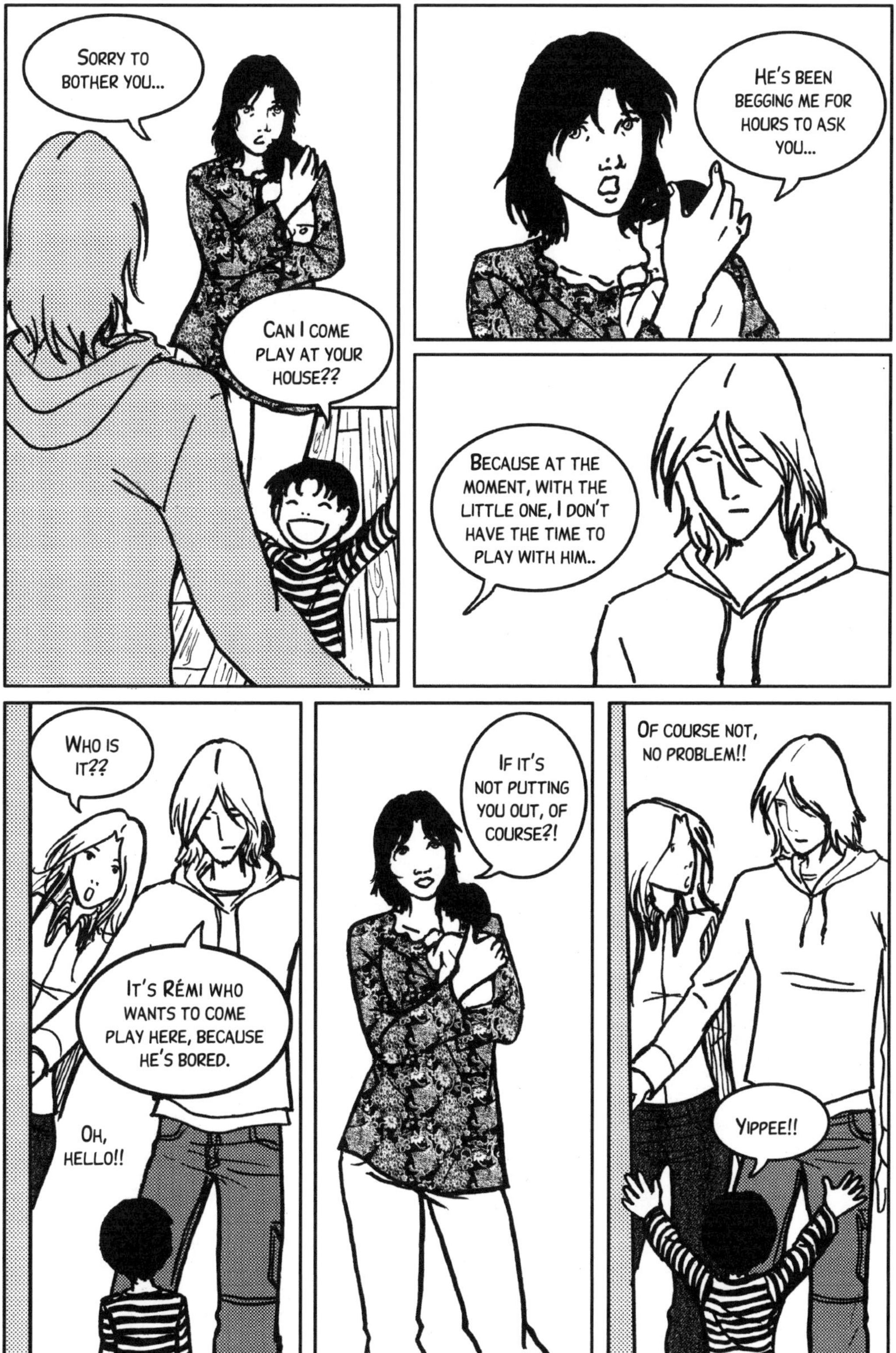
SORRY TO BOTHER YOU...
CAN I COME PLAY AT YOUR HOUSE??
HE'S BEEN BEGGING ME FOR HOURS TO ASK YOU...
BECAUSE AT THE MOMENT, WITH THE LITTLE ONE, I DON'T HAVE THE TIME TO PLAY WITH HIM..
WHO IS IT??
IT'S RÉMI WHO WANTS TO COME PLAY HERE, BECAUSE HE'S BORED.
OH, HELLO!!
IF IT'S NOT PUTTING YOU OUT, OF COURSE?!
OF COURSE NOT, NO PROBLEM!!
YIPPEE!!

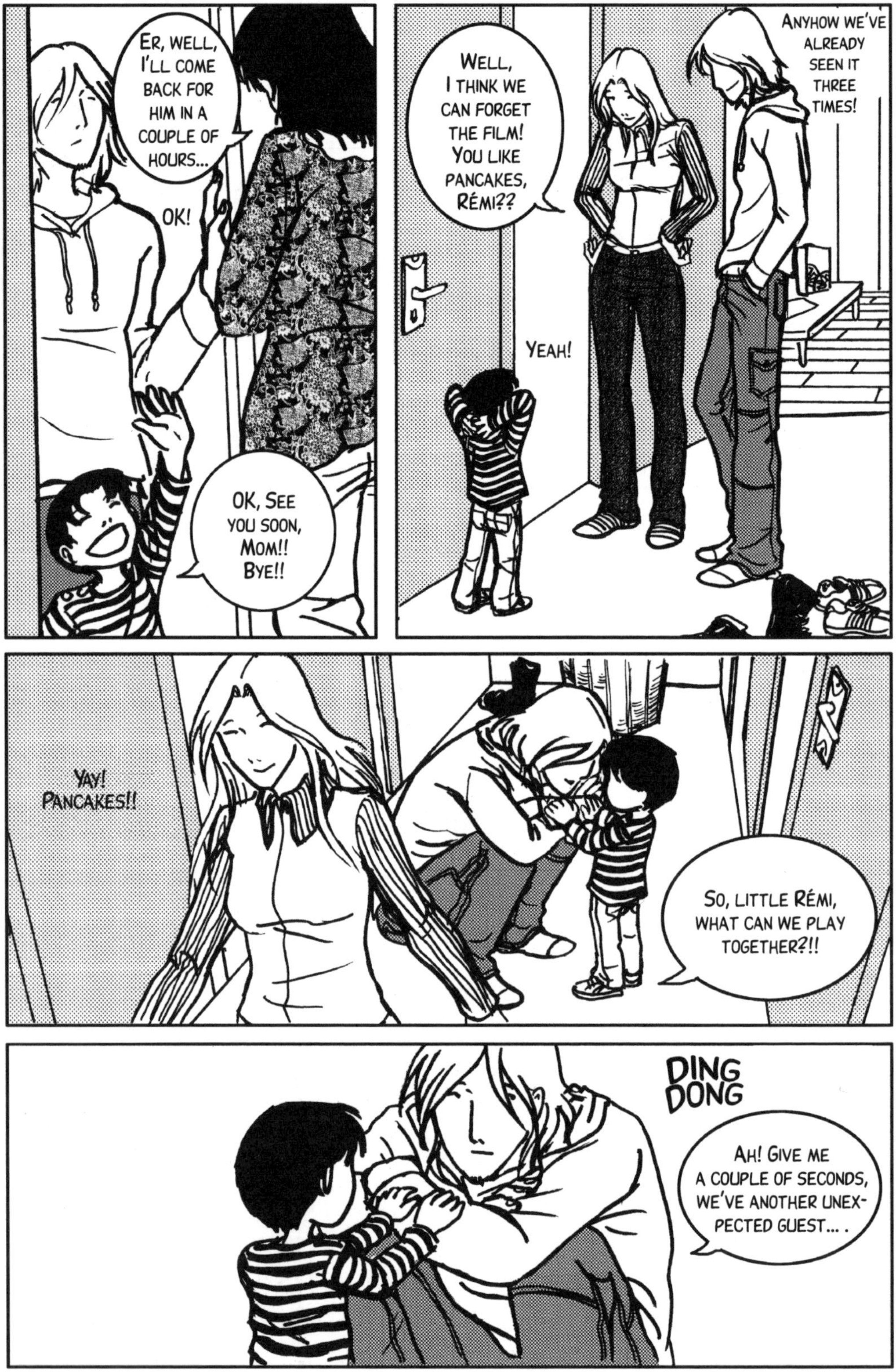
Er, well, I'll come back for him in a couple of hours...
OK!
OK, See you soon, Mom!! Bye!!
Well, I think we can forget the film! You like pancakes, Rémi??
Anyhow we've already seen it three times!
Yeah!
Yay! Pancakes!!
So, little Rémi, what can we play together?!!
DING DONG
Ah! Give me a couple of seconds, we've another unexpected guest... .

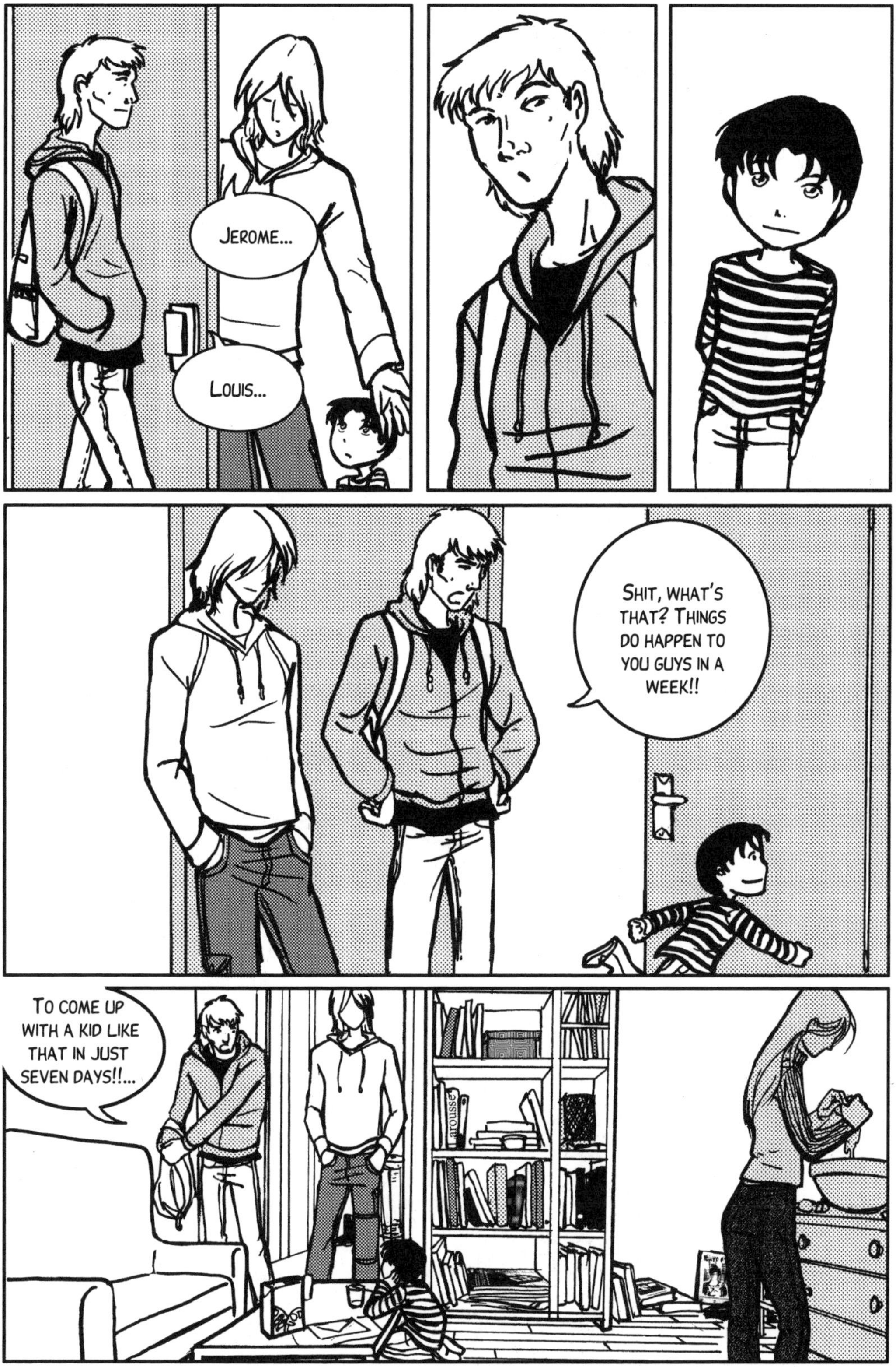
JEROME...
LOUIS...
SHIT, WHAT'S THAT? THINGS DO HAPPEN TO YOU GUYS IN A WEEK!!
TO COME UP WITH A KID LIKE THAT IN JUST SEVEN DAYS!!...

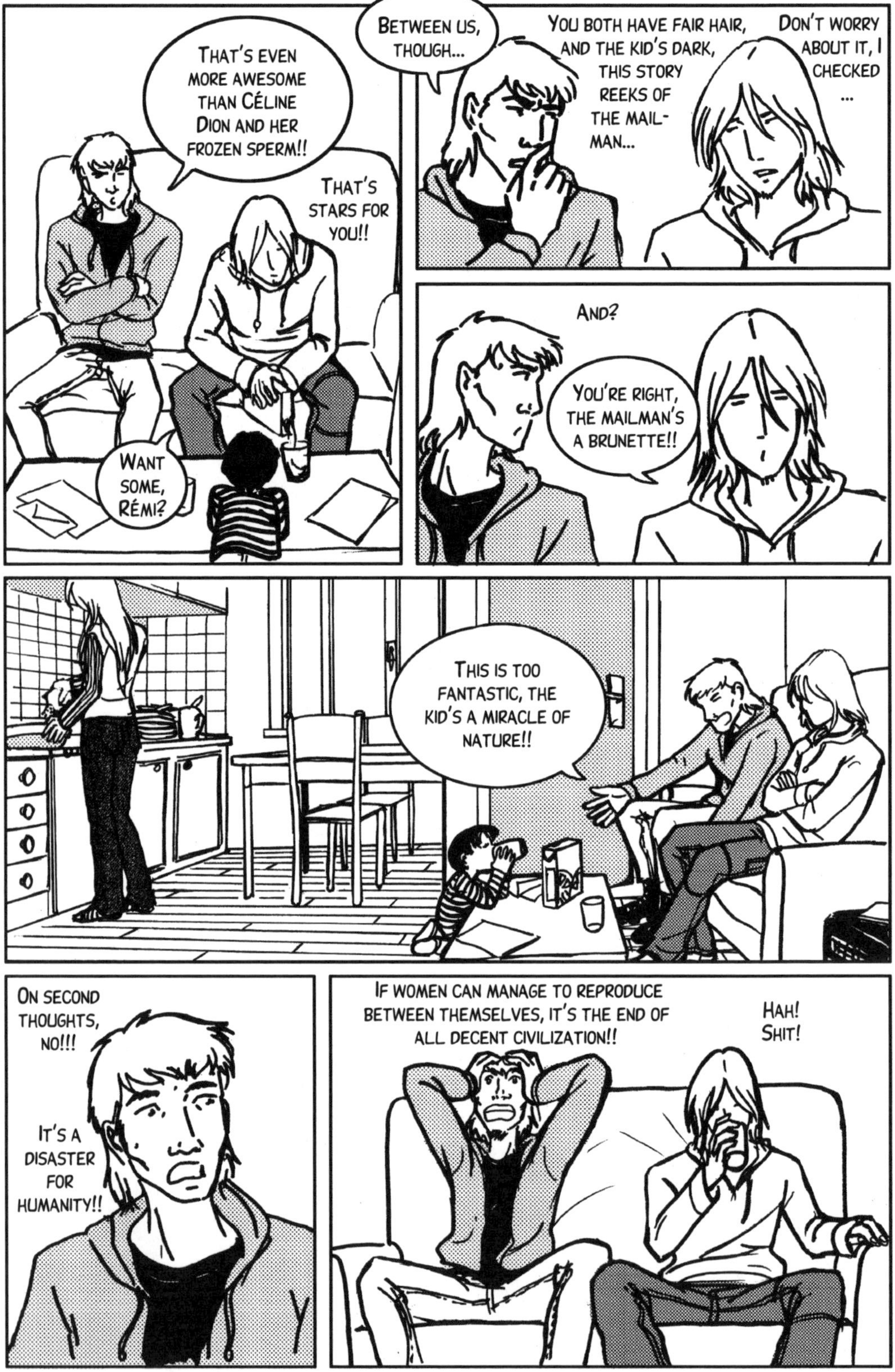

That's even more awesome than Céline Dion and her frozen sperm!!
That's stars for you!!
Want some, Rémi?
Between us, though...
You both have fair hair, and the kid's dark, this story reeks of the mail-man...
Don't worry about it, I checked ...
And?
You're right, the mailman's a brunette!!
This is too fantastic, the kid's a miracle of nature!!
On second thoughts, no!!!
It's a disaster for humanity!!
If women can manage to reproduce between themselves, it's the end of all decent civilization!!
Hah! Shit!

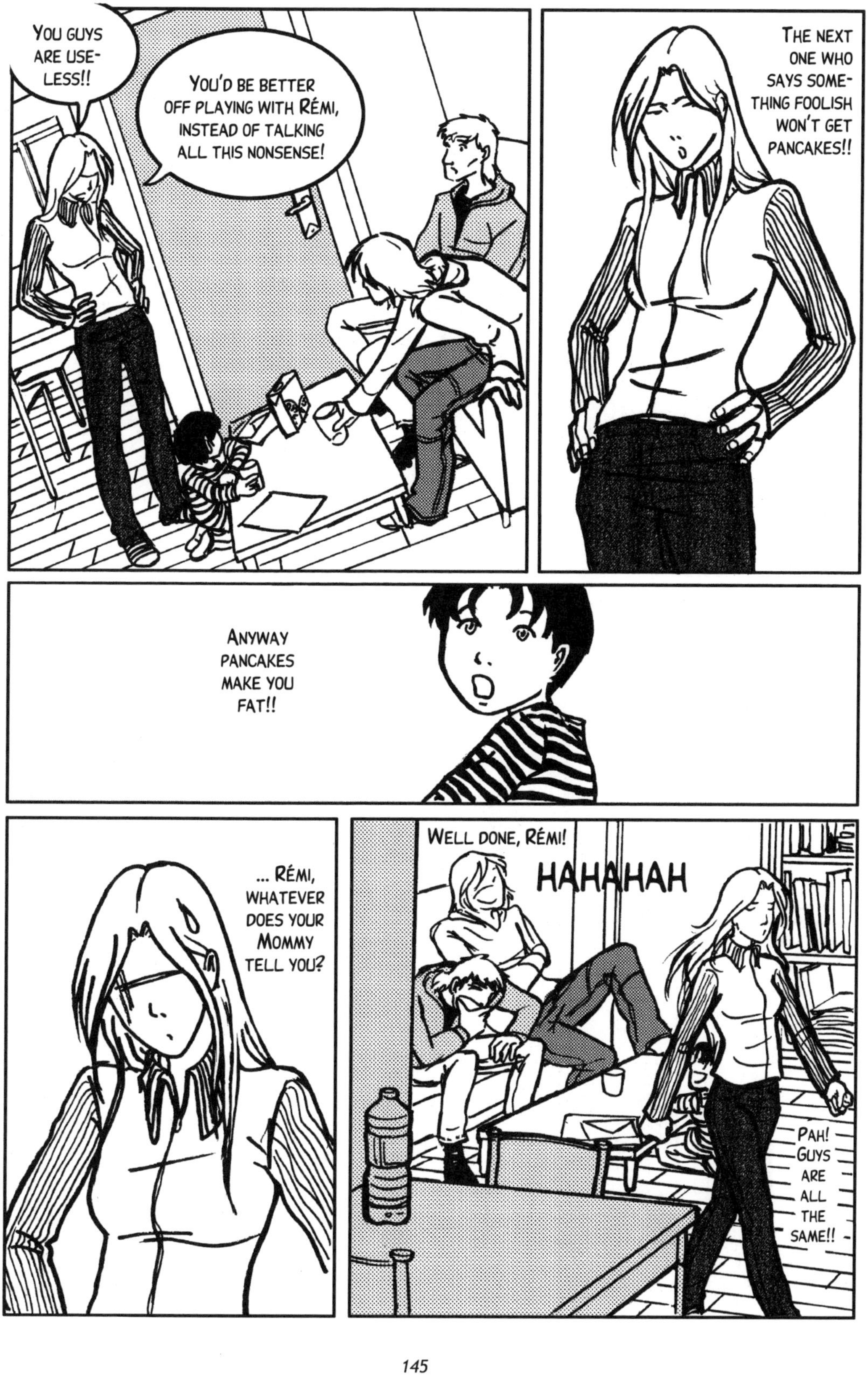
YOU GUYS ARE USE-LESS!!
YOU'D BE BETTER OFF PLAYING WITH RÉMI, INSTEAD OF TALKING ALL THIS NONSENSE!
THE NEXT ONE WHO SAYS SOME-THING FOOLISH WON'T GET PANCAKES!!
ANYWAY PANCAKES MAKE YOU FAT!!
... RÉMI, WHATEVER DOES YOUR MOMMY TELL YOU?
WELL DONE, RÉMI!
HAHAHAH
PAH! GUYS ARE ALL THE SAME!!

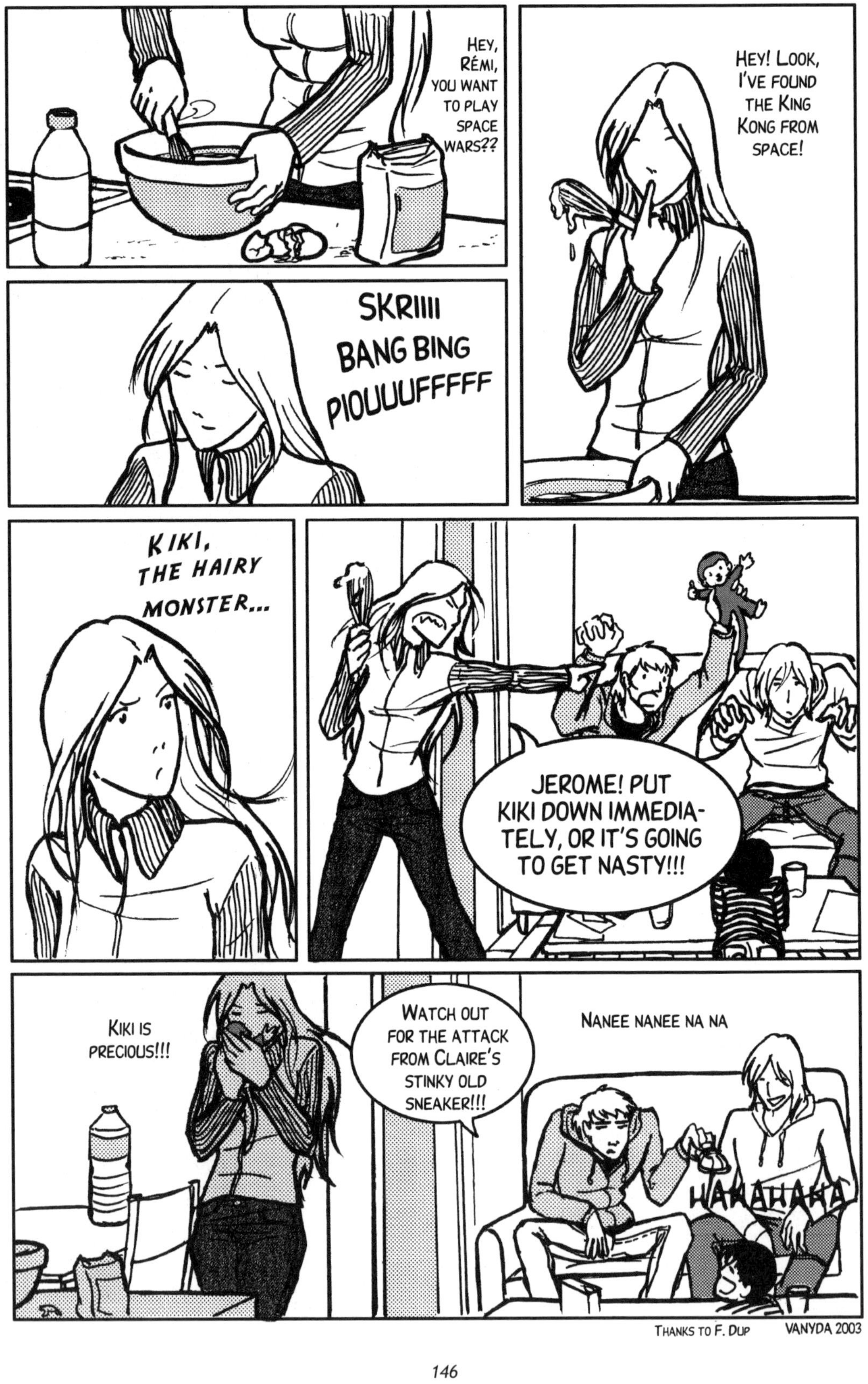

HEY, RÉMI, YOU WANT TO PLAY SPACE WARS??
SKRIIII
BANG BING
PIOUUUFFFFF
HEY! LOOK, I'VE FOUND THE KING KONG FROM SPACE!
KIKI, THE HAIRY MONSTER...
JEROME! PUT KIKI DOWN IMMEDIA-TELY, OR IT'S GOING TO GET NASTY!!!
KIKI IS PRECIOUS!!!
WATCH OUT FOR THE ATTACK FROM CLAIRE'S STINKY OLD SNEAKER!!!
NANEE NANEE NA NA
HAHAHAHA

THANKS TO F. DUP VANYDA 2003

message..

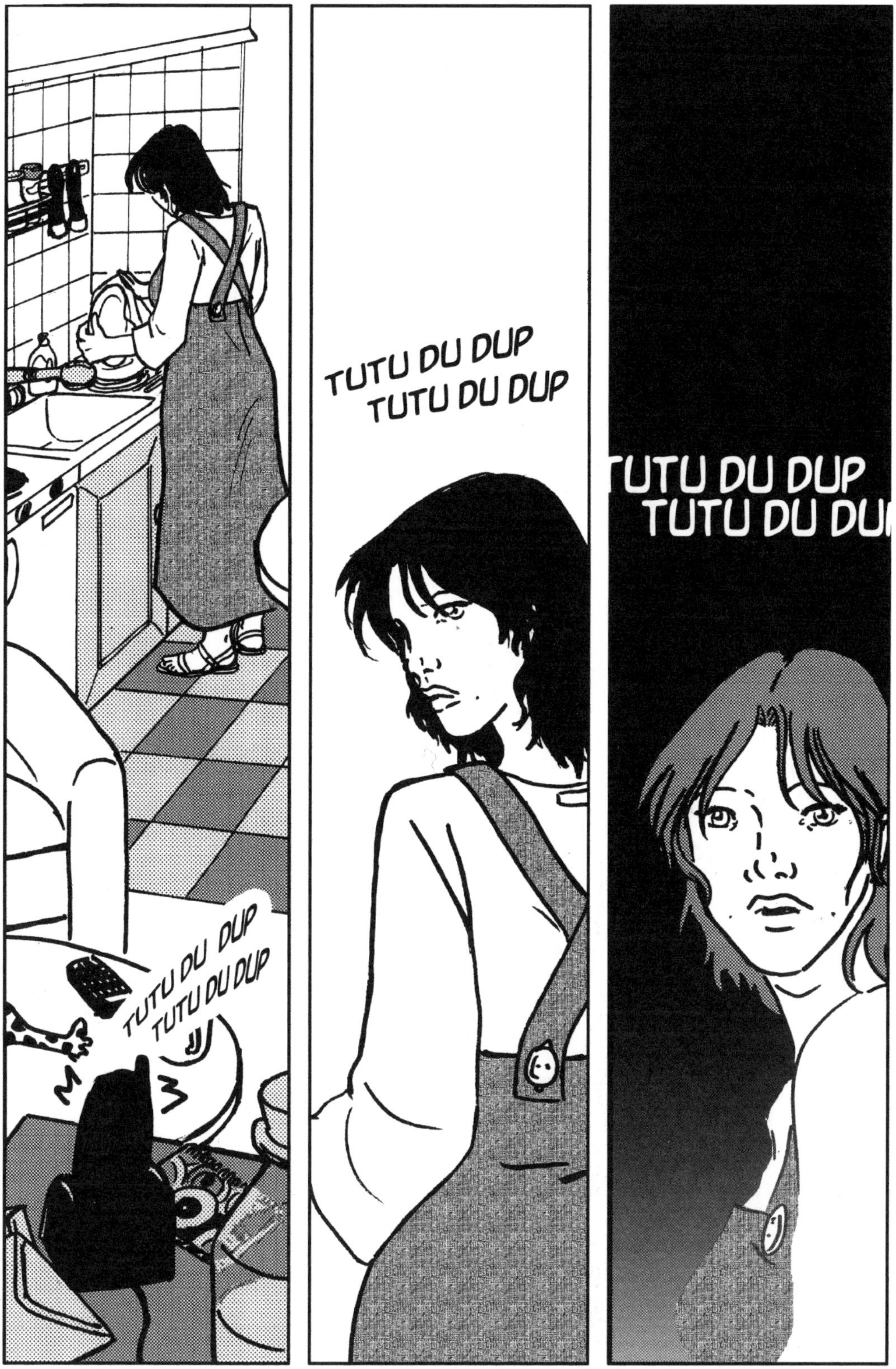
TUTU DU DUP
TUTU DU DUP
TUTU DU DUP
TUTU DU DUP
TUTU DU DUP
TUTU DU DU

Chapter 23
Monologue

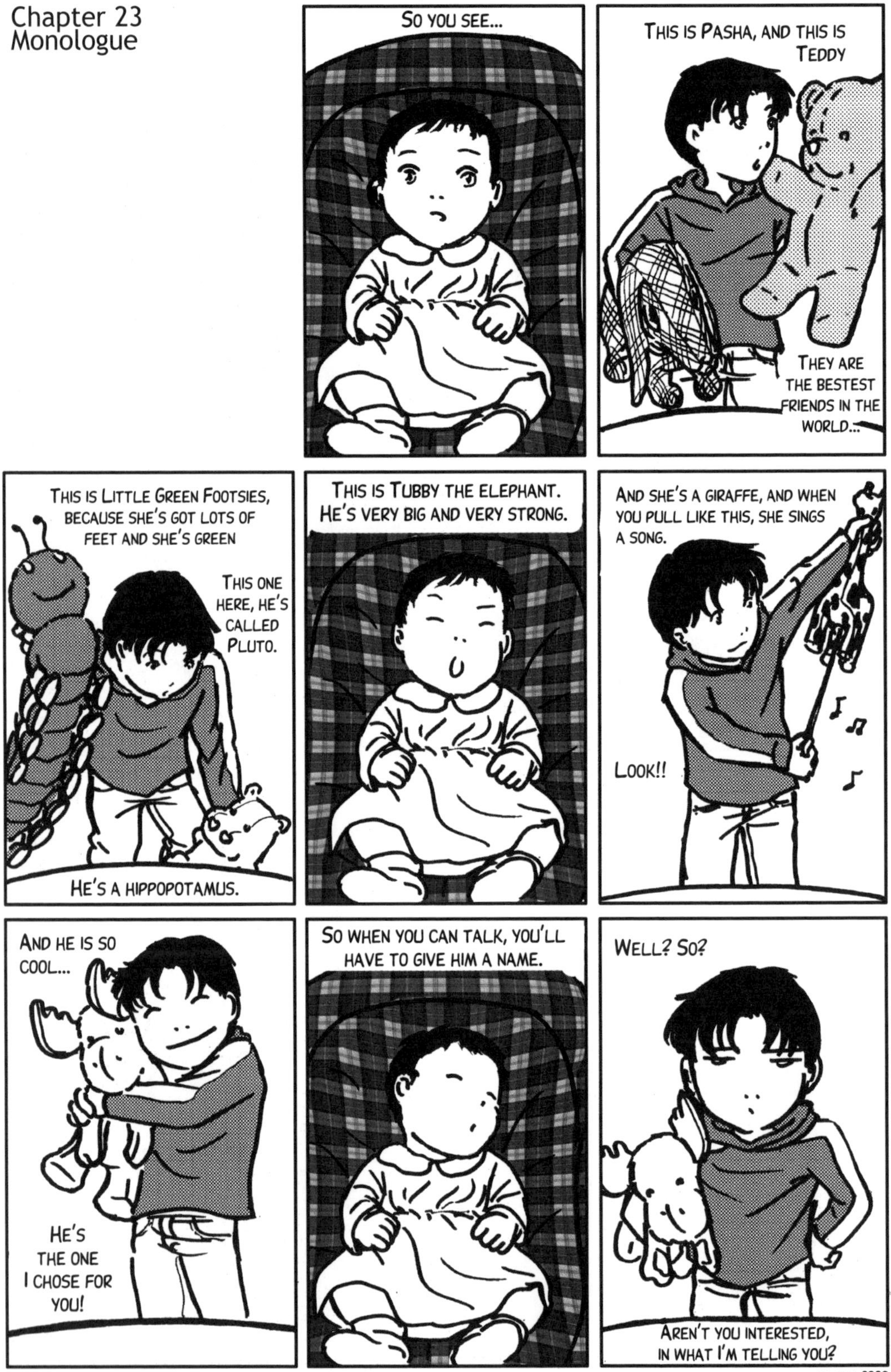

So you see...
This is Pasha, and this is Teddy
They are the bestest friends in the world...
This is Little Green Footsies, because she's got lots of feet and she's green
This one here, he's called Pluto.
He's a hippopotamus.
This is Tubby the elephant. He's very big and very strong.
And she's a giraffe, and when you pull like this, she sings a song.
Look!!
And he is so cool...
He's the one I chose for you!
So when you can talk, you'll have to give him a name.
Well? So?
Aren't you interested, in what I'm telling you?
Vanyda 2003

Chapter 24
Birthday Party

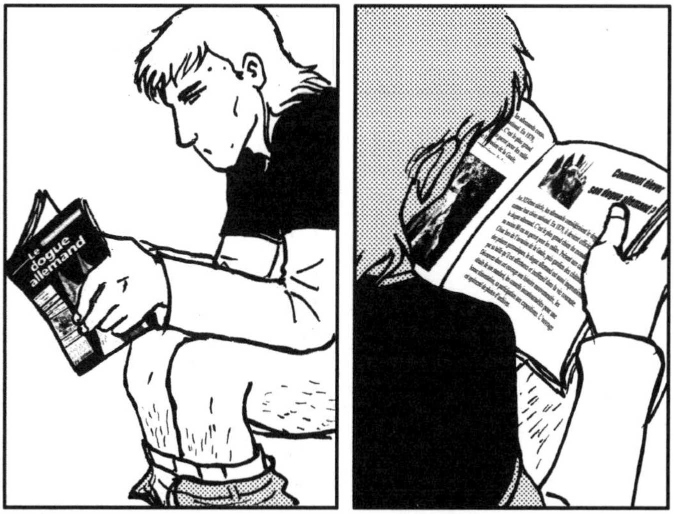

Le dogue allemand

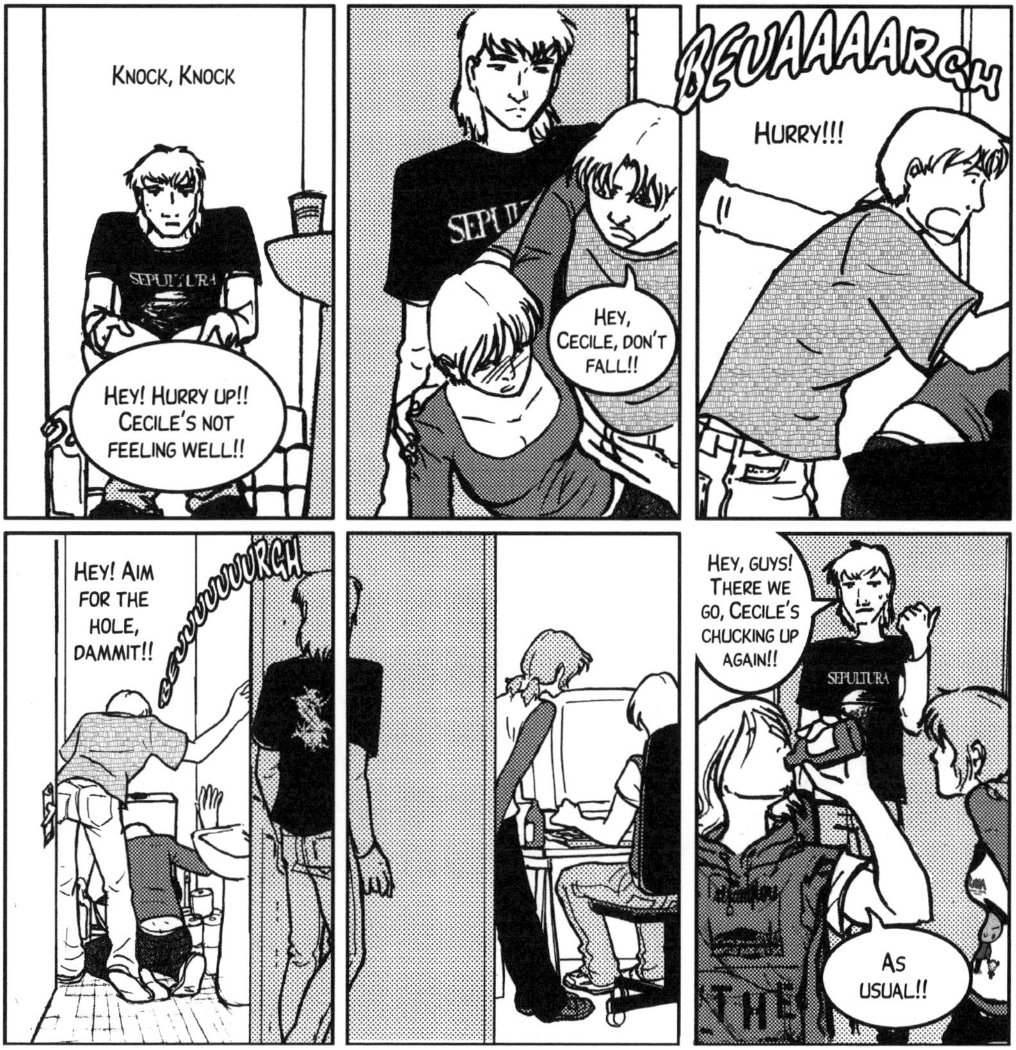

KNOCK, KNOCK
SEPULTURA
HEY! HURRY UP!! CECILE'S NOT FEELING WELL!!
HEY, CECILE, DON'T FALL!!
BEUAAAARGH
HURRY!!!
HEY! AIM FOR THE HOLE, DAMMIT!!
HEY, GUYS! THERE WE GO, CECILE'S CHUCKING UP AGAIN!!
SEPULTURA
AS USUAL!!

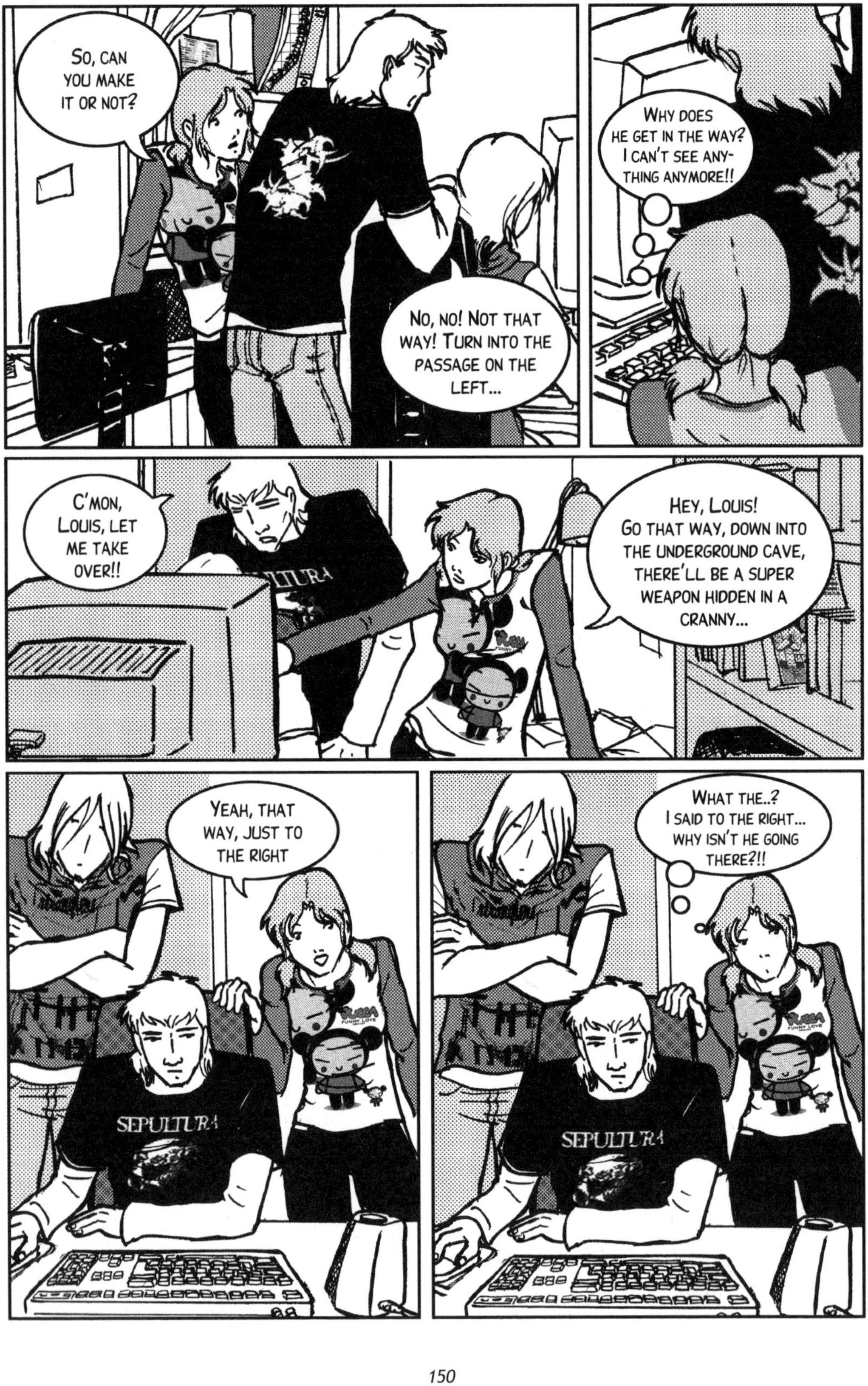

So, can you make it or not?
No, no! Not that way! Turn into the passage on the left...
Why does he get in the way? I can't see anything anymore!!
C'mon, Louis, let me take over!!
Hey, Louis! Go that way, down into the underground cave, there'll be a super weapon hidden in a cranny...
Yeah, that way, just to the right
What the..? I said to the right... why isn't he going there?!!

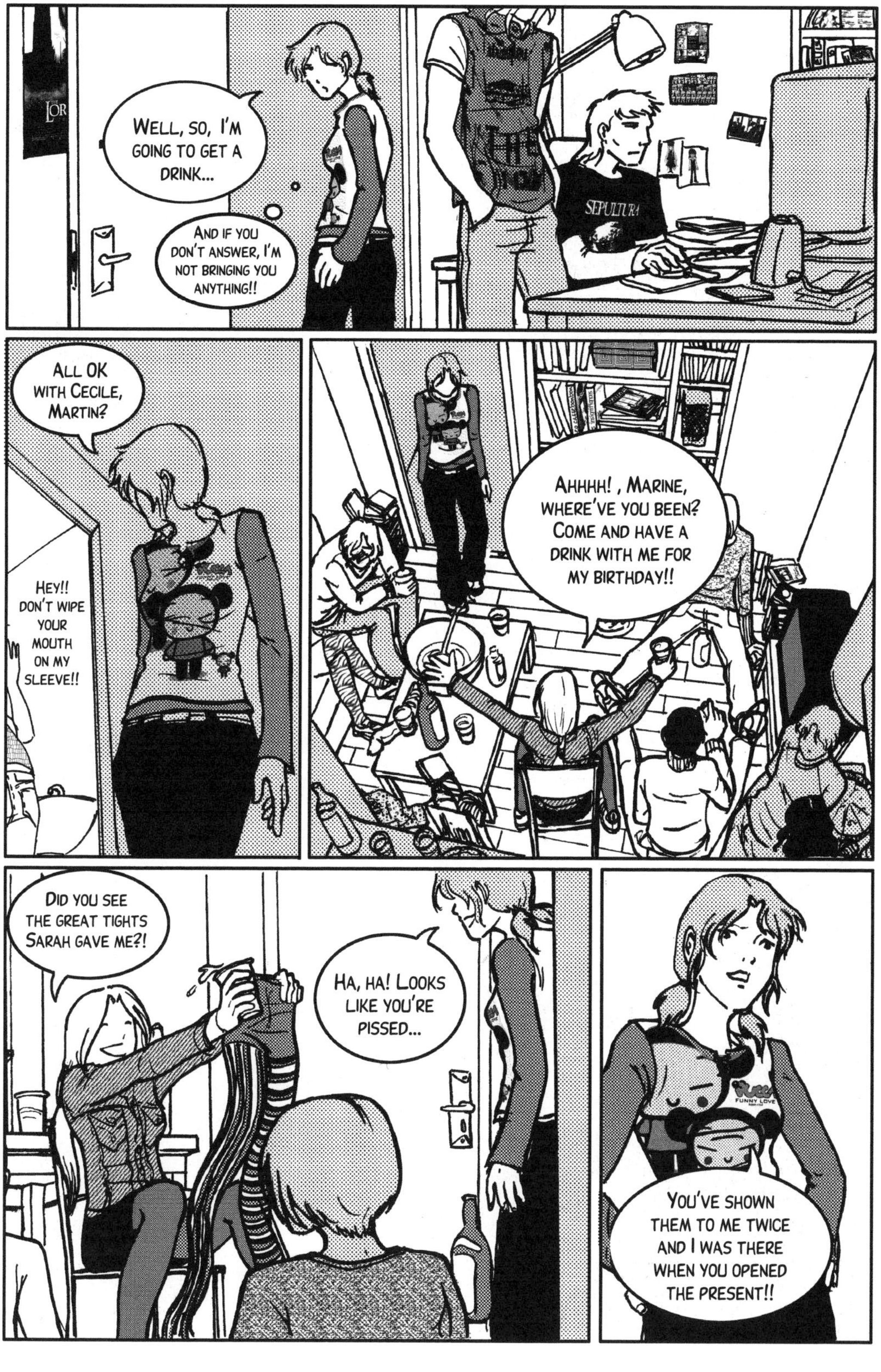
WELL, SO, I'M GOING TO GET A DRINK...
AND IF YOU DON'T ANSWER, I'M NOT BRINGING YOU ANYTHING!!
SEPULTURA
ALL OK WITH CECILE, MARTIN?
HEY!! DON'T WIPE YOUR MOUTH ON MY SLEEVE!!
AHHHH! , MARINE, WHERE'VE YOU BEEN? COME AND HAVE A DRINK WITH ME FOR MY BIRTHDAY!!
DID YOU SEE THE GREAT TIGHTS SARAH GAVE ME?!
HA, HA! LOOKS LIKE YOU'RE PISSED...
FUNNY LOVE
YOU'VE SHOWN THEM TO ME TWICE AND I WAS THERE WHEN YOU OPENED THE PRESENT!!

HEY, DON'T YOU THINK JEROME'S WEIRD?

WE HAVE THE SAME INTERESTS, BUT HE DOESN'T GIVE A SHIT ABOUT ME ...

HE DOESN'T SPEAK TO ME!! THAT GUY'S BEGINNING TO GET ON MY NERVES! HE'S OVER HERE ALL THE TIME, AND HE ACTS LIKE I'M NOT THERE!

EVERY TIME I TRY TO TALK TO HIM HE DOESN'T ANSWER ...

IT'S WEIRD... WHY'S HE LIKE THAT?

I DON'T KNOW

WELL, WHAT WITH THAT MacGYVER HAIRCUT...

I THINK THAT HE'S GOT A PROBLEM WITH GIRLS, BECAUSE AT SCHOOL, THEY USED TO MAKE FUN OF HIM BECAUSE HE WAS UGLY...

THAT PROBABLY MADE HIM HATE GIRLS!!

I REMEMBER, THEY'D RANKED ALL THE GUYS AND HE WAS LAST...

OH NO, THAT'S BAD!! POOR THING!!

OH YEAH? AND YET...

AND THEN, I THINK THAT HIS SISTER GAVE HIM A HARD TIME TOO... AT SCHOOL, SHE REALLY PISSED HIM OFF!!

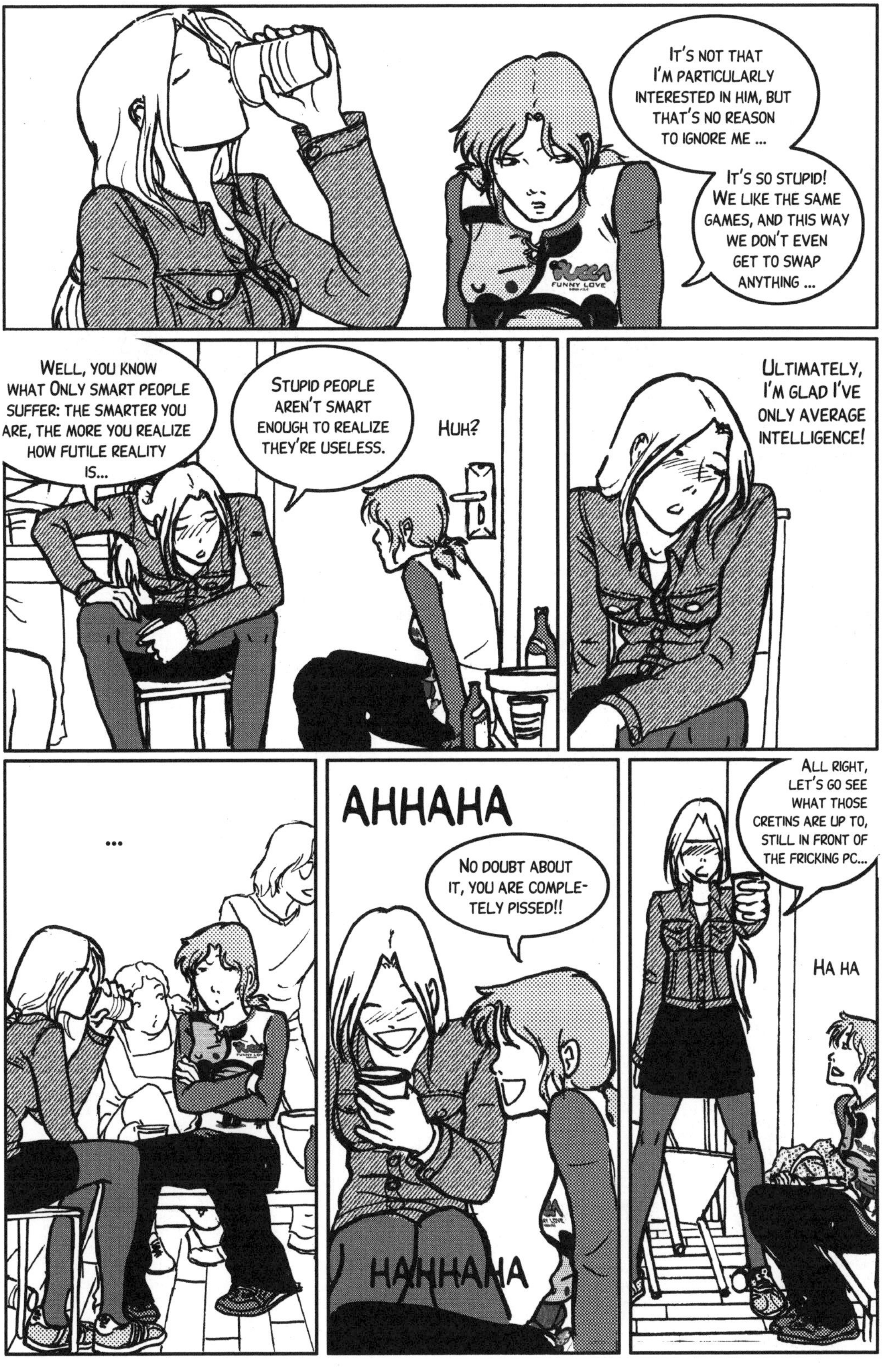
IT'S NOT THAT I'M PARTICULARLY INTERESTED IN HIM, BUT THAT'S NO REASON TO IGNORE ME ...
IT'S SO STUPID! WE LIKE THE SAME GAMES, AND THIS WAY WE DON'T EVEN GET TO SWAP ANYTHING ...
WELL, YOU KNOW WHAT ONLY SMART PEOPLE SUFFER: THE SMARTER YOU ARE, THE MORE YOU REALIZE HOW FUTILE REALITY IS...
STUPID PEOPLE AREN'T SMART ENOUGH TO REALIZE THEY'RE USELESS.
HUH?
ULTIMATELY, I'M GLAD I'VE ONLY AVERAGE INTELLIGENCE!
...
AHHAHA
NO DOUBT ABOUT IT, YOU ARE COMPLE-TELY PISSED!!
HAHHAHA
ALL RIGHT, LET'S GO SEE WHAT THOSE CRETINS ARE UP TO, STILL IN FRONT OF THE FRICKING PC...
HA HA

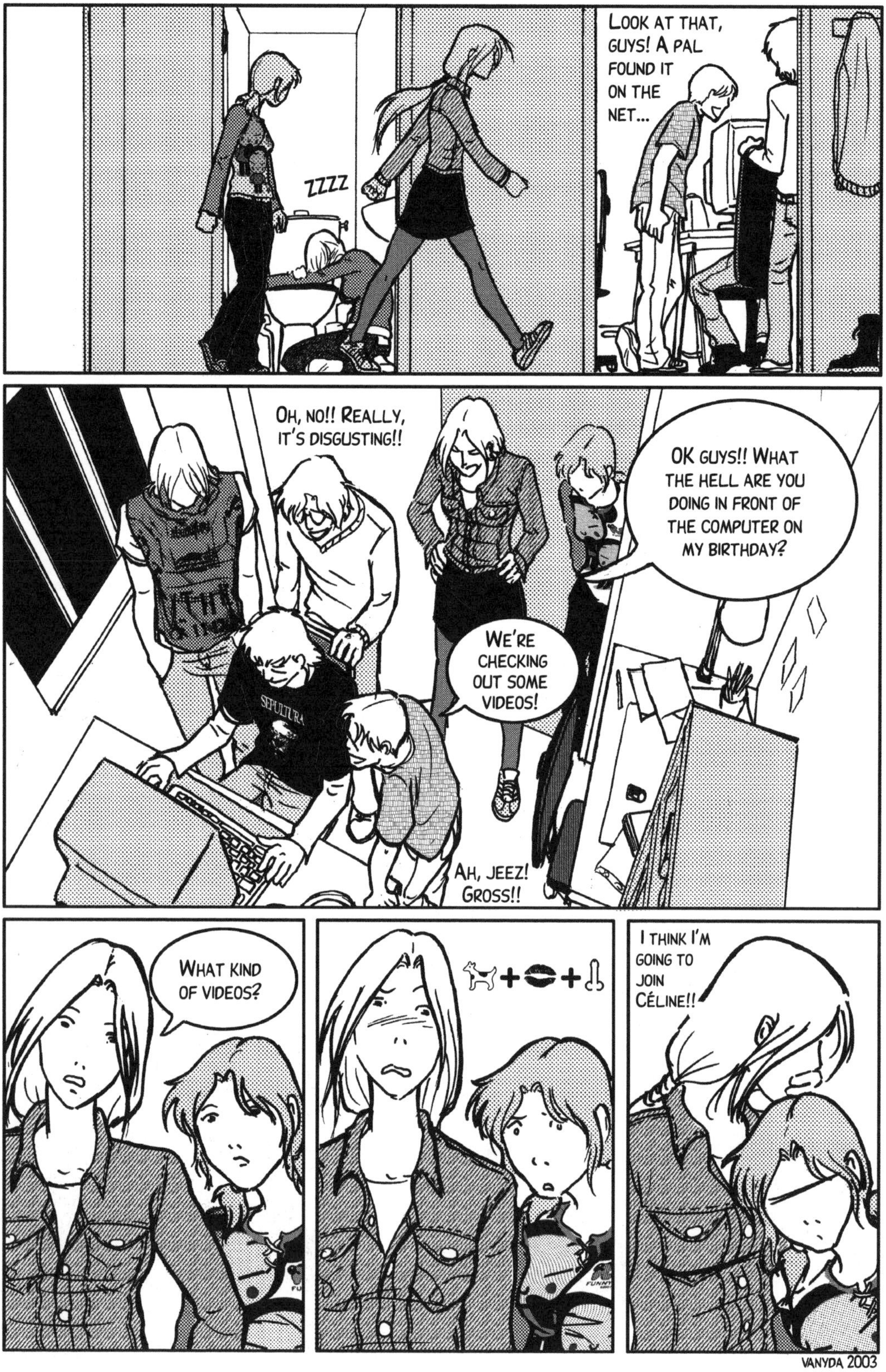
ZZZZ
LOOK AT THAT, GUYS! A PAL FOUND IT ON THE NET...
OH, NO!! REALLY, IT'S DISGUSTING!!
OK GUYS!! WHAT THE HELL ARE YOU DOING IN FRONT OF THE COMPUTER ON MY BIRTHDAY?
WE'RE CHECKING OUT SOME VIDEOS!
AH, JEEZ! GROSS!!
WHAT KIND OF VIDEOS?
I THINK I'M GOING TO JOIN CÉLINE!!
VANYDA 2003

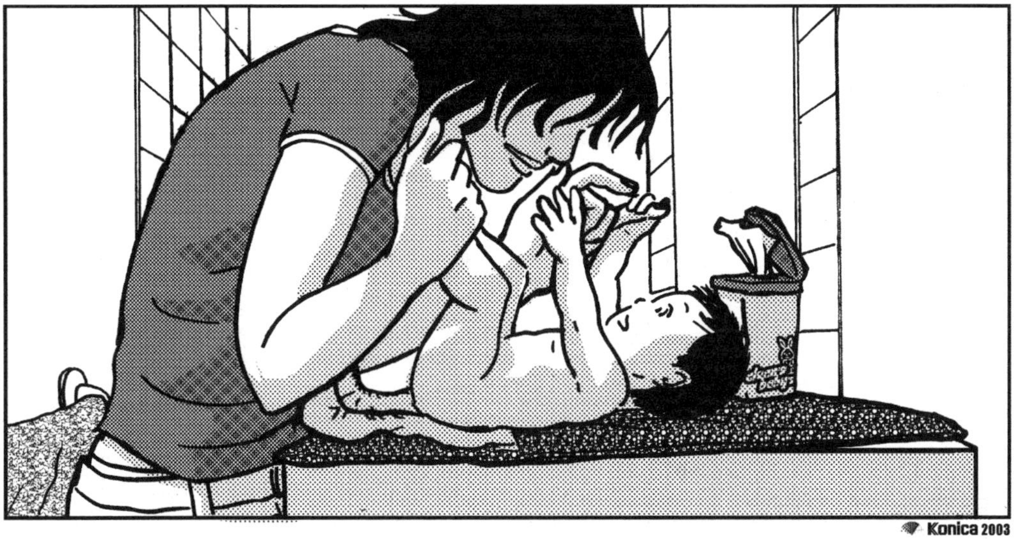

Konica 2003

Chapter 25
About to leave ...

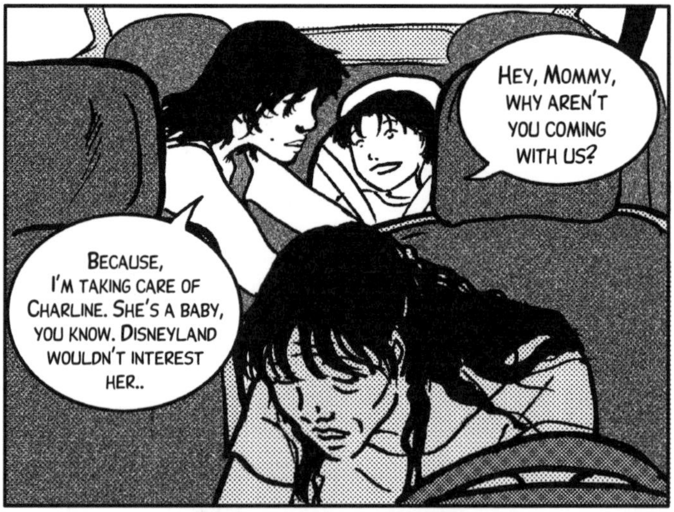

Hey, Mommy, why aren't you coming with us?
Because, I'm taking care of Charline. She's a baby, you know. Disneyland wouldn't interest her..

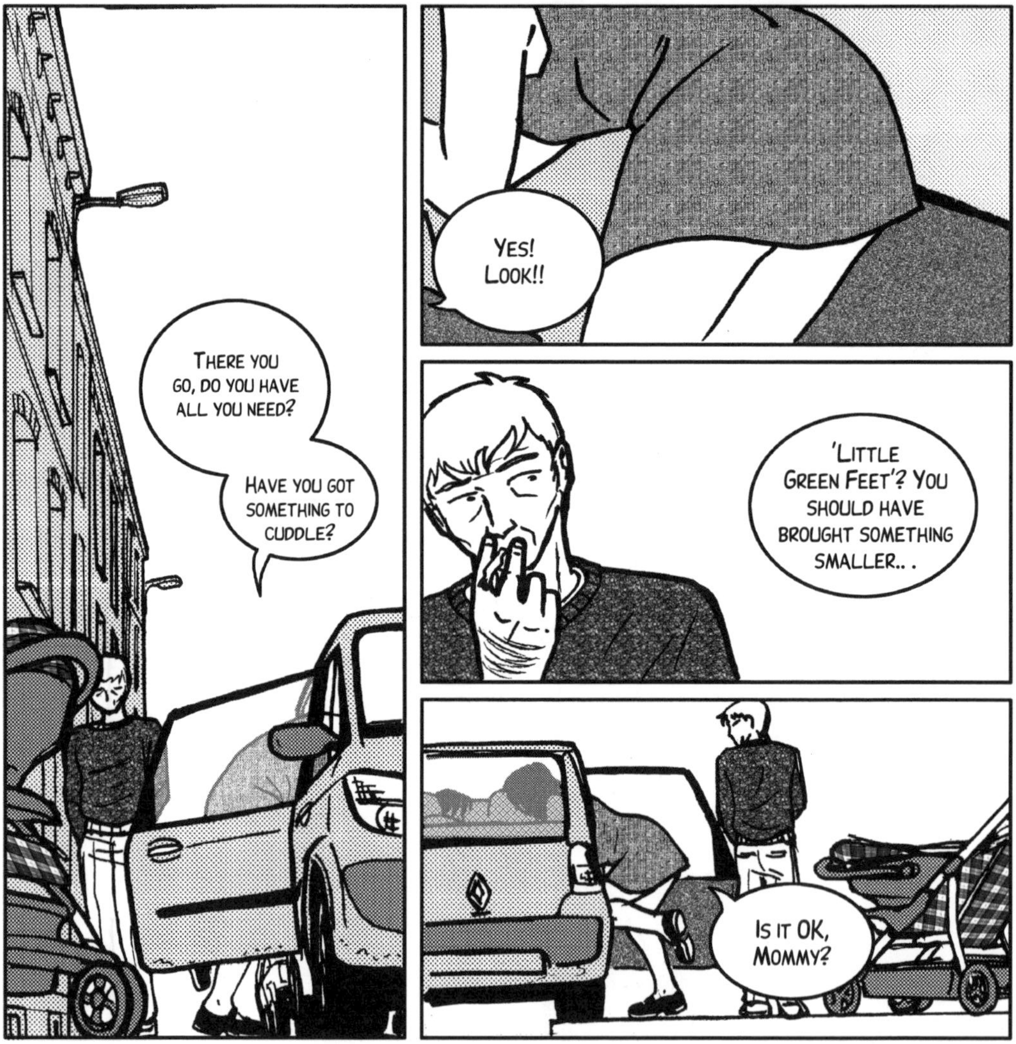

There you go, do you have all you need?
Have you got something to cuddle?
Yes! Look!!
'Little Green Feet'? You should have brought something smaller.. .
Is it OK, Mommy?

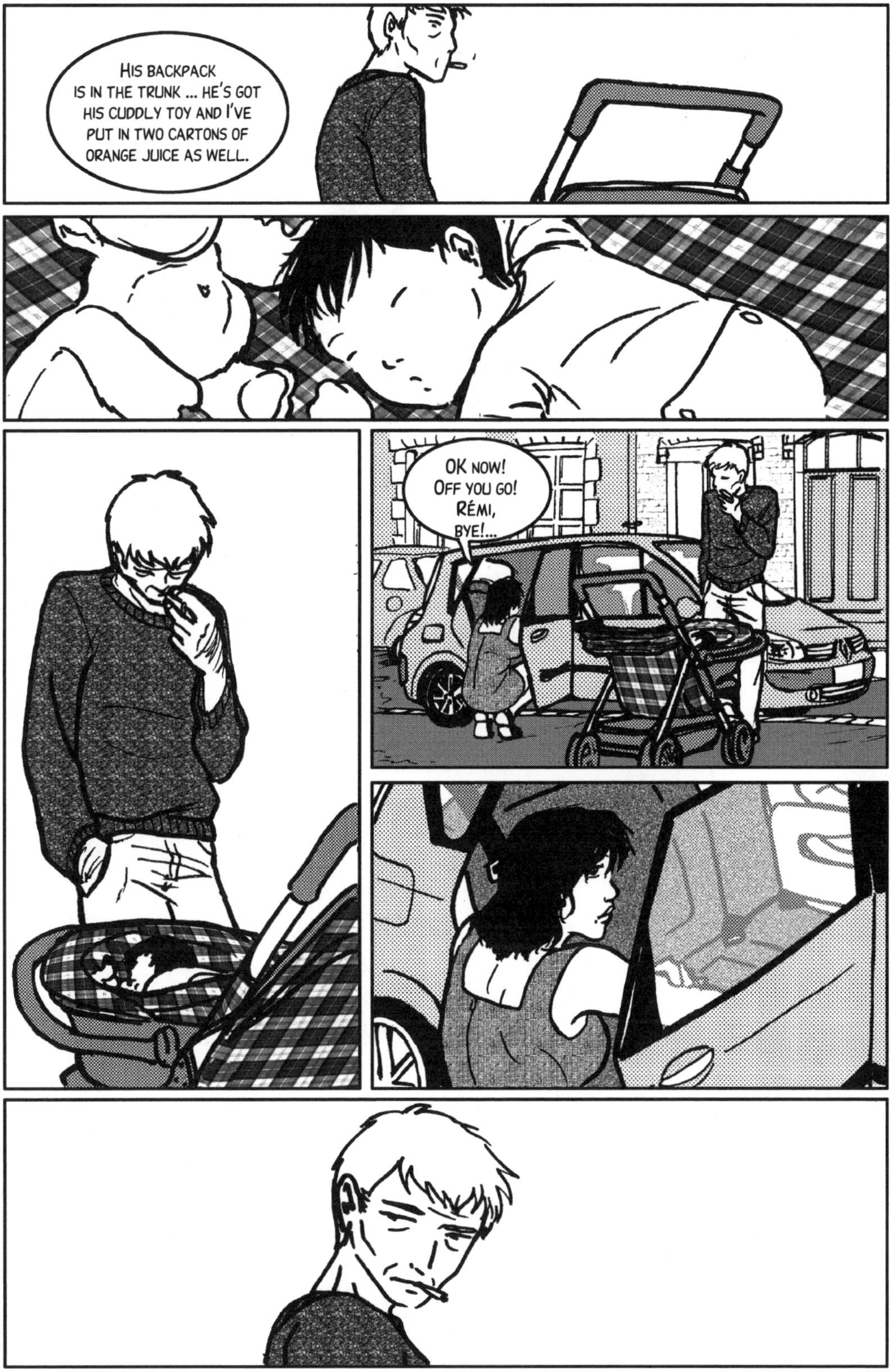
HIS BACKPACK IS IN THE TRUNK ... HE'S GOT HIS CUDDLY TOY AND I'VE PUT IN TWO CARTONS OF ORANGE JUICE AS WELL.
OK NOW! OFF YOU GO! RÉMI, BYE!...

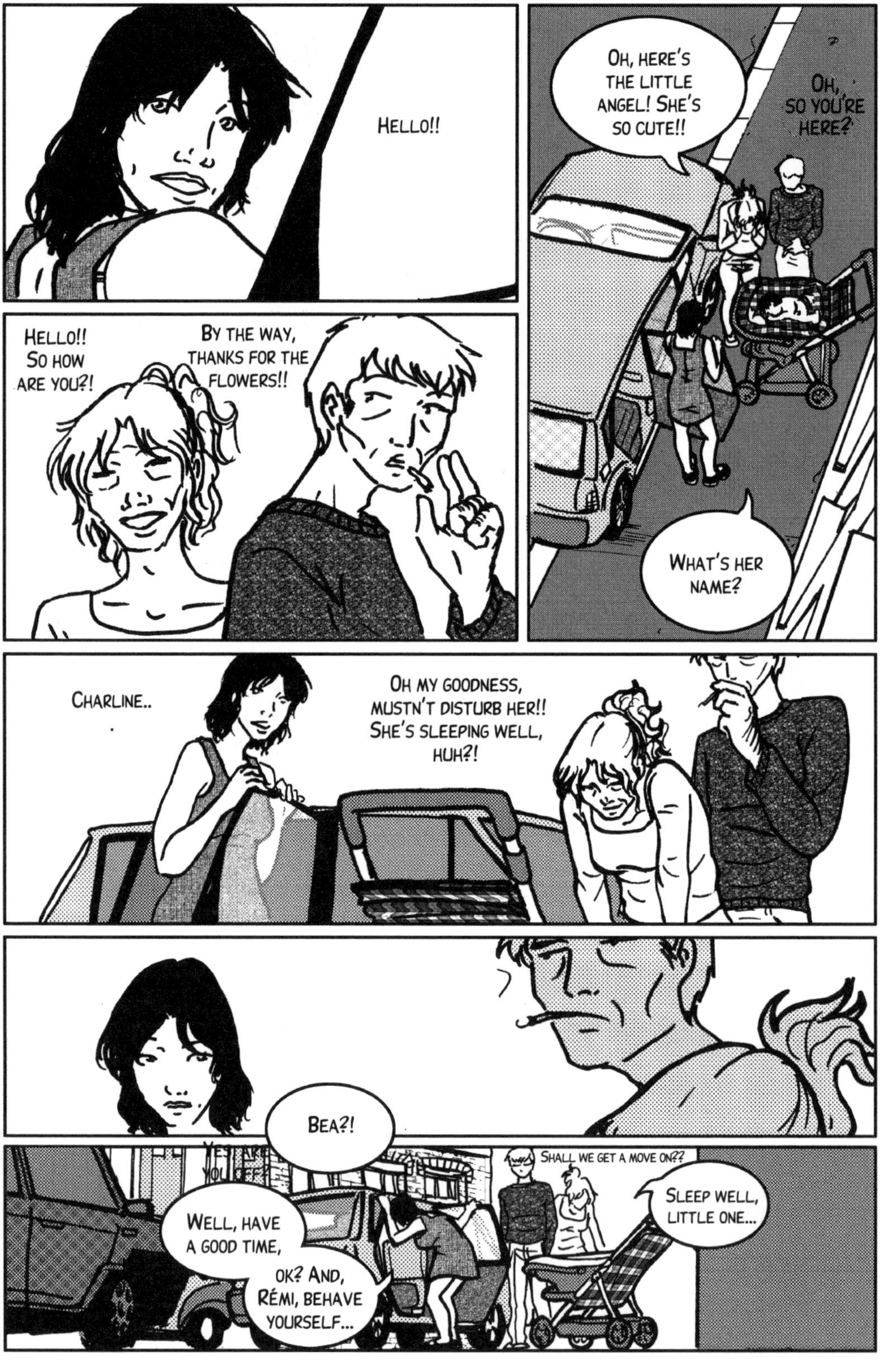
Hello!!
Oh, here's the little angel! She's so cute!!
Oh, so you're here?
Hello!! So how are you?!
By the way, thanks for the flowers!!
What's her name?
Charline..
Oh my goodness, mustn't disturb her!! She's sleeping well, huh?!
Bea?!
Yes! Are you off?
Well, have a good time,
ok? And, Rémi, behave yourself...
Shall we get a move on??
Sleep well, little one...

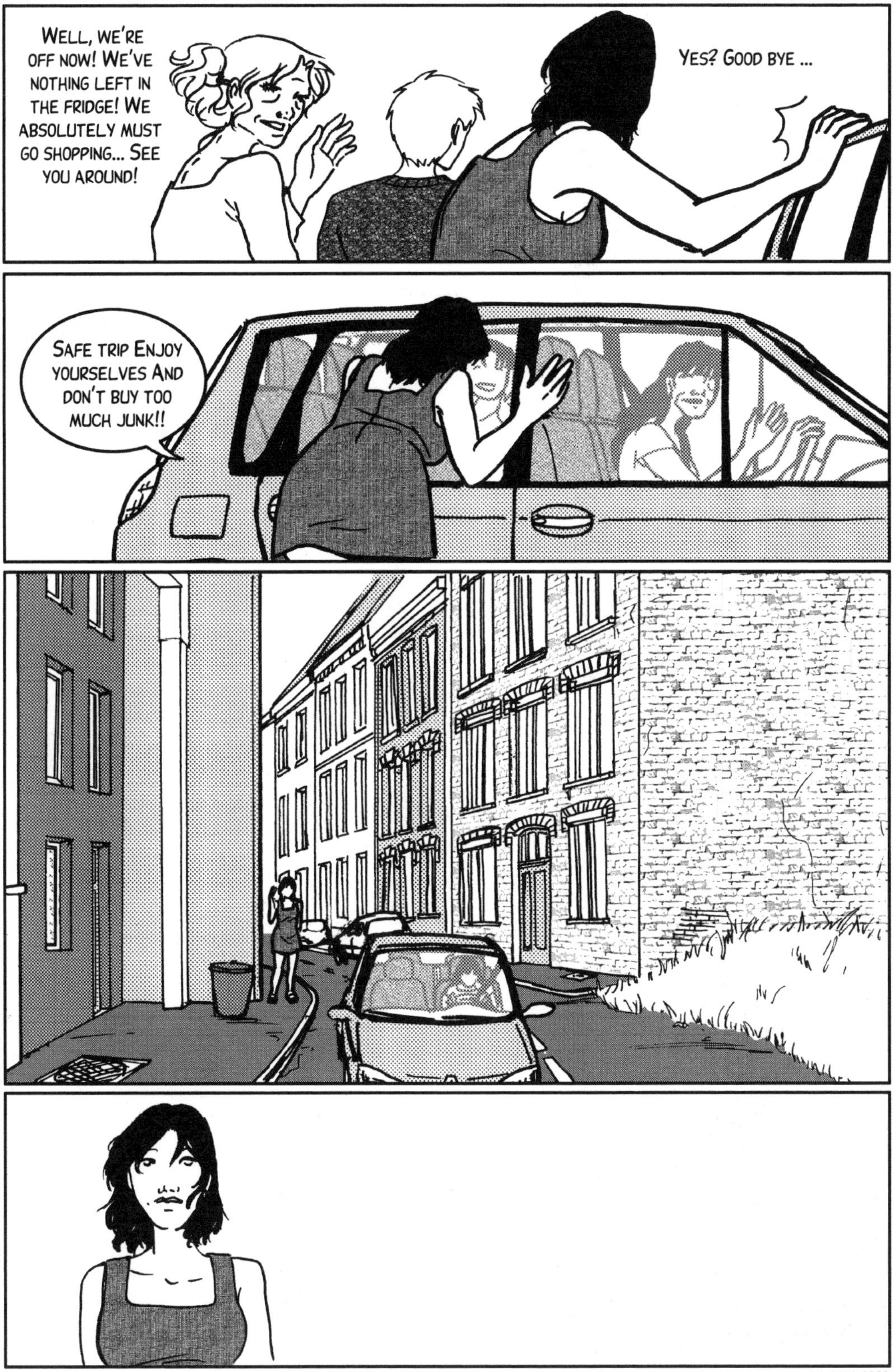
WELL, WE'RE OFF NOW! WE'VE NOTHING LEFT IN THE FRIDGE! WE ABSOLUTELY MUST GO SHOPPING... SEE YOU AROUND!
YES? GOOD BYE ...
SAFE TRIP ENJOY YOURSELVES AND DON'T BUY TOO MUCH JUNK!!

VANYDA 2003

Chapter 26
Finally...

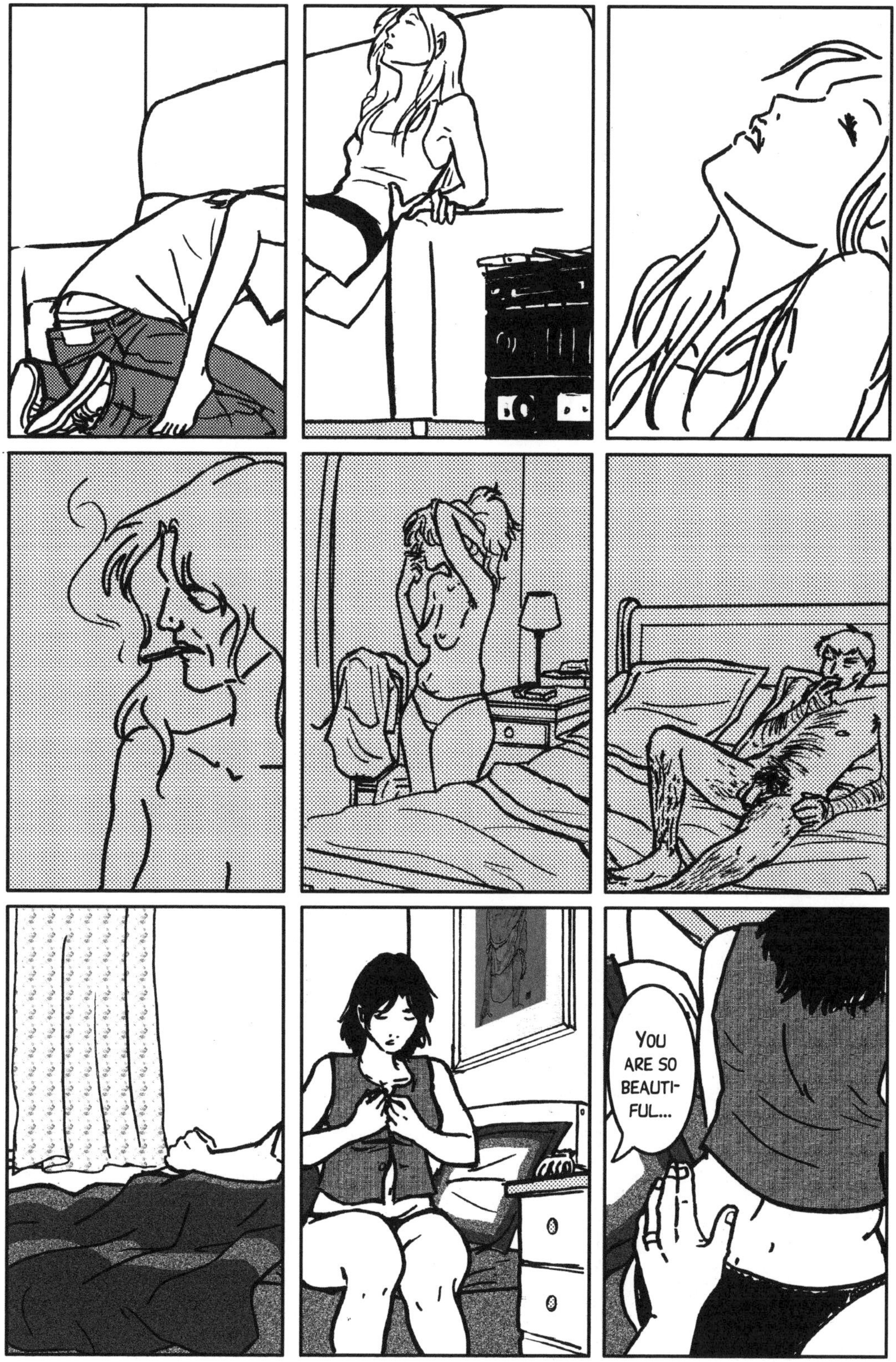
YOU ARE SO BEAUTI-FUL...

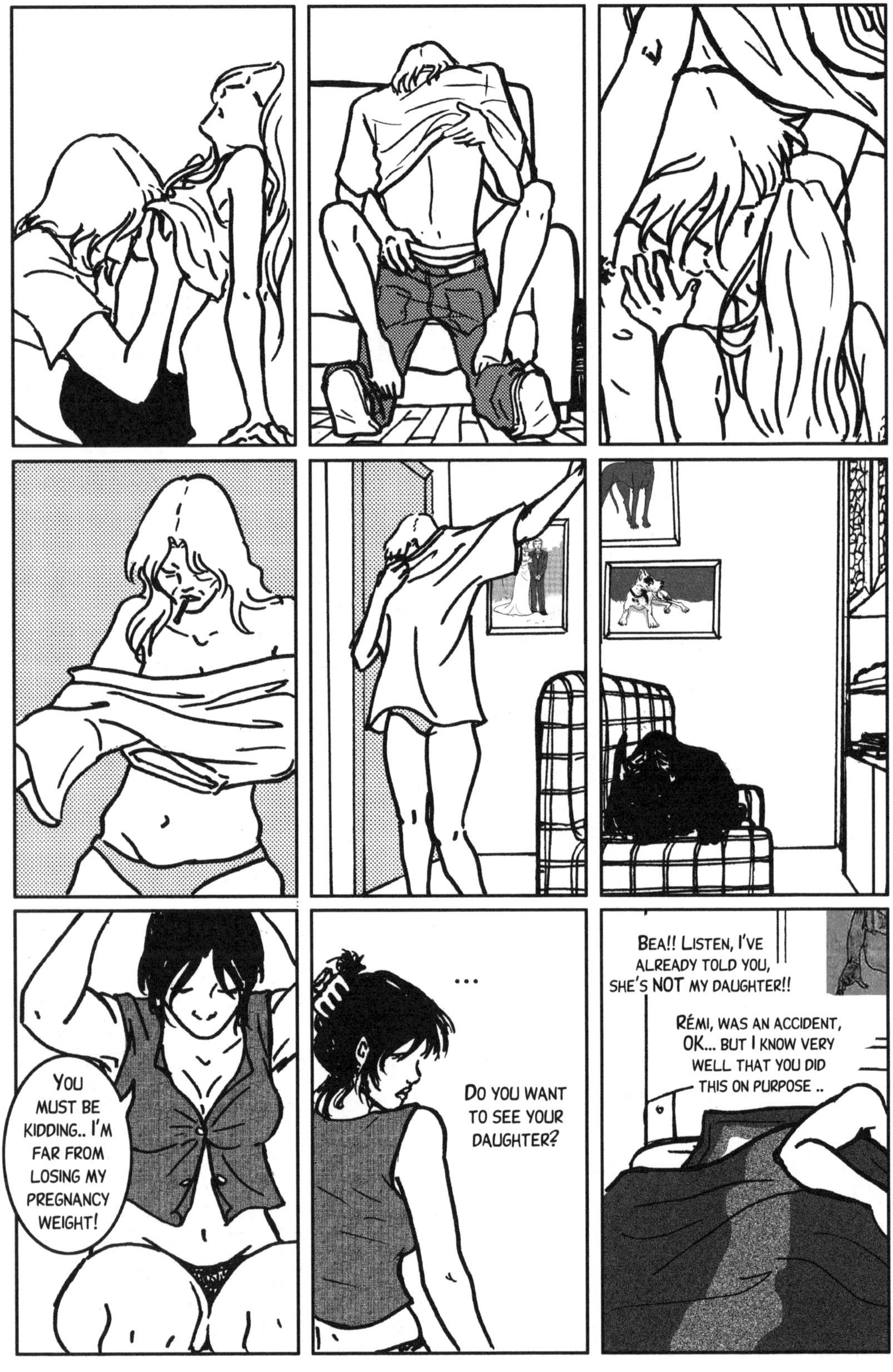
You must be kidding.. I'm far from losing my pregnancy weight!
...
Do you want to see your daughter?
Bea!! Listen, I've already told you, she's NOT my daughter!!
Rémi, was an accident, OK... but I know very well that you did this on purpose ..

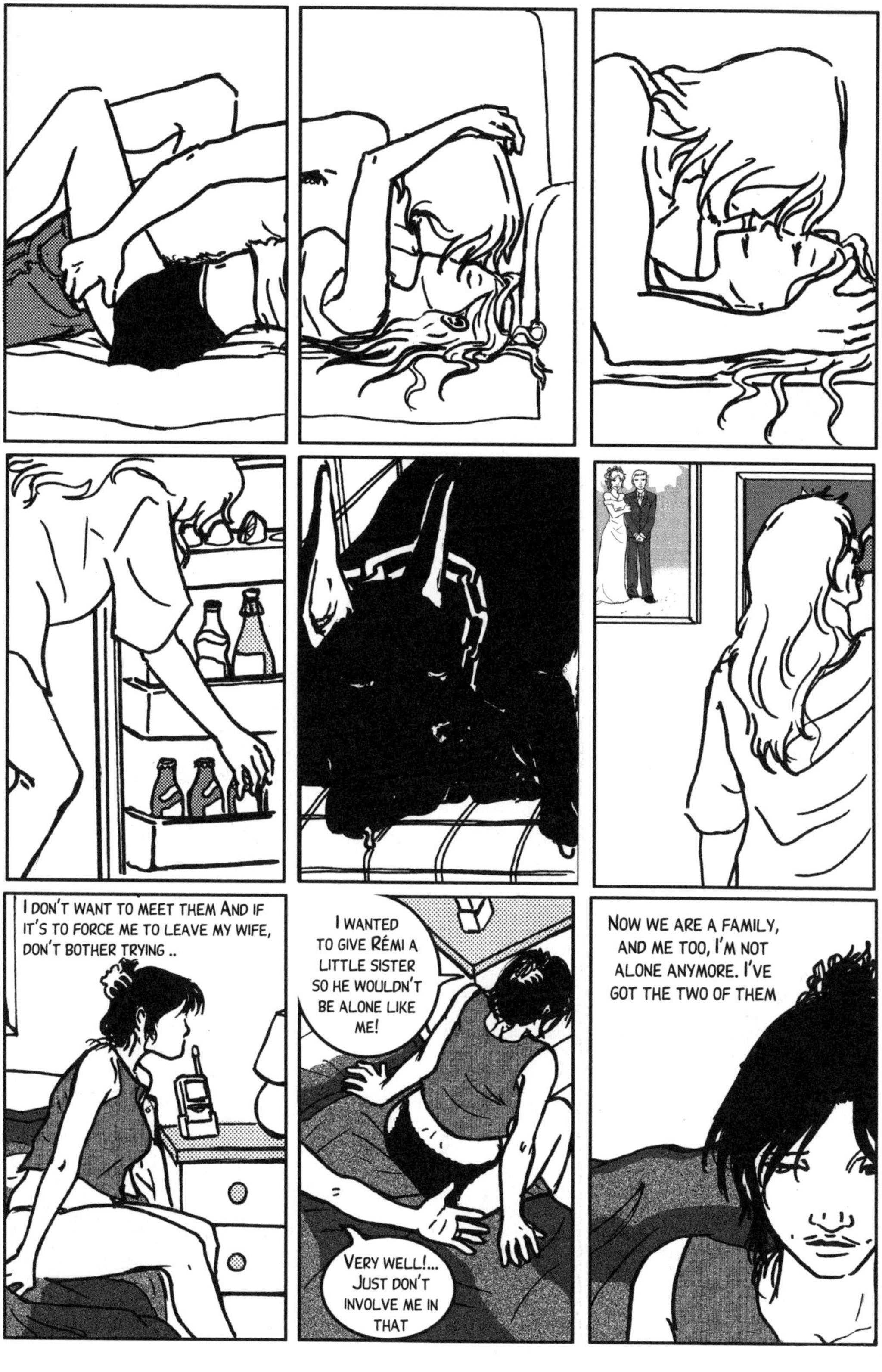
I DON'T WANT TO MEET THEM AND IF IT'S TO FORCE ME TO LEAVE MY WIFE, DON'T BOTHER TRYING ..
I WANTED TO GIVE RÉMI A LITTLE SISTER SO HE WOULDN'T BE ALONE LIKE ME!
VERY WELL!... JUST DON'T INVOLVE ME IN THAT
NOW WE ARE A FAMILY, AND ME TOO, I'M NOT ALONE ANYMORE. I'VE GOT THE TWO OF THEM

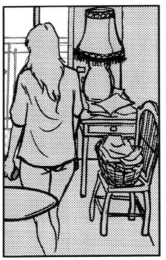

YOU
CAN LEAVE
NOW

BEA, HONEY, WHAT'S WRONG?

I'M SENDING YOU
BACK TO YOUR WIFE
AND KIDS. THAT'S
ALL.

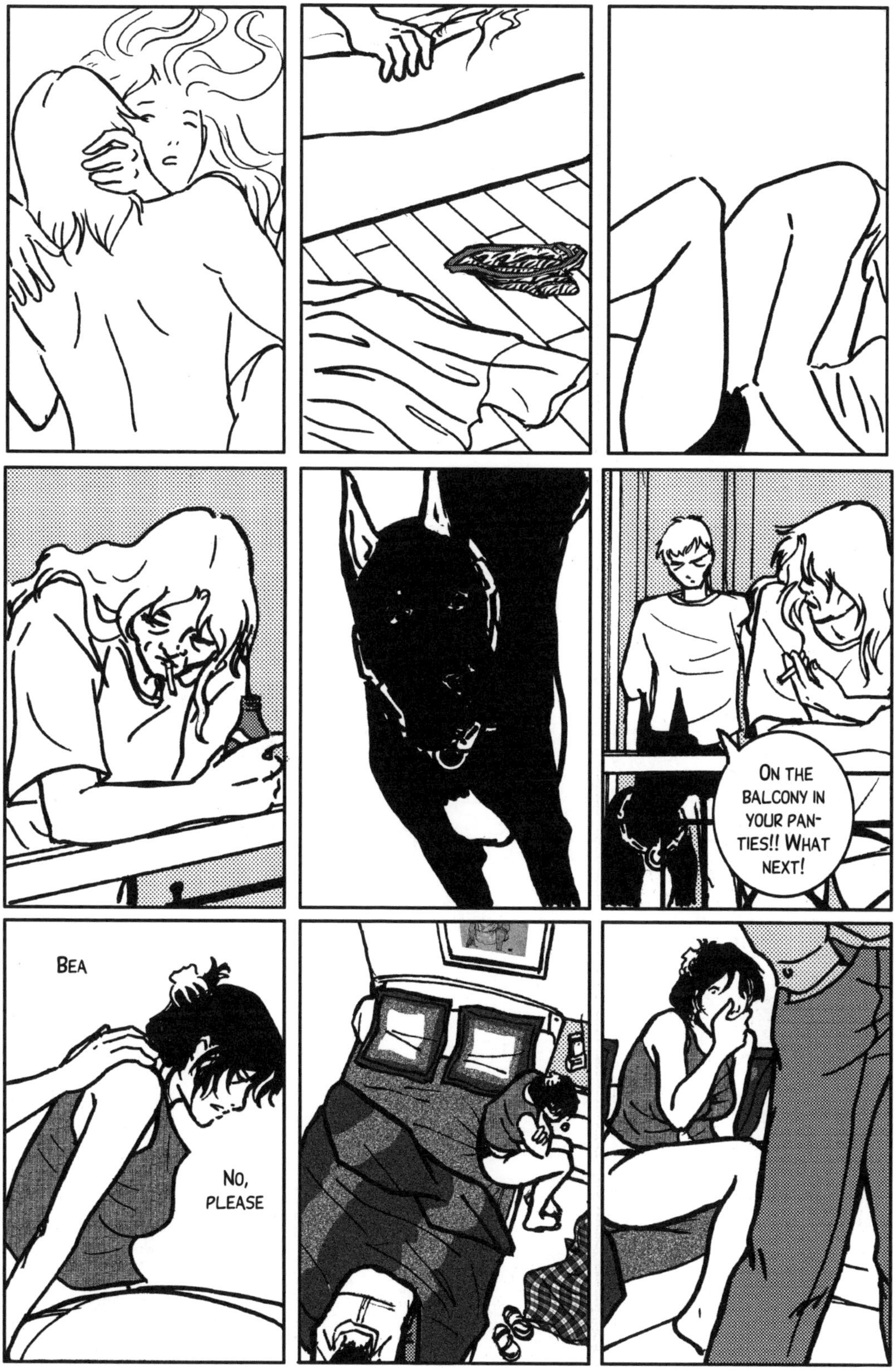
ON THE BALCONY IN YOUR PAN-TIES!! WHAT NEXT!
BEA
NO, PLEASE

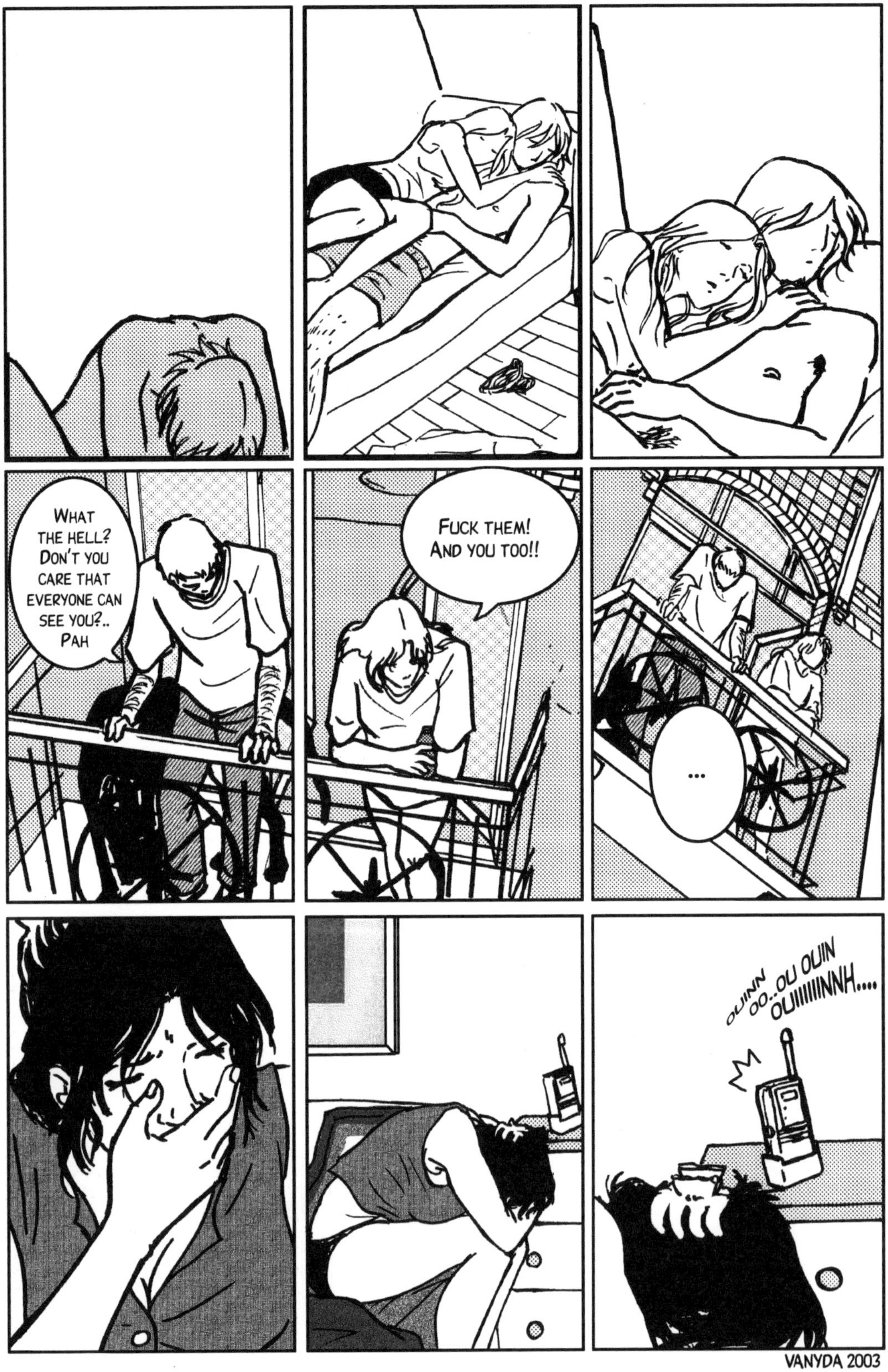
WHAT THE HELL? DON'T YOU CARE THAT EVERYONE CAN SEE YOU?.. PAH
FUCK THEM! AND YOU TOO!!
...
OUINN OO..OU OUIN OUIIIIIINNH....

VANYDA 2003

Many thanks to **Frédéric Boilet** for his work on the introduction.

Vanyda
(vanyda@free.fr)

Original French edition published in 2003 by:

La boîte à bulles
5 villa du petit valet 92160 Antony
www.la-boite-a-bulles.com
vincent@la-boite-a-bulles.com

© Vanyda 2003 / © FANFARE / Ponent Mon 2006

www.ponentmon.com

Translation: **Vanessa Champion & Elizabeth Tiernan**

Layout: **David Malvoisin & Amiram Reuveni**

ISBN: 84-933992-8-0

Printed and bound in Spain by: **Aleu S.A.**

JAN 2 8 2008